T0290096

BPE 12-1

The Beatles and Sgt. Pepper:
A Fans' Perspective

Compiled by Bruce Spizer

With additional contributions by

Bill King,
Al Sussman,
Frank Daniels,
Piers Hemmingsen
and other Beatles fans

498 Productions, L.L.C.
1010 Common Street, Suite 1964
New Orleans, Louisiana 70112
Fax: 504-299-1964
email: 498@beatle.net

The Billboard, Cash Box and Record World chart data used in this book was taken from books published by Record Research, including Billboard Pop Album Charts 1965-1969 and The Comparison Book 1954-1982. Photo credits: Beatles Book Photo Library (pages 137, 139, 141, 143, 147, 149, 153); Getty Images (page 157); Warren Hickingbottom (page 56); Rex Features/Shutterstock (page 69). The following individuals provided images of memorabilia: Pete Nash (pages vii, 88, 124); Piers Hemmingsen (pages vi, 49, 53); Rainer Mores, Beatles Museum in Germany/THINGS (pages 122, 123 advert); Alfred Ebeling, M.B.M.sp (page 123 Sgt. Pepper beer mats); Perry Cox (back cover medal); Dirk Van Damme (page 125). Other items are from the collections of Bruce Spizer and Frank Daniels.

Print edition ISBN 978-0-9832957-4-7; Library of Congress Catalog Number 2017905294.

Printed in Canada
1 2 3 4 5 6 7 8 9 0

So Let Me Introduce To You...

Well here I am again. I've twice said "I won't be writing another book on The Beatles," and both times I found a project worthy of doing. After writing eight books about the Beatles American records, I thought it was time to retire. But Frank Daniels persuaded me to join him on a Magical Mystery Tour of the Beatles British pressings. So that was definitely the last book. No need to do a book on the Beatles records issued in Gibraltar near Spain. Time to hang it up and just do expanded and revised digital editions of my sold out first four books.

Then last summer (2016), I wrote an essay on how *Sgt. Pepper* was received in America back when it first came out in 1967. As a historian, I would cover all the basics: the chart positions, radio air play, sales and reviews from that summer. But I also wanted to make it personal. I wanted to express how my friends and I experienced the album and all the excitement it generated. I sensed my memories were not unique, so I wrote the essay using the pronoun "we" rather than "I" because *Sgt. Pepper* was a communal experience.

I showed my essay to other Beatles fans to see if my memories matched theirs. The feedback I received was extremely positive, so I knew I had something worth sharing. I just had to find a place for the essay. After all, there's a place.

Although Beatlefan has published many of my articles, I felt that an essay on an album as colorful as *Sgt. Pepper* would be more effective if it went beyond the black and white columns of newsprint and was accompanied by colorful images. After all, I was painting my story in a colorful way. I thought of submitting it to magazines, but was concerned it would be edited down and would not be joined by all the images I had in my head.

So then last February I got the crazy idea to put it out myself. Why not? If I could produce extensive books on The Beatles, I surely could turn my article into a forty-page color mini-magazine timed for the big Five-O, the fiftieth anniversary of *Sgt. Pepper's Lonely Hearts Club Band*. But then I thought, I know other people have wonderful stories to tell about their *Pepper* experiences. So why not include theirs?

My initial idea was to incorporate articles written for Beatlefan by editor Bill King and fellow contributor Al Sussman. I could rerun the excellent pieces they had written to celebrate previous milestone anniversaries of *Sgt. Pepper*. And then I thought to invite Frank Daniels to add a piece on *Sgt. Pepper* influences and Piers Hemmingsen to tell us what it was like north of the border in Canada. But the real breakthrough was when I realized what the book was becoming: The Beatles and *Sgt. Pepper* from the perspective of THE FANS. So why not send out an open invitation to fans across the world and solicit their *Pepper* experiences?

As the stories came in, the 40-page magazine grew to a 170 plus page book. And what was really cool for me was that many of the stories reflected what I had written in my essay all those months ago. My *Sgt. Pepper* experience was not unique at all. So turn the pages and let me introduce to you, the act we've known for all these years, Sgt. Pepper's Lonely Hearts Club Band.

With A Little Help From My Friends

Taking on a project such as this would not have been possible without a little help from my friends. Fortunately, my many years of attending Beatles conventions, entering the world of compulsive collectors of Beatles records and memorabilia, writing Beatles articles for magazines and serving as a consultant on Beatles projects for Capitol, EMI, Universal and Apple has greatly expanded my circle of friends. I re-thank all who have helped me on my prior books.

Doing a book from the perspective of Beatles fans becomes a lot easier when you have friends at Beatlefan magazine. Bill King and Al Sussman contributed their well-researched and heartfelt memories of the Summer of Love and *Sgt. Pepper*. Not only did this save me critical time enabling me to complete this book without falling victim to the Dreaded Deadline Doom, it also gave me first-class articles from their perspective.

Frank Daniels has been a friend for well over a decade, having assisted me with all of my books written after our first telephone conference. Having him on board a project is like adding a scholar, historian, music lover and detective all in one.

If you want to know about The Beatles in Canada, you go to Piers Hemmingsen, it's what you do. Piers was kind enough to take time from the writing of his latest book to contribute a chapter on how The Beatles made Canada's centennial celebration all the more special for young Canadians.

And then there were all of the fans who shared their *Sgt. Pepper* recollections with me. When I put out the word I was looking for stories about people's initial experience with *Sgt. Pepper*, I thought I might get a dozen or so memories worth printing. I never dreamed I would receive so many wonderful and touching stories. There is no need for me to name all of those who contributed here as you will soon see their names below their remembrances. I do want to give a special thanks to some of those fans who not only sent me their story, but also asked others to contribute to the book. The list includes Jude Southerland Kessler, Gay Linvill, Lou Simon, Karen Duchaj, Kent Kotal and probably a few others who I either forgot or were unsung heroes.

As you read these fan recollections, you will see certain themes reappearing. They show the power of The Beatles influence beyond their music. Fans tell of making lifelong friends through their common love of The Beatles. Others tell of the magic of seeing that cover for the first time and being exposed to the wondrous music. But the theme that touched my heart the most was fans whose *Sgt. Pepper* experience included their parents and how the album brought them closer either from listening to the album together or appreciating the parent for having bought them the album. Having lost my mom last year, they brought tears to my eyes. She bought me my first Beatles album.

On the technical side, Diana Thornton once again served as art director, graphic designer and prepress. Kaye Alexander coordinated matters with our printer. The book was proofed by Frank Daniels and Al Sussman.

In the tradition, my thanks to my family, Sarah, Eloise, Barbara, Trish (who turned 64 this year), Big Puppy and others too numerous and crazy to name.

And in the end, I admit that I got by with a lot of help from my friends. We hope you will enjoy the show.

Life Flows On
Within You and Without You

Bruce Spizer is a lifelong native of New Orleans, Louisiana, who was eight years old when the Beatles invaded America. He began listening to the radio at age two and was a die-hard fan of WTIX, a top forty station that played a blend of New Orleans R&B music and top pop and rock hits. His first two albums were *The Coasters' Greatest Hits*, which he permanently "borrowed" from his older sisters, and *Meet The Beatles!*, which he still occasionally plays on his vintage 1964 Beatles record player.

During his high school and college days, Bruce played guitar in various bands that primarily covered hits of the sixties, including several Beatles songs. He wrote numerous album and concert reviews for his high school and college newspapers, including a review of *Abbey Road* that didn't claim Paul was dead. He received his B.A., M.B.A. and law degree from Tulane University. His legal and accounting background have proved valuable in researching and writing his books.

Bruce is considered one of the world's leading experts on the Beatles. A "taxman" by day, Bruce is a Board Certified Tax Attorney with his own practice. A "paperback writer" by night, Bruce is the author of nine critically acclaimed books on the Beatles, including *The Beatles Are Coming! The Birth of Beatlemania in America*, a series of six books on the group's American record releases and *Beatles For Sale on Parlophone Records*, which covers all of the Beatles records issued in the U.K. from 1962 - 1970. His articles have appeared in Beatlefan, Goldmine and American History magazines. He was selected to write the questions for the special Beatles edition of Trivial Pursuit. He maintains the popular website www.beatle.net.

Bruce has been a guest speaker at numerous Beatles conventions and at the Grammy Museum, the American Film Institute, New York's Lincoln Center and the Rock 'N' Roll Hall of Fame & Museum. He has appeared on Fox National News, CNN, ABC's *Good Morning America* and *Nightline*, CBS's *The Early Show* and morning shows in New York, Chicago, Los Angeles, New Orleans and other cities and is a frequent guest on radio shows, including NPR, the BBC and Beatle Brunch.

Bruce serves as a consultant to EMI, Capitol Records, Universal Music Group and Apple Corps Ltd. on Beatles projects. He has an extensive Beatles collection, concentrating primarily on American, Canadian and British first issue records, promotional items and concert posters.

"SGT. PEPPER" Souvenir Poster produced by the official Beatles Fan Club of Great Britain to mark the release of the LP Album "Sgt. Pepper's Lonely Hearts Club Band"/available on Parlophone LP in the U.K. & Capitol LP in the U.S.A.

contents

"And the jukebox kept on playin' Sgt. Pepper's Lonely Hearts Club Band…"

An American Perspective

by Bruce Spizer

During the first week of 1968, seven months removed from the release of *Sgt. Pepper's Lonely Hearts Club Band* (June 1, 1967 in the U.K. and a day later by Capitol Records in America), the album's fingerprints could still be found all over the Billboard charts. The album itself was at number five in its 29th week in the magazine's list of Top LP's, having previously held the top spot for 15 straight weeks (July 1- October 7, 1967). It would spend a total of 175 weeks on the charts, more than three and a third years. The Beatles' *Magical Mystery Tour*, containing songs recorded during and immediately following the *Sgt. Pepper* sessions, was in its first of eight straight weeks at the top. The Rolling Stones' Pepper-influenced *Their Satanic Majesties Request* was at number two, followed by The Monkees' *Pisces, Aquarius, Capricorn & Jones, Ltd.*

The Billboard Hot 100 was more of the same with The Beatles' "Hello Goodbye" and The Monkees' "Daydream Believer" holding down the top two spots. The number three song was not by a Lonely Hearts Club Band, but rather by a Playboy Band. John Fred & His Playboy Band's "Judy In Disguise (With Glasses)," a playful rocker parodying the title and lyrical wordplay of "Lucy In The Sky With Diamonds," would soon top the charts for two weeks. But the most interesting Pepper artifact was "Summer Rain," a Johnny Rivers single reaching its peak of 14. The song, written by Jim Hendricks, contains the following lyrics during its first bridge: "All summer long, we spent dancin' in the sand/And the jukebox kept on playin' Sgt. Pepper's Lonely Hearts Club Band."

These words form a wonderful image of the Summer of Love. One can visualize the youth of America dressed in brightly-colored clothes collectively dancing to the sounds of *Sgt. Pepper* flowing out of car speakers, transistor radios, record players and jukeboxes throughout the land. But there's one slight problem. None of the songs from the album were available in the singles format that summer. Nor did Capitol Records issue a Compact 33 of *Sgt. Pepper* for jukebox play. Put simply, no jukeboxes played *Sgt. Pepper's Lonely Hearts Club Band*. It just seemed that way. Everywhere you went that summer, that's what you heard. The jukebox is a metaphor for all the stereos, hi-fi record players and radios in the land.

Humanities and social sciences professor Langdon Winner, a former contributing editor for Rolling Stone, summed it up best the following year. "The closest Western Civilization has come to unity since the Congress of Vienna in 1815 was the week the *Sergeant Pepper* album was released. In every city in Europe and America the stereo systems and the radio played, 'What would you think if I sang out of tune … Woke up, got out of bed …looked much older, and the bag across her shoulder … in the sky with diamonds, Lucy in the …,' and everyone listened. At the time I happened to be driving across country on Interstate 80. In each city where I stopped for gas or food—Laramie, Ogallala, Moline, South Bend—the melodies wafted in from some far-off transistor radio or portable hi-fi. It was the most amazing thing I ever heard. For a brief while the irreparably fragmented conscious of the West was reunified, at least in the minds of the young."

This consciousness went well beyond the music. People weren't just dancing or listening to *Sgt. Pepper*. They were thinking and talking about The Beatles extraordinary new album. From its elaborate packaging to the notes in the grooves, *Sgt. Pepper's Lonely Hearts Club Band* was an experience unlike any other that had come before. It caught everyone off guard even though The Beatles' previous releases had shown remarkable growth. The clues of what lie ahead were there.

including and Eleanor Rigby

With their previous album, *Revolver*, The Beatles experimented with new sounds. In "Eleanor Rigby," Paul's haunting lyrics are sung over a backing consisting exclusively of a double string quartet. George's "Love You To" is dominated by Indian percussion and string instruments such as tabla and sitar. Ringo leads the joyous sing-along "Yellow Submarine," a children's song highlighted by sound effects, a catchy chorus and an overall party atmosphere. "Got To Get You Into My Life," later described by Paul as "an ode to pot," was embellished with brass and saxophones. But it was John's "Tomorrow Never Knows" that opened the door to the group's psychedelic phase. With its relentless tribal beat, tape loop sound effects and John's voice fed through a rotating Leslie speaker, it sounded unlike anything The Beatles or anyone else had ever recorded.

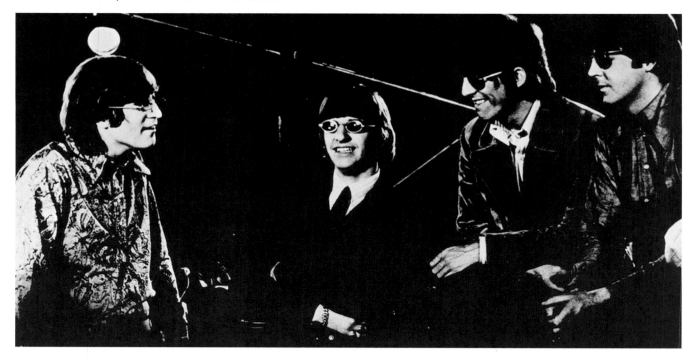

The group's next single consisted of a pair of songs recorded during the early stages of the *Sgt. Pepper* sessions that, but for the need of getting a Beatles single to market, would have been on the album. The record was released three and a half months ahead of the album in mid-February 1967. It was a fantastic double A-side disc showcasing the group's lyrical and musical development. Both songs were inspired by childhood memories of Liverpool.

"Strawberry Fields Forever" is a psychedelic opus with thought-provoking lyrics. It opens slowly with mellotron and John's dreamy vocal before building to a heavy-sounding tour-de-force of active percussion, swarmandal (an Indian harp-like instrument), guitars, trumpets and cellos, complete with a false ending that fades and comes back only to fade away again. Once again, The Beatles had challenged us with a recording unlike anything we had ever heard before.

In contrast, Paul's "Penny Lane" is an up-tempo song full of nostalgic images of the bus roundabout and surrounding suburban Liverpool neighborhood frequented by Paul and John during their youth. The song's keyboard backing track is embellished with flutes, piccolo, trumpets, flugelhorn, string bass and a distinctive piccolo trumpet solo heard towards the end of the song.

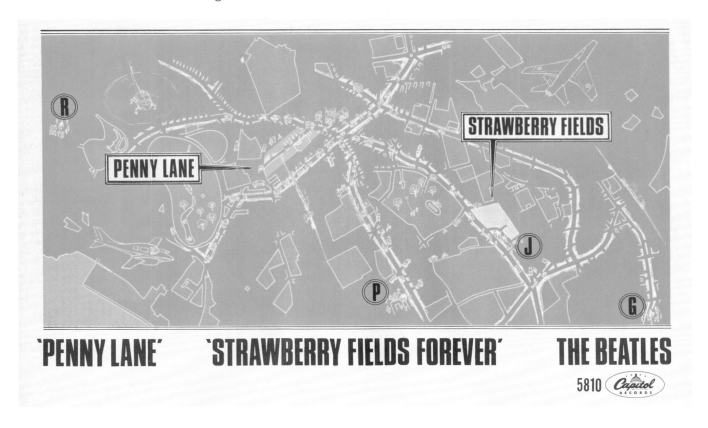

In America, the Capitol promotional copy of the single contained a seven-note piccolo trumpet flourish at the very end that is not present in the remixed version of the song appearing on the released single. The extra piccolo trumpet notes were unique to listeners of American radio stations playing the promo disc. When we played the 45 at home, some of us wondered "where did those notes go?"

Although both sides of the disc were promoted equally, disc jockeys and listeners in America responded more favorably to the more upbeat "Penny Lane," which topped the Billboard Hot 100 for one week and the Cash Box and Record World charts for two weeks. "Strawberry Fields Forever" made the top ten of all three national charts, peaking at eight in Billboard, nine in Record World and ten in Cash Box. The April 1, 1967, Billboard reported that the single had RIAA-certified sales of over one million units, giving The Beatles yet another gold record.

The Beatles, recognizing the special nature of their new release, requested that the single be issued in a custom picture sleeve prepared with their input. (Although all of Capitol's Beatles singles had been packaged in picture sleeves, this was the first Beatles U.K. single to have its own sleeve.) One side of the sleeve features a striking color photograph of the group, complete with facial hair and mod clothing, taken by Henry Grossman. Four bright lights pointing at the camera add an eye-catching star-burst effect. The photo is surrounded by a gilded frame. The other side is designed to look like a page from a photo album, complete with mounting corners and a childhood photo of each member of the group.

5810

The Beatles

The Beatles also prepared elaborate promotional films for the songs, once again boldly going where no band had gone before. Rather than being mere performance clips, the color films show images of the band and various locations to portray the feeling and mood of the songs. The films were shot in late January and early February, 1967, in Knole Park, near Sevenoaks, Kent, and Angel Lane, Stratford, London. The films were produced by Tony Bramwell and directed by Peter Goldmann.

For "Strawberry Fields Forever," close-ups of the group's faces were intercut with scenes of The Beatles romping past kettle drums in a field, playing around a large dead oak tree and pouring and brushing brightly colored paint on a piano. The "Penny Lane" video mixed places from the song (the Penny Lane sign, the barber shop and the bus shelter in the middle of the roundabout) with shots of The Beatles. The film's most telling sequence has the group, on horseback, symbolically ride past their instruments and equipment set up on risers for a performance that never takes place. It was as if The Beatles were telling us "we've gone past that."

The films made their American television debut on Saturday night, February 25, 1967, on ABC's "Hollywood Palace," a variety show broadcast in color and aimed at an adult audience. Three weeks later the clips were seen by younger viewers in black and white on the March 11 edition of "American Bandstand." After showing the videos, host Dick Clark asked members of the teenaged audience what they thought. Most of the girls had negative comments, particularly about the group's new facial hair. "Their moustaches are weird." "They're ugly." "They're like grandfathers or something." One boy observed, "They look older and it ruins their image." Towards the end, some of the teenagers clapped when one girl said, "I thought they looked good," and a boy added, "They have the right to look anyway they want." The segment ended in laughter with one of the males joking "Not much of a change."

The Beatles' radically different appearance, while offensive to some fans, let the world know that the youthful innocent four mop tops had evolved into mature, serious and innovative musicians.

The group's new image and attention to detail in the music and packaging of their records continued with *Sgt. Pepper*, which became the first Beatles album issued in America that had the same cover and songs as the British LP. The front cover is a 12" x 12" work of art, a gallery of cardboard faces and full-size wax figures of a crowd augmented with props, plants and a painted bass drum. Some of the faces were familiar, but many were a mystery to most. Just who were these people? They must be important and influential if they're on the cover of a Beatles album. And the plants at the group's feet: were those really marijuana leaves or did they just look that way? A small television set, dolls and curios. What did it all mean?

The Beatles had mustaches and were dressed in colorful military-style uniforms holding instruments associated with brass bands and symphonies. These were not your older sister's Beatles. For this album, John, Paul, George and Ringo were not even The Beatles. They were Sgt. Pepper's Lonely Hearts Club Band. And to drive home the point, this new incarnation of The Beatles was standing next to vintage 1963/1964-era figures of the boys borrowed from the London branch of Madame Tussauds Wax Museum.

The inside of the gatefold cover contained a color portrait of the group in their Sgt. Pepper uniforms. The back cover featured another picture of the colorfully-clad band, this one with Paul's back to the camera. What was that about? And, to show that the words were as important as the music, the lyrics were printed on the back cover, enabling the listener to follow along with the songs or just read the words as poetry. No rock album had done that before.

The packaging included a green background cardboard sheet containing cutout images of a moustache, a picture card of Sgt. Pepper, uniform stripes, badges of the Sgt. Pepper logo and bust of Sgt. Pepper and a standup of the group in their Sgt. Pepper uniforms. The record was housed in a custom psychedelic inner sleeve, dripping with pink and red colors. Was that what an acid trip really looked like?

And that was before even placing the record on the turntable and dropping the needle!

The Beatles previous album, *Revolver*, began with sounds of the studio—a slow, lazy count-in augmented by tape sounds and a cough. *Sgt. Pepper* places us at a concert. We hear the crowd settling in and the band warming up. And then we hear the guitars and the rest of the band falling into place. Paul quickly informs us "It was 20 years ago today/Sgt. Pepper taught the band to play." His introductory verse is followed by a change in tempo, the introduction of horns and laughter and applause from the crowd. And then The Beatles complete the illusion of the mythical brass band depicted on the cover: "We're Sgt. Pepper's Lonely Hearts Club Band/We hope you will enjoy the show."

And what a show it turns out to be. Thirteen songs interrupted only by the time needed to flip the completed first side over and place the needle at the start of the second side. The customary three to six-second gaps between tracks were eliminated by the use of segues, cross-fades and split-second breaks between songs.

But back to the title track. Forget about the gimmicks and change of identity. "Sgt. Pepper's Lonely Hearts Club Band" is a great rock 'n' roll song. Paul delivers one of his most dynamic rock vocals, right up there with "Long Tall Sally," "Kansas City" and "I'm Down." The stinging guitars are equally impressive.

The opening song ends with Paul continuing in his role as master of ceremonies: "So let me introduce to you the one and only Billy Shears and Sgt. Pepper's Lonely Hearts Club Band." This segues into the next selection with screaming fans and the group singing "Bil–ly Shears" in three ascending notes over a Hammond organ.

Ringo takes on the Billy Shears persona and delivers one of his greatest vocals. "What would you think if I sang out of tune/Would you stand up and walk out on me?" Not a chance. We're here for the show. "With A Little Help From My Friends" is a delightful song with a positive message. It is the perfect vehicle for Ringo, telling us he gets by with a little help from his friends and believes in a love at first sight. The song moves in a steady groove, propelled by Paul's piano and melodic bass lines, John's choppy rhythm guitar, George's lead guitar and Ringo's drums. The song literally ends on a high note sung by Ringo, sweetened with harmonies from his friends.

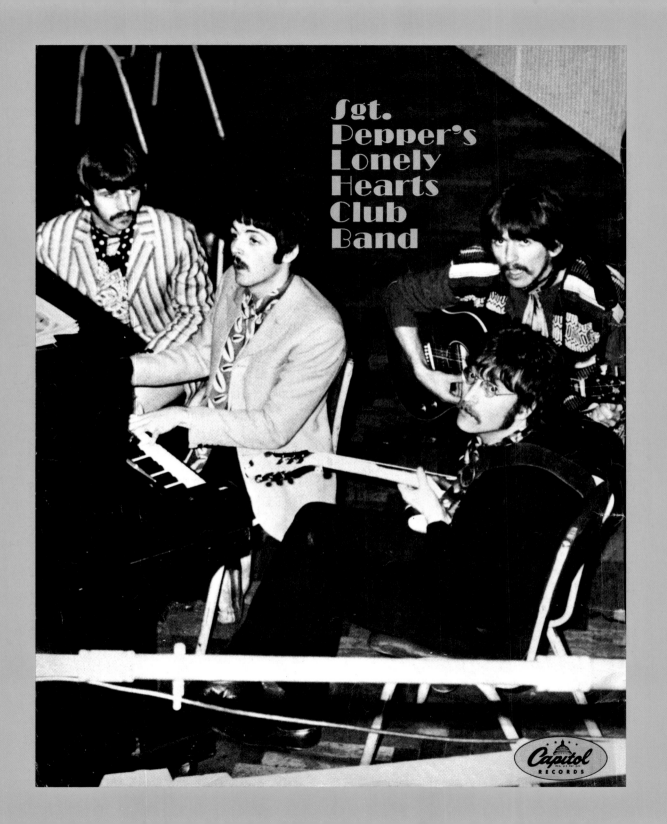

This is followed immediately by the dreamy opening notes of "Lucy In The Sky With Diamonds," a song full of lyrics dripping with psychedelic drug imagery, although actually inspired by Lewis Carroll's books "Through The Looking Glass" and "Alice's Adventures In Wonderland." John sings lead, with Paul joining him on the choruses. The backing track, full of phasing sounds, is highlighted by a catchy riff matched by Paul on organ and George on guitar, Paul's melodic bass lines and Ringo's drumming, particularly effective at the end of verses leading into the chorus.

Each of the album's opening three songs stands on its own, but together they flow seamlessly and are embedded in our consciousness as if part of a medley.

"Getting Better" shuffles along at a steady beat with Paul delivering the song's optimistic chorus that overshadows its darker side. We could all identify with the line "The teachers who taught me weren't cool," but learning of the singer beating his woman would have been tough to take had he not sung "Man I was mean, but I'm changing my scene and doing the best that I can." The musical backing includes John's steady rhythm guitar, Paul's bass, Ringo's drums and George Martin on pianette.

"Fixing A Hole" opens with George Martin on harpsichord, a keyboard instrument frequently used in Renaissance and Baroque music that had crept into American pop culture through Lurch playing it on the opening theme to the TV series The Addams Family. The backing track also includes an excellent guitar solo by George, John on rhythm guitar, Paul on bass and Ringo on drums. The song's lyrics left our minds wandering. Was it about metaphorically mending things? Fixing a hole, filling a crack. Or the freedom to do what you want? Painting a room in a colorful way. Our bedrooms were our sanctuaries, lined with colorful posters. Why not paint the walls as well?

"She's Leaving Home," like the previous track, starts with an instrument not normally heard in rock or pop songs, this time a harp. As was the case with "Eleanor Rigby," none of the Beatles plays an instrument on the song, whose backing also includes four violins, two violas, two cellos and a double-bass. Paul tells the tale of a young girl running away from home, while John provides the point of view of her parents, who sacrificed for her and don't understand why she left. Although most listeners would never seriously consider running away from home, we all knew someone who did, even if just for a little while. We could identify with her. This generation gap saga was dramatized a year later (June 23, 1968) on the premier episode of "The Summer Brothers Smothers Show," sung by host Glen Campbell and acted by Tom and Dick Smothers as the parents and guest Nancy Sinatra as the young runaway.

Side One ends with a night at the circus, courtesy of John's "Being For The Benefit Of Mr. Kite!" The song's initial backing of George Martin on harmonium, Paul on bass, Ringo on drums and George Harrison on tambourine was augmented with harmonica, guitar, organ and tape loops of steam organ music creating the atmosphere of the big tent. We all grew up with Ringling Bros. and Barnum & Bailey Circus. John gave us the mid-nineteenth century British equivalent, with words pulled from a poster promoting the February 14, 1843, performance of Pablo Fanque's Circus Royal.

SGT. PEPPER'S
LONELY HEARTS CLUB BAND
THE BEATLES

STEREO   SMAS-2653
(SMAS-X-1-2653) 1

1. SGT. PEPPER'S LONELY HEARTS CLUB BAND (BMI-1:59)
(Lennon-McCartney)
2. WITH A LITTLE HELP FROM MY FRIENDS (BMI-2:46)
(Lennon-McCartney)
3. LUCY IN THE SKY WITH DIAMONDS (BMI-3:25)
(Lennon-McCartney)
4. GETTING BETTER (BMI-2:47) (Lennon-McCartney)
5. FIXING A HOLE (BMI-2:33) (Lennon-McCartney)
6. SHE'S LEAVING HOME (BMI-3:24)
(Lennon-McCartney)
7. BEING FOR THE BENEFIT OF MR. KITE
(BMI-2:36) (Lennon-McCartney)
Produced in England by
George Martin

SGT. PEPPER'S
LONELY HEARTS CLUB BAND
THE BEATLES

STEREO   SMAS-2653
(SMAS-X-2-2653) 2

1. WITHIN YOU WITHOUT YOU (BMI-5:03)
(George Harrison)
2. WHEN I'M SIXTY-FOUR (BMI-2:38)
(Lennon-McCartney)
3. LOVELY RITA (BMI-2:43)
(Lennon-McCartney)
4. GOOD MORNING GOOD MORNING
(BMI-2:35) (Lennon-McCartney)
5. SGT. PEPPER'S LONELY HEARTS CLUB
BAND - REPRISE (BMI-1:20)
(Lennon-McCartney)
6. A DAY IN THE LIFE (BMI-5:03)
(Lennon-McCartney)
Produced in England by
George Martin

Side Two opens with George Harrison's "Within You, Without You." We have left the childhood innocence of the circus far behind, heading for something mystical and meaningful. The song blends Indian instruments with symphonic strings. George plays sitar and sings "We were talking about the space between us all." We would soon be talking about the song and what it meant, along with the rest of the album. "With our love we could save the world, if they only knew." We took it seriously, but to make sure we didn't take it too seriously, the track was followed by laughter.

Paul's "When I'm Sixty-Four" is a bouncy tune featuring his bass and piano, Ringo on drums with brushes and strategically placed chimes, and John on guitar, augmented by two clarinets and a bass clarinet. Its nostalgic vaudeville sound sets the song apart from the psychedelic and mystical sounds of the album's other tracks. To us, being sixty-four with grandchildren on our knees seemed so far away, but we could still appreciate the humor ("Will you still need me? Will you still feed me?") and the imagery in the lyrics. If The Beatles were poking fun at growing old, they were doing it in a charming and loving way. And lest we laugh too hard, the song contains a somewhat ominous warning: "You'll be older too."

The tongue-in-cheek mood continues with "Lovely Rita," Paul's tale about a sexy meter maid. Although the song contains a vaudeville touch or two, it is a return to rock 'n' roll with Paul on piano and bass, John and George on acoustic guitars and Ringo on drums. George Martin adds a honky-tonk style piano solo. The song's climatic ending is highlighted by Ringo's energetic drumming and John's vocal shenanigans with moans and sighs. Maybe Paul made it with Rita after all.

"Good Morning, Good Morning" opens with the sound of a crowing rooster, horns and the "Good Morning" chorus. While John sings of mundane suburban life, the song's music is far from mundane. It is full of energy, led by Paul's hyperactive yet melodic bass, Ringo's pounding drums, hard-driving horns (three saxophones, two trombones and a French horn), George's rhythm guitar and a stinging guitar solo by Paul. Towards the end of the song, the rooster returns, followed by animal sound effects of cats, dogs, horses, sheep, lions and elephants. The sounds escalate into a fox hunt, complete with pursuing bloodhounds and horses that gallop across the room on stereo systems. The song ends with a clucking hen that blends into George's bending guitar note leading into a reprise of the title track.

We had all heard Paul's energetic "One, two, three, faaa!" count-in to "I Saw Her Standing There" numerous times in early 1964 (Spring 1963 if you lived in the U.K.). Here he was again, counting-in another great rocker, "Sgt. Pepper's Lonely Hearts Club Band (Reprise)." Between the "two" and the "three" we heard John tell us "bye" in a dreamy voice. There was applause and laughter and great rock 'n' roll, with John and George on guitar, Paul on bass, overdubbed Hammond organ (John) and Ringo on drums. The band told us they were sorry but it was time to go. They graciously thanked us and sang "We hope you have enjoyed the show." They needn't have worried. We certainly enjoyed the show. But it wasn't over yet. The album's final track is *Sgt. Pepper*'s most memorable and most provocative.

"A Day In The Life" opens simply enough with John's acoustic guitar and Paul's piano, soon joined by John's wonderful opening line "I read the news today, oh boy." The first verse is about a man who "blew his mind out in a car." We knew he had died in a car crash, but wasn't that also a drug reference? "A crowd of people stood and stared." Well that was human nature, wasn't it? The second verse was about a film in which the English army had just won the war. This time, the crowd turned away, but John had to look having read the book. John and Paul then sing "I'd love to turn you on." As we were absorbing that message, the song builds to a chaotic climb of piano and symphonic noise interrupted by a ringing alarm clock leading into the middle part of the song. This time, it's Paul's turn. "Woke up, fell out of bed, dragged a comb across my head." After catching the bus, he climbs the stairs to the upper deck and has a smoke. Paul then sings "Somebody spoke and I went into a dream," leading into a vocal dream sequence that brings it all back home to "I read the news today, oh boy" and John's final verse about 4,000 holes in Blackburn, Lancashire filling the Albert Hall. At the time we had no idea what that was all about, but it sounded cool. After a repeat of "I'd love to turn you on," the song once again spirals into symphonic chaos before coming to an abrupt halt followed by a long-fading chord played on multiple keyboards.

George Martin had concerns over whether he and The Beatles "were being a bit pretentious, a bit clever-clever" with the album, but he gained confidence after a visit from Capitol Records president Alan Livingston.

According to Martin: "I played him 'A Day In The Life.' It knocked him sideways. He was completely flabbergasted by it. He was in no way perturbed by any aspect of the song, by its relatively bizarre lyrics or its avant-garde production— only speechless with admiration. I knew then we were home and dry. I suppose I had been worried that we might be leaving our public behind, getting a bit too far in front. If Alan Livingston liked it, though...."

Livingston recalled George Martin and Paul playing that tape of "A Day In The Life" at Abbey Road. "I was fascinated with it. Absolutely delighted with what I heard."

Capitol did not add the high-pitched tone and inner groove gibberish placed at the end of the fading chord of "A Day In The Life" on British and some of the other pressings of the album. And looking back, it's just as well. Perhaps The Beatles got a little bit too cute on that one. For us in America, that chaotic orchestral climb and ominous ending chord sounded like the end of the world. It was seared into our minds, the somber mood uninterrupted, leaving us in awe.

At the time of the album's release, AM was king, with the ears of America's youth glued to Top 40 stations. The popular radio format placed the most popular 40 or so songs of the week in moderate to heavy rotation, sneaking in a small sampling of oldies and just-released potential hits. The rise of FM stations and their AOR (album-oriented radio) format was still in its embryonic stage. With none of *Sgt. Pepper*'s songs available on 45s or appearing on the national singles charts, one would have expected Top 40 stations to ignore the album. But, as was often the case, an exception was made for The Beatles.

At least two New York stations played a tape of "A Day In The Life" originating from an acetate source in mid-April 1967. WABC's April 18 All American Survey listed "I Read the News Today" by The Beatles as a "First and Exclusive on WABC!" In an interview appearing in the June 24, 1967 issue of The New Yorker, WMCA disc jockey Joe O'Brien claimed his station was the first to play "A Day In The Life," also citing an April 18 air date. The song was quickly removed from rotation by both stations after they received complaints from Beatles attorney Nat Weiss, who was based in New York. Other stations in other cities also played the song.

Los Angeles radio station KRLA obtained a vinyl pressing of *Sgt. Pepper* in late April 1967, more than a month ahead of the album's release, from a Capitol Records employee working in the company's LA pressing plant. Disc jockey Dave Hull played songs from the unreleased LP as "KRLA exclusives" for a few days until being temporarily fired by the station's program director, who was concerned about retribution from Capitol.

WMCA began playing selected tracks from *Sgt. Pepper* on May 4, starting with "She's Leaving Home," after obtaining an advance pressing of the LP from the U.K. Although the American reporter for Britain's New Musical Express reported that disc jockey Gary Stevens had smuggled the album out of England, Stevens later admitted it was not quite that exotic. He only recalls playing tracks from the LP for a few days until the station was ordered to stop by attorney Weiss. When the album became available for radio airplay towards the end of May, WMCA temporarily wandered from its top 40 format by playing all of its songs, with a heavy emphasis on "When I'm Sixty-Four."

WABC played several songs from *Sgt. Pepper* starting late May and continuing throughout June, but did not include them in the numerical listings of its weekly survey, which was based more on record sales than listener requests. Instead, "Lucy In The Sky With Diamonds," "Getting Better," "Lovely Rita" and "She's Leaving Home" appeared under the heading "Album Cuts." Seattle's KJR, whose charts focused more on requests, assigned numbers to several of the songs, including the following peak listings: "She's Leaving Home" (26); "When I'm Sixty-Four" (23); "Sgt. Pepper's Lonely Hearts Club Band" (17); and "Lovely Rita" (5).

While "A Day In The Life" was banned by BBC radio for its alleged drug references, some American stations, particularly on the West Coast, embraced the song. The KRLA surveys dated July 1 and July 8, 1967, showed "A Day In The Life" at number two, behind "Light My Fire" by The Doors, a local LA band that was exploding onto the national scene. KJR had the song at number six for two weeks in June.

Although jukeboxes weren't playing *Sgt. Pepper's Lonely Hearts Club Band*, AM radio stations throughout the United States were.

When we in America heard the songs from *Sgt. Pepper* on the radio, they were the mono versions. But when we listened to the album at home or at a friend's house, it was almost always the stereo disc. By mid-1967, mono was on its way to being completely phased out by most U.S. record companies. Radio stations still received mono records for air play, but by then most consumers were purchasing stereo albums. If you didn't yet have a stereo player, you hoped or expected to get one soon. Those who bought *Sgt. Pepper* in mono didn't do so because they thought it sounded better, they did so because mono albums cost a dollar less than stereo albums. Within a year of the album's release, it didn't matter. Capitol Records was no longer pressing mono discs. If you were late in buying *Sgt. Pepper* or were replacing your trusty worn-out original copy, your only option was stereo.

While listeners in the British Isles were almost exclusively experiencing *Sgt. Pepper* in mono, for us it was stereo. Years later we were told that you hadn't really heard *Sgt. Pepper* unless you heard it in mono. We learned that The Beatles spent most of their time on the mono mixes, which had subtle touches not present in the stereo mixes. But to our ears, the stereo version of the album was pretty damn cool. And dare it be said, in some cases a more interesting listening experience.

In the stereo "Good Morning, Good Morning," the animal effects at the end of the song move from the right to the left speaker, giving the effect of the animals running across the room. At the end of the song, the stereo edit of the clucking hen and George's bending guitar note is smoother than the mono edit, which is awkward, giving the guitar note a jerky sound. On "A Day In The Life," John's lead vocal is in the right channel for the first five lines, but pans to the center during the next five. For the verse about the film, it pans from center to left and stays there for "I'd love to turn you on." Paul's vocal in the song's midsection is in the left channel, while the transitional "ahs" pan between channels. John's voice appears in the left for the final verse, but is double-tracked right at the end of the verse. "I'd love to turn you on" is heard from both sides. The shifting vocals add to the other-worldliness of the song.

Back on our world, we, the fans, knew The Beatles had given us something special. But would the critics and others take notice?

The June 10, 1967 Billboard contained a Pop Spotlight review of *Sgt. Pepper* that made the following obvious prediction: "This inventive album by the inventive Beatles should zool [zoom] to the top of the charts in short order." The review listed the top cuts as the title song, "Getting Better," "Fixing A Hole" and "Good Morning." George Harrison's "Within You, Without You" was called "another gem."

Sgt. Pepper debuted at number eight in the Billboard Top LP's chart dated June 24, 1967. At the time, the top albums included: greatest hits collections from The Lovin' Spoonful (#14), Bob Dylan (#12) and Paul Revere & The Raiders (#11); soundtracks from *The Sound Of Music* (#15), *A Man And A Woman* (#13) and *Dr. Zhivago* (#10), along with the Roger Williams album *Born Free* (#5) featuring the title song from that film; The Mamas and The Papas' latest album, *Deliver* (#9); Jefferson Airplane's *Surrealistic Pillow* (#6); Aretha Franklin's *I Never Loved A Man The Way I Love You* (#4); comedian Bill Cosby's *Revenge* (#3); and *Sounds Like* by Herb Alpert and The Tijuana Brass (#2).

However, the main competition for The Beatles was The Monkees, who had three of the top albums with their debut LP, *The Monkees*, still high on the charts at 16, *More Of The Monkees* at seven and their new *Headquarters* LP at number one. The Monkees had become what The Beatles once were. They were four long-haired individuals with unique personalities, stylishly-dressed in matching outfits. While we in America had formed our images of The Beatles from The Ed Sullivan Show and two movies, The Monkees had a television series that aired every Monday night. The Beatles politely made fun of authority in their films and press conferences; The Monkees did it every week in our living rooms. We knew their names and their traits. Although Micky and Davy handled most of the lead vocals, Mike and Peter also took their turns. Young girls had their favorite Monkee and pictures of the group on their walls. The Monkees were the darlings of teen magazines. They were four likeable young lads who were releasing catchy well-produced hit singles every few months and selling tons of records.

The Beatles had moved beyond their boy band days. Many of their younger fans had welcomed or even defected to The Monkees. Were The Beatles still on top or had The Monkees taken over? It was *Sgt. Pepper* head-to-head with *Headquarters*. Who would prevail?

Sgt. Pepper knocked *Headquarters* down to the second spot in short order on the July 1 Billboard Top LP's chart. For 11 weeks, it was The Beatles at one and The Monkess at two, before The Doors pushed The Monkees down to three. It was a similar story in Cash Box and Record World, with *Headquarters* also being replaced by *Sgt. Pepper* after only one week at the top. The Beatles album remained in the top spot for 15 straight weeks in Billboard, holding off not only The Monkees, but also The Doors (self-titled debut LP), Jefferson Airplane (*Surrealistic Pillow*), The Young Rascals (*Groovin'*) and The Rolling Stones (*Flowers*), before giving way to Bobbie Gentry's *Ode To Billie Joe* LP. *Sgt. Pepper* was number one for 14 weeks in Cash Box and 13 in Record World. The Beatles were still number one.

As reflected by the charts, U.S. sales of the album were brisk, with 1.5 million copies sold in its first two weeks. *Sgt. Pepper* was certified gold by the Recording Industry Association of America on June 15, 1967. After three months, sales were reported at over 2,500,000 copies. By its 30th anniversary, the album had surpassed diamond status of 10 million units and was at certified sales of 11 million.

Sgt. Pepper was issued prior to the emergence of American music magazines such as Rolling Stone and Creem. Crawdaddy!, which billed itself as "The Magazine of Rock," was in its infancy at the time, founded in February 1966 by Swarthmore College student Paul Williams. Issue #10, cover dated July-August 1967, contained a "Preliminary Review of Sergeant Pepper" that was nothing more than a single-page collage by Bhob Stewart containing the lyrics "Good Morning, Good Morning" and "I have to admit it's getting better" and the message "WE LOVE the BEATLES— friends and crawdaddy." The issue also referenced Sgt. Pepper in an article on the San Francisco music scene and in its current events section titled "What Goes On," which commented on the way the mass media covered Sgt. Pepper "not as a phenomenon, but as a work of art to review."

Crawdaddy Issue #11, dated October [1967], featured a green color-saturated photo of Paul taken by his future wife, Linda Eastman. The issue did not contain a conventional review of Sgt. Pepper, but had five items pertaining to the album.

Richard Meltzer wrote a rambling piece dated July 4, 1967, and titled "My Sergeant Pepper Trip," which opens with "I feel like I just woke up on a different planet." Meltzer goes on to say that "Sgt. Pepper has more than 49 focal points, maybe even 50, or 242 million and five, and they're all grabbing at you and you're a great big data freak taking it all in and it's hard. And when you see it all you know there's more and more."

Don McNeill wrote a "Report on the State of the Beatles," in which he proclaimed: "The Beatles are dead! Long live the Beatles! There they are, the metamorphosis complete, standing on the flowered grave of their former selves... The end has become the beginning."

Gary Blackman conducted a faux interview between Crawdaddy and the group, which allegedly took place "Between the Floors" in a stalled London elevator. Most of the Beatles' answers were lyrics from the album. Paul Williams contributed "Sergeant Pepper As Noise" and Rafael Black drew a Toulouse-Lautrec-influenced picture of a cosmic-looking nude woman titled "Lucy in the Sky."

CRAWDADDY!
october   50¢

ROCK

Sgt PEPPER NOISE

-13-

GIRL WITH

OSCOPE EYES

Crawdaddy

WE LOVE the BEATLES-
friends and crawdaddy

I HAVE TO ADMIT IT'S GETTING BETTER.

GooD MORNing GooD MORNing

REPORT
ON THE STATE OF THE BEATLES

The Beatles are dead! Long live the Beatles! There they are, the metamorphosis complete, standing on the flowered grave of their former selves. There they are, in solid flesh,
evidence as indisputable as the rock rolled away from the cave. There they are, in butterfly
brilliance, their waxen images set nearby like the larva of a former life. Consider the im-
plications. Is it true what acid can do?

One is tempted to call it a comeback. Throughout the winter, there was a sense of the
inevitability of the downfall of the Beatles, highlighted by Lennon's Christ comment. They've
gone too far! They can't go farther! And they said they were breaking up. Suddenly, with
Sgt. Pepper, all this is over. The end became the beginning.

The American news weeklies, Time, Life and Newsweek, provided coverage of Sgt. Pepper that was more conventional than Crawdaddy's free-spirit approach. In these June 1967 magazines, we were reading the news on how Israel had just won the Six-Day War in the Middle East at the same time we were listening to John sing "the English army had just won the war."

In its issue dated June 14, 1967, Time paid tribute to Beatles producer George Martin in its story titled "Mix-Master to the Beatles," which began "George Martin's new LP was out last week." While Martin's role was significant, the Time piece seemed to ignore the contributions of John, Paul, the other George and Ringo. This oversight was rectified three months later when Time placed The Beatles on the cover of its September 22 issue and proclaimed the group as "The Messengers." The magazine noted that, "Without having lost any of the genial anarchism which helped them revolutionize the life style of young people in Britain, Europe and the U.S., they have moved on to a higher artistic plateau" and "have exercised a compulsion for growth, change and experimentation." Time recognized that the Beatles were "creating the most original, expressive and musically interesting sounds being heard in pop music" and noted that "'Serious musicians' are listening to them and marking their work as a historic departure in the progress of music—any music."

Newsweek's review of Sgt. Pepper was written by the magazine's drama and film critic, Jack Kroll, who titled his piece "'It's Getting Better...'" Kroll stated that The Beatles should be chosen as Britain's new Poet Laureate. He described Sgt. Pepper as a "rollicking, probing language-and-sound vaudeville, which grafts skin from all three brows—high, middle and low—into a pulsating collage about mid-century manners and madness." He commented on the group's lost innocence, citing comparisons to the writings of British poets Edith Sitwell, William Wordsworth and Alfred Lord Tennyson, British playwrights John Osborne and Harold Pinter and American author Donald Barthelme. The orchestral buildup of "A Day In The Life" is described as a "growling, bone-grinding crescendo that drones up like a giant turbine struggling to spin new power into a foundered civilization." Kroll recognizes the song as the Beatles equivalent to T.S. Eliot's massive masterpiece poem "The Waste Land," calling the album's closing track "a superb achievement of their brilliant and startlingly effective popular art."

SHOW BUSINESS

RECORDS

Mix-Master to the Beatles

George Martin's new LP was out last week, and U.S. record dealers had placed orders for more than 1,000,000 copies before it was even released. So it has already been awarded the record industry's coveted gold disk—the 23rd for Martin. Of course, the album is not actually under Martin's name, although he produced it, scored all the arrangements for it, performed on several tracks, and served as its mad electronic scientist. It is called *Sgt. Pepper's Lonely Hearts Club Band*, and it features the group whose sound Martin has

more than three mo...
six in...
left...
wi...
ab...
M...
sc...
N...

DEREK BAYES

MARTIN AT RECORDING SESSION
The head behind the hair...

helped to create and shape sin...
first recording session five ye...
the Beatles.

Martin, 41, is a lean, precise...
er with short hair and a back...
second oboist in the old Sad...
orchestra. He was a senior p...
England's EMI records whe...
unknown Beatles—already...
several recording firms, inc...
—pleaded for an audition...
any double somersaults,...
"The material wasn't very...
he liked them well enough...
a recording contract, and...
out with a firm hand: "I t...
much what to do."

Pillow to Pot. Things...
considerably since the...
George Harrison puts it...
the freedom to please o...
this means for Martin is...
place far greater dema...
dio than any other grou...
Where their first albu...
songs they had evolved...
corded in a single day...

ALAN CLIFTON

Gerald Scarfe

THE BEATLES / Their New Incarnation

VOL. 90 NO. 12
(REG. U.S. PAT. OFF.)

Life ran a story titled "The New Far-Out Beatles," which detailed the recording of some of the album's songs, complete with pictures of the group at Abbey Road. The magazine proclaimed "They're grown men now and creating extraordinary musical sounds." Life wondered whether The Beatles were "stepping far ahead of their audience, recording music too complex and so unlike the music that made them successful that they could very likely lose the foundation of their support." While this seemed to be a legitimate concern, Life failed to realize that we were growing and expanding our cultural tastes along with The Beatles. And, equally important, the music was so damn good that we were willing to keep up with them. The evolving depth, complexity and maturity of their recordings gained The Beatles new fans who could no longer try to dismiss their work as teenybopper music.

While most critics praised the album, a notable exception appeared in The New York Times courtesy of Richard Goldstein, who found the album's overall effect "busy, hip and cluttered." Referring to the unprecedented four months and $100,000 spent on the album, he compared it to "an over-attended child," calling the LP "spoiled." Goldstein complained of the "surprising shoddiness in composition" and stated that "the Beatles have given us an album of special effects, dazzling but ultimately fraudulent." He did, however, recognize the brilliance of "A Day In The Life," devoting nearly half of his review to the song, calling it a terrifying glimpse of modern city life and a "historic Pop event." He lamented that "A Day In The Life" was "only a coda to an otherwise undistinguished collection of work."

The New Yorker covered the release of *Sgt. Pepper* in its "The Talk of the Town" section as if it were an event, focusing on interviews with disc jockeys and reactions of record store customers. Murray the K, who in 1964 dubbed himself as the Fifth Beatle, proclaimed, "The Beatles had the guts to go ahead and do something different from anything they've ever done before." He indicated he was playing the entire album, non-stop, on his show on WOR-FM. WMCA's Joe O'Brien observed that "college students are now the hard-core Beatles fans." O'Brien's son, who was a freshman at Yale, told his father that the day the album was issued, the entire student body of Yale went out and bought it. His son further reported that exactly the same thing happened at Harvard.

LIFE

ASIA EDITION

The New Far-out Beatles

MARIJUANA'S TURNED-ON MILLIONS

**WHY MA SITSON
FLED CHINA, PART II**

The Beatles

BURMA...........K 1.25
CEYLON..........Rs 1.25
GUAM/OKINAWA......25¢
HONG KONG...HK$ 1.80
INDIA...........Rs 2.25
INDONESIA......Rp 25
JAPAN..........100 Yen
KOREA..........70 Won
LAOS...........K 150
MALAYSIA......M$ 0.75
NEPAL........N.Rs 2.00
PAKISTAN......Rs 1.25
PHILIPPINES....P 1.00
SINGAPORE....S$ 0.75
TAIWAN........NT$ 10
THAILAND......B 5
U.S. ARMED FORCES 25¢
VIET NAM......VN$ 30
WAKE ISLAND....25¢

JULY 24 · 1967

Comments from New York record stores ranged from a shoeless guitar carrier declaring, "It's like a show! It stones you," to a dark-suited lover of classical music calling the album "technically interesting and imaginative." The star of the piece was Lawrence LeFevre, who was actually the magazine's 59-year old editor, William Shawn. He rattled off superlative similarities between jazz great Duke Ellington and The Beatles and compared the album's release to a "notable new opera or symphonic work," observing that "The Beatles have done more to brighten up the world in recent years than almost anything else in the arts."

When it came time for the 10th Annual Grammy Awards for recordings released in 1967, we were apprehensive. Back then, the Grammys had yet to evolve into the hip extravaganza it is today. It was run by the music industry establishment that had yet to recognize the artistic integrity of rock 'n' roll. To us, it seemed more like the Granny Awards. Our generation wasn't being represented.

For the past two years, Frank Sinatra LPs had been voted Album of the Year. Prior winners included Judy Garland, Barbra Streisand and comedian Bob Newhart. These were great adult records, but what about us? No rock album had ever won a Grammy for musical achievement (although *Help!* and *Revolver* had at least been nominated).

But *Sgt. Pepper* could not be ignored. Artists Peter Blake and Jann Haworth won the Grammy for Best Album Cover—Graphic Arts (as Klaus Voormann had done the year before for his combination pen and ink drawing and photo collage on the *Revolver* cover). Geoff Emerick received a Grammy for Best Engineered Recording—Non-Classical. The album won the Grammy in a newly-created category, Best Contemporary Album. And to top it all off, *Sgt. Pepper's Lonely Hearts Club Band* was proclaimed the Album of the Year. The Grammys, with a little help from our friends, The Beatles, at long last recognized our music was legitimate.

But what is there about *Sgt. Pepper* that makes people care today? Was it The Beatles' best collection of songs? No. Not by a long shot. Several Beatles albums have better songs. *Rubber Soul* might win that poll. Was it their best overall album? No. Fans and critics often give that honor to *Revolver*. Do Beatles fans consider it their favorite

Beatles album? Nope. *The White Album* and *Abbey Road* are more likely to hold that distinction. Was it the first concept album? No. Frank Sinatra's *In The Wee Small Hours* preceded it by over a decade. Some would argue *Sgt. Pepper* wasn't even a concept album to begin with. Then what was it? Put simply, *Sgt. Pepper's Lonely Hearts Club Band* was The Beatles most important album. And, according to Rolling Stone magazine, the most important rock 'n' roll album ever made. It elevated rock music to an art form. But it was far more than art for art's sake. It was then and still remains a great listening experience.

Even now, in every city in Europe and America (and throughout most of the world), stereo systems, broadcast radio, satellite radio, iPods, iPads, iPhones and streaming services play: "It was twenty years ago today...What would you think if I sang out of tune?...Picture yourself in a boat on a river...Wednesday morning at five o'clock as the day begins...For the benefit of Mr. Kite there will be a show tonight...We were talking...When I get older losing my hair... Nothing to do to save his life...I read the news today, oh boy." And everyone listens.

As for "Summer Rain," it remains a staple of oldies radio, a reminder of that special time when all you needed was love. The words of the song's second bridge differ slightly from the first: "All summer long, we spent groovin' in the sand/Everybody kept on playin' Sgt. Pepper's Lonely Hearts Club Band." Dancing is replaced with grooving and the jukebox is gone. But the message is the same.

50 years on and for as long as humans have ears and souls, it shall be that way.

Everybody keeps on playin'
Sgt. Pepper's Lonely Hearts Club Band...

Remember Sgt. Pepper's Lonely Hearts Club is The Beatles

On Friday, June 2, 1967, the latest issue of New Musical Express hit the British newsstands. Below the magazine's upper banner was a near full-page message form EMI: "Remember Sgt. Peppers Lonely Hearts Club Band is The Beatles." Looking back 50 years later, it seems strange that the world's largest recording organization felt the need to inform or remind the public of the connection between Sgt. Pepper and The Beatles. After all, by the time the ad ran in the music publications, the album had been out for over a week, rushed into stores on May 25 ahead of its scheduled June 1 official release date.

That same NME issue debuted the new Beatles album at the top of its LP chart, where it would remain for several months. The following week the *Sgt. Pepper* album charted at number 21 in the magazine's singles chart!

It was more of the same in the other music mags. *Sgt. Pepper* debuted at number eight in the June 1 Record Retailer. The following week it moved up to number one, a position it held for 27 out of the next 35 weeks, being temporarily replaced at times by the perennial chart-topping soundtrack to *The Sound Of Music* and the album *Val Doonican Rocks, But Gently*. It remained on the charts for an entire year, including 37 weeks in the top five and 43 in the top ten. Melody Maker debuted *Sgt. Pepper* in its June 3 issue at number one, where it remained for 22 straight weeks. The LP charted for 43 weeks, including 11 at number two and a total of 39 weeks in the top five. Disc and Music Echo also reported the album at number one for several months.

The first news of the new Beatles album came in the music magazines. The April 8, 1967, Disc and Music Echo ran an interview with producer George Martin about *Sgt. Pepper*. Martin stated: "The boys have been working very long and very hard on it. I shall be glad to get it finished myself. Really, we have worked every night, right through the night." The April 22 Melody Maker reported the new Beatles album was titled *Sgt. Pepper's Lonely Hearts Club Band.*

The April 27 Record Retailer reported that The Beatles first album in nine months was finished, and that EMI was expected to rush press the LP for May 19 release. The magazine listed the album's songs and stated that EMI and NEMS were planning special trade and consumer promotion to exploit the album. The May 4 issue reported that the disc's release had been pushed back to June 1 and that the album was virtually continuous with no pauses between tracks. The May 18 issue reported that the album's fold out double wallet sleeve would include a post card of Sgt. Pepper, a false moustache, a pair of military stripes, two badges and a standup picture of The Beatles portrayed as Sgt. Pepper's Lonely Hearts Club Band. EMI stated that "this is one of the most expensive give-away promotions ever mounted with an album in this country." EMI was also distributing a Sgt. Pepper poster to record dealers.

Members of the Official Beatles Fan Club and others purchasing The Beatles Monthly Book learned bits and pieces about the new Beatles album in the May 1967 (No. 46) issue. Beatle People were told that the album was completed after nearly four months of solid session work and that it would be titled *Sgt. Pepper's Lonely Hearts Club Band*. The May Newsletter contained tantalizing Beatle Bits about the wide variety of folks that Beatle People would meet via the LP songs, including Sgt. Pepper himself, Lucy ("the girl with the kaleidescope eyes"), lovely Rita (who was a female traffic warden) and Mr. Kite (whose name appeared on an old theatre poster John bought at Sevenoaks, Kent). The newsletter also reported that Lucy was the subject of a school painting done by Julian Lennon. (This May 1967 reference to the song being inspired by Julian's painting shoots down the theory that John later invented the Julian painting story only after some listeners of the album surmised that the title "Lucy In The Sky With Diamonds" stood for LSD.) Readers also learned that Ringo's track for the new LP, originally called "Bad Finger Boogie," had been re-titled "A Little Help From My Friends" and that three saxes, two trombones and one French horn from the band Sounds Inc. had been recruited to provide backing on the song "Good Morning, Good Morning."

The magazine's Beatle News section reported that George Martin had finished the LP, completing the marathon task of editing and balancing all the tracks. This was quite a job, because, unlike their earlier sessions, The Beatles were now recording so many bits and pieces to be added afterwards. Readers learned that the boys had a special, very secret photo session for which lots of unusual costumes were delivered, and that it was extremely likely that one of the pictures from the session would turn up on the cover. The cover-up story ended with a prediction that would soon come true in spades: "the new cover will be one of the best and most elaborate ever!"

The May issue also featured 17 pictures of the group taken during the recording sessions for the new album. Paul was shown with George Martin conducting a horn session overdub and playing an electric guitar. John was shown blowing into a French horn. Ringo was pictured at the keyboard of a Hammond organ. George was shown playing keyboards in the presence of an Indian man identified as Ravi Shankar's brother. There were also shots of the group at the mixing board in Abbey Road Studio Two's control room.

The June 1967 issue of The Beatles Monthly Book (No. 47) was a Sgt. Pepper Special sporting a wrap-around color cover featuring The Beatles wearing the uniforms of their alter-ego band. The portrait is an alternate shot of the picture used for the album cover's open gatefold inside spread. The issue contains numerous photos of the group in the studio (primarily from the "With A Little Help From My Friends" session) and on the set where the album cover photograph was taken. Of particular interest is a wide shot that shows the group getting familiar with the set and their band instruments. In the foreground is the dirt box garden filled with flowers and props. Off to the far right side is a full standup cardboard figure of Adolph Hitler, which was removed from cardboard crowd of dignitaries before the picture was taken.

Editor Johnny Dean reminds the readers that "The release of a new Beatles' album is a big event in the world of entertainment" and that "Their records always have that vital ingredient which is so hard to achieve—originality." In discussing the different things the group does in the studio, he assures the readers that "they never do anything just to be gimmicky."

Fans were treated to an article about the recording of the album written by Beatle assistants Mal Evans and Neil Aspinall, in which they provide details about each song and the extra bits added between the end of the last track and the record label in the run-out groove. They warn us that the 18 kilocycles high frequency note was added for dogs and that you will not hear it unless you have very unusual ears. As for the inner groove gibberish, they suggest its translation might be "Thank you for listening. That's all for now. Please come to our next LP—you're all invited."

The issue also contains an article on the creation of the album's cover. It was written by Beatles public relations man Tony Barrow under his Frederick James pseudonym. Barrow discusses the custom tailoring of the uniforms, the montage of pictures and the props, as well as describing its physical side. "It wasn't just made like any ordinary sleeve—it was built. Planned with much ingenuity, the materials gathered together from all sorts of sources........and then BUILT. Into a cardboard house worthy of Sgt. Pepper and of his four famed architects!"

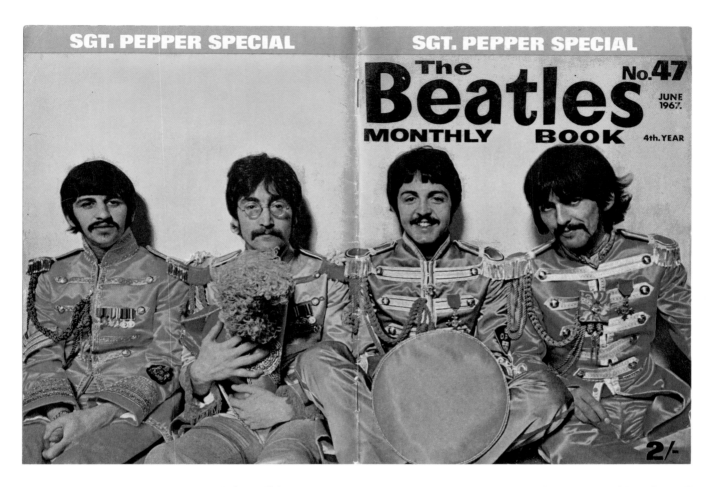

SGT. PEPPER SPECIAL

SGT. PEPPER SPECIAL

The Beatles MONTHLY BOOK

No.47 JUNE 1967. 4th. YEAR

2/-

The Beatle News section reported that offshore pirate station Radio London claimed a "Beatles World Exclusive" at 5:00 p.m. on Friday, May 12, when it began playing tracks from *Sgt. Pepper* as its Album of the Week, a full two weeks ahead of the LP's release. Radio London took out a full-page ad in the issue, touting itself as "Your Number 1 Beatles Station." At that time, pop music on the BBC received minimal air play on its Light Programme. But for *Sgt. Pepper*, BBC disc jockey Kenny Everett (who had recently been stolen by the BBC from pirate station Radio London) played tracks from the album, along with interviews with The Beatles. He did not play "A Day In The Life," which was banned by the BBC for its alleged drug references.

The May 6 issue of Record Mirror provided readers with a list of the album's tracks, including the name of the lead singer for each song. That week's Disc and Music Echo went through the entire LP, song by song. The coverage in the music magazines coupled with premature unauthorized air play gave fans tantalizing previews of what to expect when they finally purchased and listened to their own copy of the album. Although there was no Internet, Facebook, Twitter or other form of social media back in the sixties, there was a tremendous buzz about *Sgt. Pepper* taking shape that eliminated any need for EMI's "Remember Sgt. Pepper is The Beatles" advert.

The album was also receiving stellar reviews prior to its release. The May 18 Record Retailer called *Sgt. Pepper* their best by far. "A sensational album which will be their biggest seller yet." The magazine observed that "All 13 songs are good enough to be released as singles."

The May 20 Disc and Music Echo called *Sgt. Pepper* another masterpiece, using words such as genius, brilliant, beautiful, potent, unique, clever and stunning. The magazine observed that while the first listen leaves listeners perplexed, subsequent hearings reveal multi-layered sounds and incredible intricacies that made it obvious that no one had ever done anything like it before. It predicted that the record would flatten the rest of the pop world.

The May 20 New Musical Express contained Allen Evans' review, which was written after only one hearing of the album. He found the tunes all varied and interesting, with "Within You Without You" being the most memorable. While he wasn't sure *Sgt. Pepper* was their best or even whether it was worth the five months it took to make, he described it as very good and said it would sell like hot cakes. Evans called the title track a beat-raver, with Paul shouting out the lyrics. "She's Leaving Home" was a "very clever musical essay on a real life drama," while "Being For The Benefit of Mr. Kite!" was fascinating. He called "A Day In The Life" eerie, with final sounds that were really frightening. Evans concluded that "The Beatles have provided us with more musical entertainment, which will both please the ear and get the brain working a bit, too!" His review was accompanied by a fascinating cartoon drawn by Neil Smith, who was an internationally-renowned skin pathologist who served as the resident cartoonist for NME.

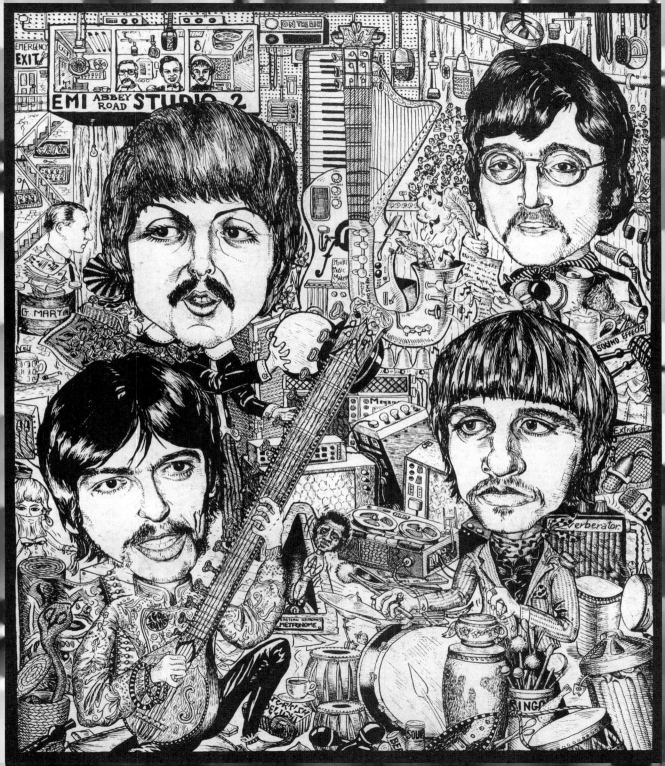

The May 27 Record Mirror contained a review by Peter James, who called the album clever and brilliant, both musically and lyrically, as it moved from raucous to poignant and back again. He found the production advanced and the arrangements original. The same issue ran an interview with George Martin, who called *Sgt. Pepper* "the most ambitious Beatles album yet," one whose aim "is to sound like a complete programme, ostensibly by the club band." Martin elaborated: "It took a long time because they're perfectionists and wanted to get the LP exactly the way they had it in their minds. They've always wanted to be one step ahead, a policy that is courageous, dangerous but inevitable, too, if they wanted to survive."

Norrie Drummond was among the dozen or so journalists and disc jockeys invited to the *Sgt. Pepper* launch party held on May 19, 1967, at Brian Epstein's four-story Georgian home at 24 Chapel Street, near Buckingham Palace. Drummond wrote about his experience in the May 27 New Musical Express in an article titled "Dinner with the Beatles." Upon arrival, guests were ushered into a large room with a table laden with salads, fruit, cheeses, eggs, hams and other goodies. Beatle associates handed out glasses of champagne and cigarettes. The Beatles, dressed in flamboyant clothes, posed for the photographers and then made themselves available for interviews, all the while trying to sneak in some food. After allowing sufficient time for the guests to mingle with each other and the band, press assistant Tony Barrow asked everyone to find their way upstairs to the lounge, where the *Sgt. Pepper's Lonely Hearts Club Band* album was played. For a couple of hours everyone drank and chatted.

According to Drummond, John viewed the new album as one of the most important steps in the group's career. "It just had to be right. We tried and I think succeeded in what we set out to do. If we hadn't then it wouldn't be out now." Asked if the new recordings were too far ahead of record buyers, George didn't think so. "People are very, very aware of what goes on around them nowadays. They think for themselves and I don't think we can ever be accused of under-estimating the intelligence of our fans." John agreed. "The people who have bought our records in the past must realize that we couldn't go on making the same type forever. We must change and I believe those people know this."

Jack Hutton also reported on the *Sgt. Pepper* launch in the May 27 Melody Maker. Paul told him that it was "exciting to see the way an LP goes. To see how many different things can be taken from it." John proclaimed, "No more tours, no more mop tops," leading Hutton to observe that The Beatles now "wanted to give to their fans through their albums, without all the fuss [of touring]." He noted that Lennon and McCartney were constantly expanding the scope of their musical ideas, embracing a whole new world of sound.

The May 27 Disc and Music Echo ran an extensive interview by Ray Coleman with each member of the group. Coleman praised the album, calling *Sgt. Pepper* as relevant to 1967 as "She Loves You" was to 1963. He observed that The Beatles and their music both had grown and matured. They were no longer four mop tops; they were maturing creative artists. Regarding the BBC's decision to ban "A Day In The Life," Paul called it rubbish to say the song was about drugs. "We were just trying to reflect a day in anybody's life…Going upstairs on a bus and having a smoke. Does that have to be about drugs?" As for the new album, George thought it was "the best we've done, but only the best we could do at this time. The next one ought to be better. That's always got to be the goal."

Chris Welch's article in the June 3 Melody Maker speculated on who influenced The Beatles. Older, classically trained musicians came up with names like German composer Richard Strauss, English Renaissance composer William Byrd and sitar master Ravi Shankar. Others found associations with skiffle singer Lonnie Donegan, British entertainer George Formby and perhaps an ancient schoolteacher etched in their childhood memories. Welch compared Paul's singing on the title track to that of James Brown. He noted that The Beatles "have always loved telling a tale, sometimes sadly, sometimes with a wry humour, often mixing depressing sentiments with a chirpy bounce in the grand music hall tradition." He cited "Lovely Rita" and "Good Morning, Good Morning" as examples. Welch observed that wherever their inspiration comes from, "The lads have brought forth yet another saga of entertainment and achievement that will keep the British pop industry ticking over securely for another six months at least." Even with all of its new sounds, the music "retains the Beatles stamp of humour, sorrow, sympathy and cynicism." Welch called *Sgt. Pepper* an extraordinary, valuable and meaningful contribution to the world's music.

The mainstream British press also had praise for the album. William Mann, the chief music critic for The Times (of London), responded to *Sgt. Pepper* with an article titled "The Beatles Revive Hopes of Progress in Pop Music." Mann spent about 70% of his "review" discussing the state of pop music and its various genres before turning to The Beatles latest offering. "Fixing A Hole" was described as a cool, anti-romantic quasi-ballad, while "She's Leaving Home" was "a slow waltz reminiscent of old musical comedy, but with a classically slanted accompaniment for harp and string quartet, and with ironical words about a domestic tragedy." "When I'm Sixty-Four" was a neat vaudeville number, while "Within You Without You" carried the manner of Indian music farther into pop music than ever before. Mann diagnosed psychedelia in the fanciful lyrics and intriguing asymmetrical music of "Lucy In The Sky With Diamonds," the sound effects of "Lovely Rita" and the hurricane glissando of "A Day In The Life." He also enjoyed the five-bar phrases of "Good Morning, Good Morning" and the tidy simplicity and shapely bass-line of "With A Little Help From My Friends." Mann opined that the latter song was the only track on the album that would have been conceivable in pop songs five years ago. Mann concluded that any of the album's songs was more genuinely creative than anything currently heard on pop radio stations. In relation to what other groups were doing, he found *Sgt. Pepper* significant as "constructive criticism, a sort of pop music master class examining trends and correcting or tidying up inconsistencies and undisciplined work, here and there suggesting a line worth following." Drama critic Kenneth Tynan later wrote in The Times that the release of *Sgt. Pepper* was "a decisive moment in the history of western civilization." The Times Literary Supplement called the album a "barometer of our times."

Scotland's nation newspaper, The Scotsman, lauded the album, with Alastair Clark calling *Sgt. Pepper* "a brilliant exercise in pop-song and poetry." He had particular praise for "A Day In The Life," saying that the recording "lifts pop to a creative level it has rarely reached before."

In its first week of release, *Sgt. Pepper* sold over 250,000 units in the U.K. Within a month of hitting the stores, sales exceeded a half million copies. Its songs were bombarding the British Isles via air waves dominated by off-shore floating radio stations. Everyone knew Sgt. Pepper's Lonely Hearts Club Band was The Beatles.

But the question remained, "Is Sgt. Pepper too advanced for the average pop fan to appreciate?" That very question appeared in red uppercase letters at the top of page 24 of the August 1967 Beatles Book (No. 49). Tony Barrow, once again writing under his Frederick James pseudonym, took on the task of providing the answer.

Barrow indicated that his desk was buried somewhere beneath a mountain of mail about *Sgt. Pepper's Lonely Hearts Club Band*, with Beatle People (nearly all female) from all over Britain having written to say what they thought of the album. From these letters, he compiled a cross-section of opinions to answer the article's title question and the equally important question of whether there was brilliance in *Sgt. Pepper* or whether the true musical artistry of The Beatles was concentrated in their earlier recordings? He then quoted from two letters to present the extremist views. Karen Baird of Long Eaton, Derbys, lamented, "I really enjoyed everything The Beatles recorded before *Revolver*, but it's impossible to understand half the stuff they do today." Peggy Franklin of Loughton, Essex had the opposite view. "I'm not a true pop fan and I never used to collect top 20 records. A year ago, The Beatles became part of my life. They are the greatest music talent the world has ever known. *Sgt. Pepper* contains words and ideas which are far above anything anyone else is capable of creating."

Sometimes initial impressions stuck, while others changed their minds. Joanne Tremlett of Welling, Kent said she was one of the first in her neighborhood to buy the album and was disappointed when she played it through, finding only "When I'm Sixty-Four" and the title track up to standard. "Everything else is over our heads and The Beatles ought to stop being so clever and give us tunes we can enjoy." Valerie Samuel of Chertsey in Surrey admitted that "The first time I heard the LP I was brought down." She eventually changed her tune. "Then I listened again and again. Finally I was overwhelmed by what I heard. Not just impressed but overwhelmed. Particularly 'A Day In The Life' and 'Lucy In The Sky With Diamonds.' It's all marvelous music. But it's no good just half-listening. You've got to concentrate hard and let The Beatles hypnotize you. Then you're under the spell of *Sgt. Pepper* and a splendid time IS guaranteed for all!" Pam Thorn of Doncaster in Yorkshire praised its variety of styles. Wendy East of Ealing, London wondered, "How can people accuse The Beatles of progressing too far? That's what their talent is all about."

Nancy Ryan of Cheshunt, Herts was 15 when she first heard the group and now was approaching 20, soon be to married. "I've grown up with The Beatles and The Beatles' music has grown up with me. So we're still together— with The Beatles getting just a bit ahead now and again. I can learn things from The Beatles that I can't learn from the majority of other pop records. It's fun trying to keep up with The Beatles." Sylvia Wilton of Bristol believes that "*Sgt. Pepper* demonstrates just how good pop music can be if a group is willing to do a bit more work and not just churn out new records which say the same old things." Susan Walker of Dorking, Surrey observed that "The progress The Beatles have made in just 4 years is amazing! Compare their first LP with *Sgt. Pepper*. I still play both and I like both for different reasons."

Of course there were fans who were turned off by *Sgt. Pepper* and appeared to give up on The Beatles. Judy Conn of Leytonstone, London used to play the group's early albums, but now she had put them away and loved The Monkees. Ann Turnbull of Bognor Regis, Sussex felt cheated having spent two pounds to buy *Sgt. Pepper* and only finding three songs worth hearing. Jan Williams of Caernarfon in North Wales was equally blunt. "I was looking forward to *Sgt. Pepper* but the title song is the only one I really like. It's The Beatles we used to know before they went stark raving mad and started to write rubbish."

Barrow observed that while a few letters condemned *Sgt. Pepper* as rubbish, the vast majority of readers said everything on the LP was fantastic, fabulous and groovy. Addressing his original question of whether *Sgt. Pepper* was too advanced for the average pop fan to appreciate, Barrow answered that "some of you feel quite happy about keeping up with *Sgt. Pepper* and a lot more of you are prepared to listen and learn, to make an effort to find out what The Beatles' 1967 music is all about, because you admire what the group is achieving and you want them to stay an important part of your lives." These fans were comfortable with the transition and accepted that...

Sgt. Pepper's Lonely Hearts Club is The Beatles

Canada's Centennial Celebration Gets A Present From The Beatles

By Piers Hemmingsen

1967 was a special year for Canadians—a year-long celebration of Canada's 100th birthday. It was a chance to look back at Canada's first 100 years of history. And a chance to look forward to another 100 years. To look ahead to a new century that many said would be "Canada's century." Celebration plans had been in the making for at least five years prior to January 1st, 1967. Canada had adopted a new national flag in January 1965 and Montreal would play host to the world with its wonderful exposition called "Expo '67." There was a dizzying array of other important Centennial events all across the country. Every town and city had organized its own Centennial projects and events. There was a real sense of excitement in the air for all Canadians. And just six weeks into this exciting Centennial year was launched the greatest single recording of all time: The Beatles' "Strawberry Fields Forever" backed with "Penny Lane." Some who were alive then will say that 1967 was Canada's greatest year, and the five new Beatles disc releases that year made it all extra special for Beatles fans of the period.

I had been a Beatles fan since I had first seen the "scruffy" group performing "Please Please Me" on television in England in early 1963. Just one year later in Canada I had seen them looking much more "sanitized" performing live during their first appearance on CBC's Ed Sullivan Show. By the summer of 1966, I was a far more serious fan of their newest recordings. I had bought the "Nowhere Man" and "Paperback Writer" singles as soon as they had entered the charts, and I had purchased the *Yesterday And Today* and *Revolver* LPs within weeks of their release.

The NEW Beatles album *Sergeant Pepper's Lonely Hearts Club Band* was released in Canada in the first week of June 1967, just in time to kick off the "Summer of Love." By the summer of 1967, all four Beatles had travelled the globe and their new album was the clear evidence of the huge gap between their new worldly music in 1967 and their fans. The previous year's *Revolver* had been a top selling album, but it would be the final "formula" Beatles album with the requisite hits on each side. *Sergeant Pepper* would have no singles. With the exception of some unusual audio clips in the run out areas, this was the same audio package that was issued in England.

Capitol of Canada began its hype for the album over two months in advance of its release. Capitol's national promotion manager, Paul White, authored a weekly flyer called The Sizzle Sheet in which he plugged the company's future and new releases. The flyer was sent to Canada's radio stations in hopes of getting disc jockeys to give extra spins to the Capitol discs.

The March 23, 1967, Sizzle Sheet broke the news in Canada: "What's with the new Beatles LP? Every day we here receive numerous phone calls from Beatles fans asking for the latest news on their new LP—We are sure that radio people receive the same requests and we will keep passing on any information we learn of it—The last report we have is that six tracks have now been recorded for their next album, which will not probably be released before May—even possibly June. Ringo Starr and George Harrison will each be featured and one track in the can has a 41-piece orchestra backing. Should be well worth waiting for."

Paul White's last words would prove to be an understatement. Three weeks later he had more news, courtesy of the weekly British music papers such as Melody Maker and New Musical Express, which were shipped from England to Canada and sold in news outlets such as W.H. Smith. In the April 14 Sizzle Sheet he informed readers of the following discoveries: "According to the Sunday Times the group has now spent 525 hours recording it!! The tentative title is 'Sergeant Pepper's Lonely Hearts Club Band'—the group have worked for the past four months a five day week— often nights and dawns—producing the new album with a wealth of sounds. It will feature solo tracks by all four Beatles. Their producer, George Martin, has stated that the new album once again explores new avenues of sound."

In the following week's Sizzle Sheet, Paul White discussed radio air play of a tape of an EMI acetate of "A Day In The Life" that was being played on radio stations in Toronto, Ottawa and Vancouver: "You hear it here...You hear it there... But the kids can't buy it anywhere! We mean naturally THAT track by The Beatles that somehow sneaked out of the U.K. and raised another wild scramble for exclusives by stations all over North America. A Beatles track from their latest sessions—'A Day In The Life' started to get airplay this week—and naturally the rush was on from fans who wanted it! We don't have it—and after listening to the song on a local stations, it sounds like an album track more than a single content. Anyway, somehow the cut was leaked out but has nothing to do with Capitol Records. As soon as we have more news on the selection in question, and indeed the release date for the new album, we'll let you know! So please don't call us 'cause we don't have that 'scoop track'—and please—those stations who get it—tell your listeners it isn't available yet!"

Vancouver's CKLG for the week of April 22, 1967, listed the following "Hitbound" disc in its Boss 30 chart: Day In A New Life/Bumble Bee (The Beatles—Capitol). It was a strange non-release which oddly referenced the Peter Cook & Dudley Moore single from early 1967 titled "L.S. Bumble Bee," which was a sort-of Beatles parody and a play on the letters L.S.D. The fact that a non-existent 45 would be listed as a new release indicates how many rumors were in circulation in advance of the release of *Sgt. Pepper*. Three weeks later, Ottawa's CFRA listed "A Day In The Life" as its number one "Chart Bound" disc in its May 12 survey. At least they got the title right.

Meanwhile, Canada's version of the World's Fair, Expo '67, opened in Montreal on April 27. The British Pavilion featured large photo images of The Beatles as part of its display of cutting edge British pop culture.

Paul White used the May 5 Sizzle Sheet to promote the May 9 Canadian Broadcasting Company's radio special "How The Beatles Changed the World" and pay tribute to the group: "Pop songs became tuneful, loaded with 'message' and IN. Mod clothing became a permanent part of the fashion scene. The teenager became a human being. Long hair gained an acceptance long denied it. And the radio and movie industry took on a new lease of imaginative life. Thanks to the Beatles."

RADIO CK73LG
BOSS 30
Vancouver's Official Radio Record Survey

CKLG BOSS 30 — APRIL 22nd, 1967

This Week	Title	Artist Label	Last Week
1	SOMEBODY TO LOVE	Jefferson Airplane/RCA	4
2	BLUE'S THEME	Arrows/Capitol	3
3	SOMETHING STUPID	Nancy and Frank Sinatra/Reprise	7
4	THE HAPPENING	Supremes/Motown	2
5	NO MILK TODAY/KIND OF A HUSH	Herman's Hermits/Quality	9
6	MY BACK PAGES	Byrds/Columbia	18
7	YELLOW BALLOON	Yellow Balloons/Canterbury	8
8	CAN'T SEEM TO MAKE YOU MINE	Seeds/GNP	20
9	NEVER LOVED A MAN	Aretha Franklin/Atlantic	6
10	GIRL YOU'LL BE A WOMAN SOON	Neil Diamond/Bang	12
11	AT THE ZOO	Simon & Garfunkel/Columbia	16
12	BERNADETTE	Four Tops/Motown	5
13	SHE'S LOOKING GOOD	Rodger Collins/Galaxy	17
14	ANIMAL CRACKERS	Gene Pitney/Columbia	10
15	SUNSHINE GIRL	The Parade/A & M	25
16	WHEN I WAS YOUNG	Animals/MGM	19
17	OUT OF LEFT FIELD	Percy Sledge/Atlantic	30
18	ON A CAROUSEL	Hollies/Capitol	8
19	YOU'VE GOT WHAT IT TAKES	Dave Clark 5/Capitol	23
20	HIM OR ME/WHAT'S IT GONNA BE	Paul Revere/Columbia	—
21	LITTLE GAMES	Yardbirds/Capitol	29
22	LIVE	The Merry Go Round/A & M	—
23	LOVE EYES	Nancy Sinatra/Reprise	14
24	I GOT RHYTHM	Happenings/S. T. Puppy	28
25	GET ME TO THE WORLD ON TIME	Electric Prunes/Reprise	26
26	BUY FOR ME THE RAIN	Nitty Gritty Dirt Band/Liberty	—
27	THE LOVE I SAW	Miracles/Motown	13
28	I WAS KAISER BILL'S BATMAN	Whistling Jack Smith/Deram	—
29	GROOVIN'	Young Rascals/Atlantic	—
30	MY BABE	Ronnie Dove/Diamond	—

HITBOUND

1	SIX O'CLOCK	Lovin' Spoonful/Kama Sutra
2	OOGUM BOOGUM SONG	Brenton Wood/Double Shot
3	100 OR TWO	Springfield Riflers/Jerden
4	WHEN YOUR YOUNG AND IN LOVE	Marvellettes/Motown
5	ROUND ROUND	Jonathon King/Parrot
6	DAY IN A NEW LIFE/BUMBLE BEE	Beatles/Capitol

BOSS
MUCH...

THE SIZZLE SHEET

FAST TALK ABOUT HOT Capitol RECORDS

SIZZLE #225 WEEK ENDING APRIL 21/67

FROM THE DESK OF Paul White

YOU HEAR IT HERE . . . YOU HEAR IT THERE . . .

BUT THE KIDS CAN'T BUY IT ANYWHERE . . . !

We mean naturally THAT track by The Beatles that has somehow sneaked out of the U.K. and raised another wild scramble for exclusives by stations all over North America. A Beatle track from their latest session - "A Day In The Life" started to get airplay this week - and naturally the rush was on from fans who wanted it! We don't have it - and after listening to the song on a local station, it sounds like an album track more than a single content. Anyway, somehow the cut was leaked out but it was nothing to do with Capitol Records. As soon as we have more news on the selection in question, and indeed the release date for the new album, we'll let you know!

Some of the cuts recorded by The Beatles for the new package are: - the aforementioned A DAY IN THE LIFE - a John Lennon solo with a 41 piece orchestra backing; WHEN I'M 64 - featuring Paul McCartney and done in the early phonograph style; GOOD MORNING, GOOD MORNING - a duet of John and Paul with musical accompaniment by the excellent group, Sounds Incorporated. SHE'S LEAVING HOME (with strings) SERGEANT PEPPERS BLUES and METER RITA are three other numbers. METER RITA is a John Lennon solo incorporating three four-track machines, and we are told, a comb and paper played backwards is also used!!

So, please don't call us 'cause we don't have that "scoop track"- and please - those stations who did get it - tell your listeners it isn't available yet!

THE CLASSIEST ACT IN OUR BIZ!

CFRA SWING SET FOR THE WEEK OF MAY 12, 1967

1.	I Think Were Along Now (6)	Tommy James
2.	When I Was Young (14)	Eric Burdon
3.	Kind Of A Hush (1)	Herman's Hermits
4.	On A Carousel (2)	The Hollies
5.	Yellow Balloon (16)	The Yellow Balloons
6.	Here Comes My Baby (16)	The Tremeloes
7.	Something Stupid (3)	Nancy and Frank Sinatra
8.	My Back Pages (12)	The Byrds
9.	Girl, You'll Be A Woman Soon (23)	Neil Diamond
10.	Happy Jack (10)	The Who
11.	This Is My Song (6)	Petula Clark
12.	Happy Together (5)	The Turtles
13.	No Milk Today (1)	Herman's Hermits
14.	You Got What It Takes (19)	The Dave Clark Five
15.	I'm A Man (8)	The Spencer Davis Group
16.	Him or Me, Who's It Gonna Be (35)	Paul Revere
17.	Sweet Soul Music (31)	Arthur Conley
18.	Little Bit Me, Little Bit You (7)	The Monkees
19.	The Happening (22)	The Supremes
20.	Merry Go Round (21)	The Youngbloods
21.	Creeque Alley (37)	The Mamas & The Papas
22.	I Was Kaiser Bill's Batman (27)	Whistling Jack Smith
23.	Half Past Midnight (23)	The Staccatos
24.	Me Minus More (9)	The Skaliwags
25.	Your Place In My Heart (28)	Don Norman & The Other Four
26.	At The Zoo (33)	Simon & Garfunkel
27.	I Got Rhythm (39)	The Happenings
28.	The Way I Feel (36)	Gord Lightfoot
29.	My Girl Josephine (30)	Jerry Jaye
30.	Lovin' Sound (32)	Ian & Sylvia
31.	Who Do You Love (28)	The Woolies
32.	What A Woman In Love Won't Do (29)	Sandy Posey
33.	Jimmy Mack (34)	Martha & The Vandellas
34.	Ha! Ha! Said The Clown (-)	Manfred Mann
35.	Little Games (-)	The Yardbirds
36.	Too Many Fish In The Sea (-)	Mitch Ryder
37.	My Friend Jack (-)	The Smoke
38.	Somebody Told My Girl (-)	Those Naughty Boys
39.	Six O'Clock (-)	The Lovin' Spoonful
40.	Release Me (-)	Engelbert Humperdinck

CFRA Chart Bound

1.	A Day In The Life	The Beatles
2.	Do It Again, A Little Bit Slower	Jon & Robin
3.	Groovin'	The Young Rascals
4.	She'd Rather Be With Me	The Turtles
5.	Mirage	Tommy James & The Shondells
6.	Sound Of Love	The 5 Americans
7.	My Old Car	Lee Dorsey
8.	Pictures Of Lilly	The Who
9.	Girls In Love	Gary Lewis
10.	All I Need	The Temptations

Swing Set Hit	Swing Set Album
Bowling Green The Everly Brothers Warner Bros.	The Youngbloods R.C.A.

1961! for CHINA, it's the year of the ram.......it's the year of the big blast in CANADA..... and for OTTAWA??? (cont'd back page)

by gunn

debut
and
ence.
e
oosh
eek,

apitol
esday
er
sday
l
es
ir

Bon".

The May 19 Sizzle Sheet stated that the new Beatles album would be released around June 1. The following week, White was finally able to provide more definitive information: "Here come The Beatles! It's on the presses…The greatest Beatles' album of them all! You've heard that line before, but this time it's The Truth!" White then gave a track by track description of the album. He predicted that "A Day In The Life" would get plenty of air play, even if the BBC found the words offensive, stating "frankly, we don't think they get the story right to make that assumption," a reference to the BBC's banning of the track due to its alleged drug references.

The album was finally released in Canada on June 1, 1967. My friend James Deeks provided the following recollection of his being one the first Canadians to buy the album: "CHUM 1050 had been playing selected songs from *Sgt. Pepper* from early May '67 on… TANTALIZING us listeners with the most exciting music we'd ever heard (or heard, at least, since *Revolver* came out the previous summer). The actual *Sgt. Pepper* album wasn't planned for Canadian release until June 1st. The wait was excruciating. When Thursday, June 1 arrived, I thought I'd better get down to Music World early and join what I figured would be a lengthy lineup, prior to opening at 9:00 a.m. I got there at about 7:45, to find a raccoon chewing on an apple core, and nothing else. No lineup, no crazed Beatle-nuts demanding their new fix, no CHUM remote waiting to interview breathless fans. Weird. The first employee arrived at about 8:00. He told me he had to get the store's van and drive down to the Capitol Records warehouse to pick up the *Pepper* albums, and invited me to come along. I did. The guy at Capitol told us we were the first store to arrive for the pickup, and Toronto was the first city in Canada getting the record. Whether any of what we were told was true, I know not. But I, of course, demanded the first copy from the first box, thereby ensuring that I was therefore presumably the first person in Canada to obtain a (bought) copy of *Sgt. Pepper*. I've been "dining out" on this story for some 50 years now. Well, not exactly dining out. No one really cares, actually (except my friend Piers Hemmingsen). But the memory, for me… it's getting better all the time."

As for me, I "experienced" my first copy of *Sgt. Pepper's Lonely Hearts Club Band* two months later in Montreal, Quebec (and I'll get to that story in a little while).

The first Canadian review of Sgt. Pepper ran in the June 8 Toronto Telegram in its After Four section. Tim Elia opined that the album was even better, if that seems possible, than the group's previous two albums, *Rubber Soul* and *Revolver*. He stated that the "triumph of insanity" began with the jacket itself: "How about an impossible collage on the front, a cut-out page in the middle, and a sing-along song sheet on the back. Sheer madness to start." As for the recording, it continued the Beatle trend for experimentation, using the English music hall concert as its format and providing numbers that showed every conceivable style and orchestration. He singled out "Lucy In The Sky With Diamonds" ("dazzling lyrics into the dream-like world of hallucinations"), "She's Leaving Home" (similar in style to "Eleanor Rigby," but with lyrics "eventually questioning the values of the girl leaving home as well as her parents" that are "far more searching and evocative") and "Within You Without You" ("a remarkably successful experiment in using Western instruments in the Eastern musical idiom").

Elia concluded with the following praises: "They're just the best popular writers and *musicians* around. Period. They are happiness throughout, laughing in words and music, at the Establishment, the older generation, the younger generation, even at themselves. Space runs out before the superlatives. The Beatles remain the most important pace-setters in popular music because they refuse to be satisfied with old worn out forms. They are constantly trying to find new means of expression, new combinations of words and rhythms. They accomplish this in many ways, among them using established instruments, in new ways, and by introducing special electronic effects. All there is to be said is this: if you like the best music – originality, technical perfection, and fun – this is your record. In the words of Sgt. Pepper, 'A splendid time is guaranteed for all.'"

The June 10 RPM Music Weekly contained the following rambling review, which made reference to Paul wearing an OPP (Ontario Provincial Police) badge on his uniform. "Prepare to blow your mind. Here they are for real. You don't have to put up with any more bootlegged sound from your local ear ache. The Beatles are here along with half a hundred of their friends, thanks to Madame Tussauds. She's really English, you know? Anyway, ain't that a gas of an album cover? I got so excited I played the cover and smoked the record. Besides a new Beatle portrait, you get Sgt.

Pepper cut-outs, printed lyrics and get this, 13 new Beatle songs. Ooh, I'm so glad I'm 13. Imagine, Sgt. Pepper cut-outs. Just what will the English think of next? Paul's wearing an OPP crest on his left arm, you know."

More insights into the effect The Beatles were having in Canada came in the June 23 Sizzle Sheet: "Out less than a month and already on its way to becoming the best seller to date by The Beatles, 'Sgt. Pepper's Band' is also proving a tremendous success in stereo. Reports coming show a sudden upsurge in stereo sales whenever stores demonstrate the album for customers. Shipments of the album are reaching for the 70,000 mark in Canada." These promotional notations by Paul White around the time of Sergeant Pepper's release in Canada provide a unique view of a period when Beatles fans were getting a little older and some of them were investing in more expensive equipment to play their records. More Beatles fans were buying stereo LPs and this was great news for Capitol – between 1963 and 1967, it was standard practice to charge an extra $1.00 for stereo albums over the standard "mono" price. For example, a monaural copy of *Sgt. Pepper* could be purchased in the summer of 1967 in Montreal for $4.98 while the stereo version was priced at $5.98. This was also a period when FM stations in Canada were starting to hit the airwaves – it would be another year or so when "underground FM" stations would be flying the flag "high" for an album-oriented format in late night slots. In June of 1967, Capitol of Canada would have seen revenues increase from sales of the stereo version of the new Beatles LP, but the real fact was that the LP was a major leap forward for stereo sound reproduction. In 1967 with the advent of *Sgt. Pepper*, Beatles fans and teenagers in general were becoming hooked on the stereo format. In the "summer of love", Paul White was spotting a new trend for sure. Although *Revolver* had been a break-through in recording techniques (backward recordings, tape loops, etc.), the majority of copies of *Revolver* sold in Canada were monaural.

By the time Canada celebrated its 100th birthday on July 1, 1967, Sgt. Pepper had overtaken The Monkees' *Headquarters* album to rise to the top of the RPM Music Weekly 25 Top LPs chart, where it remained for eight straight weeks before switching placing with *Headquarters*. Other high-charting albums at the time were Herb Alpert's *Sounds Like* and Jefferson Airplane's *Surrealistic Pillow*. The Beatles album spent two more weeks in September at number one ahead of the new Rolling Stones LP, *Flowers*.

June 24, 1967

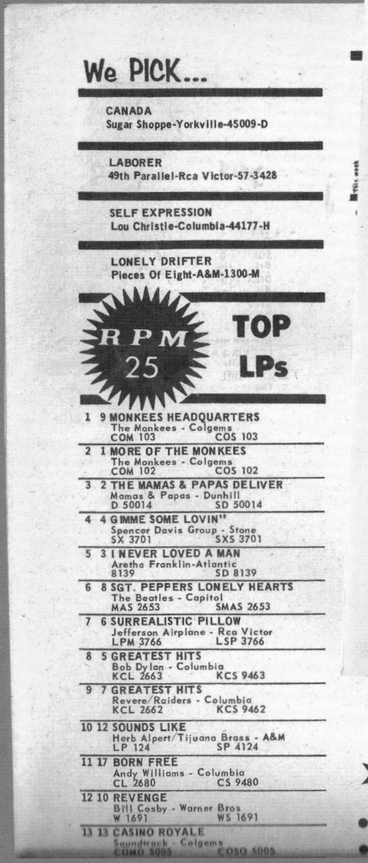

We PICK...

CANADA
Sugar Shoppe-Yorkville-45009-D

LABORER
49th Parallel-Rca Victor-57-3428

SELF EXPRESSION
Lou Christie-Columbia-44177-H

LONELY DRIFTER
Pieces Of Eight-A&M-1300-M

RPM 25 TOP LPs

1 9 MONKEES HEADQUARTERS
The Monkees - Colgems
COM 103 COS 103
2 1 MORE OF THE MONKEES
The Monkees - Colgems
COM 102 COS 102
3 2 THE MAMAS & PAPAS DELIVER
Mamas & Papas - Dunhill
D 50014 SD 50014
4 4 GIMME SOME LOVIN''
Spencer Davis Group - Stone
SX 3701 SXS 3701
5 3 I NEVER LOVED A MAN
Aretha Franklin-Atlantic
8139 SD 8139
6 8 SGT. PEPPERS LONELY HEARTS
The Beatles - Capitol
MAS 2653 SMAS 2653
7 6 SURREALISTIC PILLOW
Jefferson Airplane - Rca Victor
LPM 3766 LSP 3766
8 5 GREATEST HITS
Bob Dylan - Columbia
KCL 2663 KCS 9463
9 7 GREATEST HITS
Revere/Raiders - Columbia
KCL 2662 KCS 9462
10 12 SOUNDS LIKE
Herb Alpert/Tijuana Brass - A&M
LP 124 SP 4124
11 17 BORN FREE
Andy Williams - Columbia
CL 2680 CS 9480
12 10 REVENGE
Bill Cosby - Warner Bros
W 1691 WS 1691
13 13 CASINO ROYALE
Soundtrack - Colgems
COMO 5005 COSO 5005

August 12, 1967

We PICK...

THERE IS A MOUNTAIN
Donovan-Epic-10212-H

GET TOGETHER
The Youngbloods-Rca Victor-9264-N

SIXTEEN TONS
Tom Jones-Parrot-40016-K

(We'll Meet In The) YELLOW FOREST
Jay/Americans-Apex-50196-J

RPM 25 TOP LPs

1 1 SGT PEPPERS LONELY HEARTS BAND
The Beatles-Capitol
MAS 2653 SMAS 2653
2 2 MONKEE HEADQUARTERS
The Monkees-Colgems
Com 103 COS 103
3 4 SURREALISTIC PILLOW
Jefferson Airplane-Rca Victor
LPM 3766 LSP 3766
4 6 SUPREMES SING RODGERS & HART
Supremes-Motown
M 659 S 659
5 3 SOUNDS LIKE
Herb Alpert/Tijuana Brass-A&M
LP 124 SP 4124
6 11 UP UP AND AWAY
5th Dimension-Soul City
SCM 91000 SCS 92000
7 8 GIMME SOME LOVIN'
Spencer Davis Group-Stone
SX 3701 SXS 3701
8 9 GREATEST HITS
Bob Dylan-Columbia
KCL 2663 KCS 9463
9 10 GREATEST HITS
Paul Revere/Raiders-Columbia
KCL 2662 KCS 9462
10 5 REVENGE
Bill Cosby-
W 1691
11 12 CASINO RO...
Soundtrack-...
COMO 5005
12 13 RELEASE ...
Engelbert H...
PA 61012
13 21 FLOWERS
Rolling Sto...
LL 309

CANADA'S ONLY OFFICIAL 100 SINGLE SURVEY

Compiled from Record Company, Record Store and Disc Jockey reports.

RPM 100

◆ - BOTH SIDES
☆ - MONSTER
● - BIG MOVER

DISTRIBUTOR CODES
Allied -C
Arc -D
C.M.S. -E
Capitol -F
Caravan -G
Columbia -H
Compo -J
London -K
Phonodisc -L
Quality -M
Rca Victor -N
Sparton -O

This week / 1 week ago / 2 weeks ago

1 3 5 A WHITER SHADE OF PALE
Procol Harum-Deram-7507-K
2 2 2 LIGHT MY FIRE
Doors-Elektra-45615-C
3 1 1 WHITE RABBIT
Jefferson Airplane-Rca Victor-9248-N
● 4 19 32 PLEASANT VALLEY SUNDAY
The Monkees-Rca Victor-66-1007-N
5 5 9 I WAS MADE TO LOVE HER
Stevie Wonder-Tamla-54151-L
● 6 18 28 A GIRL LIKE YOU
Young Rascals-Atlantic-2424-M
7 4 10 MERCY MERCY MERCY
Buckinghams-Columbia-44182-H
● 8 16 22 SILENCE IS GOLDEN
Tremeloes-Epic-10184-H
● 9 26 49 ALL YOU NEED IS LOVE
Beatles-Capitol-5964-F
10 11 11 FOR YOUR LOVE
Peaches & Herb-Date-1563-H
11 8 15 MORE LOVE
Smokey Robinson-Tamla-54152-L
12 6 16 I TAKE IT BACK
Sandy Posey-MGM-13744-M
13 9 19 CARRIE ANN
Hollies-Columbia-5-10180-H
14 14 20 EVERY LITTLE BIT HURTS
Spencer Davis Group-Stone-708-G
15 13 17 SOUL FINGER
Bar Kays-Volt-148-M
16 22 31 MAMMY
Happenings-B.T.Puppy-530-J
17 20 24 JACKSON
Sinatra/Hazelwood-Reprise-0595-J
● 18 31 56 TO LOVE SOMEBODY
Bee Gees-Atco-6503-M
● 19 44 63 BABY I LOVE YOU
Aretha Franklin-Atlantic-2427-M
20 7 3 UP UP AND AWAY
5th Dimension-Soul City-756-K
21 24 37 THE BOAT THAT I ROW
21 29 36 DING DO...
Fifth Est...
22 30 48 SEVEN F...
Four Top...
23 32 56 COME T...
Harpers ...
☆ 42 53 WINDY
Associa...
25 27 39 GIRLS I...
Gary Le...
● 26 40 59 SOUND...
Five A...
● 27 39 45 BOWLI...

● 35 48 58 DON'T LET THE RAIN FALL....
Critters-Kapp-838-L
36 36 39 PICTURES OF LILY
Who-Decca-32156-J
● 37 57 71 (I Wanna) TESTIFY
Parliaments-Revilot-207-G
38 40 51 SHOWBUSINESS
Lou Rawls-Capitol-5941-F
39 39 50 YOU ONLY LIVE TWICE
Nancy Sinatra-Reprise-0595-J
● 40 65 73 IT'S A HAPPENING WORLD
Tokens-WB-7056-J
41 49 62 PAPER SUN
Traffic-Island-CB-1302-G
42 46 57 BLUEBIRD
Buffalo Springfield-Atco-6499-M
43 51 55 THE HAPPENING
Herb Alpert-A&M-860-M
● 44 54 77 COLD SWEAT
James Brown-King-6110-L
45 47 65 WASHED ASHORE
Platters-Columbia-MU-4-1251-H
● 46 60 82 COME BACK WHEN YOU GROW UP
Bobby Vee-Liberty-55964-K
● 47 64 87 CRY SOFTLY LONELY ONE
Roy Orbison-MGM-13764-M
● 48 62 ---- DARLING BE HOME SOON
Bobby Darin-Atlantic-2420-M
49 41 42 THIS TIME LONG AGO
Guess Who-Quality-1874-M
50 52 52 LABORER
49th Parallel-Rca Victor-57-3422-N
51 53 68 LONELY DRIFTER
Pieces of Eight-A&M-854-M
● 52 79 ---- RIVER IS WIDE
Forum-Sparton-1612-O
53 58 80 EVERYBODY NEEDS LOVE
Gladys Knight/Pips-Soul-35034-L

67 70 93 I'LL TURN TO STONE
Four Tops-Motown-1110-L
68 74 94 THE LOOK OF LOVE
Dusty Springfield-Philips-40465-K
● 69 ---- ---- HEROES AND VILLAINS
Beach Boys-Capitol-1001-F
● 70 92 ---- JACKRABBIT
BTB4-Yorkville-45011-D
● 71 99 ---- JILL
Gary Lewis/Playboys-Liberty-55985-K
72 81 100 THOUSAND SHADOWS
Seeds-GNP-394-J
● 73 95 98 PENNY ARCADE
Cyrkle-Columbia-44224-H
74 76 78 WHY GIRL
Precisions-Stone-712-G
● 75 90 ---- YOU'RE MY EVERYTHING
Temptations-Gordy-7063-L
76 59 60 LOVE IS A BEAUTIFUL THING
Gettysbyrg Address-Franklin-0100-G
● 77 86 ---- RUNNIN' 'ROUND IN CIRCLES
Five D-Sir John A-1-N
78 68 46 I'LL FORGET HER TOMORROW
Witness Inc-Apex-77044-J
79 78 95 I'LL NEVER FIND ANOTHER YOU
Sonny James-Capitol-5914-F
80 80 86 CORNFLAKES AND ICE CREAM
Lords of London-Apex-77054-J
81 82 96 SLIPPIN' & SLIDIN'
Willie Mitchell-Hi-2125-K
82 85 97 LONESOME ROAD
Wonder Who-Philips-40471-K
● 83 96 ---- MY ELUSIVE DREAMS
Houston/Wynette-Epic-5-10094-H
● 84 94 ---- FUNKY BROADWAY
Wilson Pickett-Atlantic-2430-M
85 91 ---- BLUES THEME
Arrows-Capitol
86 93 ---- SLIM JENKIN'S PLACE
Booker T/MGs-Stax-224-M
● 87 ---- ---- YOU KNOW WHAT I MEAN
Turtles-White Whale-254-M

RPM PICKS

JUST ONE LOOK
Hollies-Imperial-66258-M

ODE TO BILLIE JOE
Kingpins-Atco-6516-M

CHILD OF CLAY
Jimmie Rodgers-A&M-871-M

LIGHTNING'S GIRL
Nancy Sinatra-Reprise-0620-J

RPM 25 TOP LPs

1 1 SGT. PEPPERS LONELY HEARTS BAND
The Beatles-Capitol
MAS 2653 SMAS 2653
2 2 FLOWERS
The Rolling Stones-London
LL 3509 PS 509
3 7 GROOVIN'
Young Rascals-Atlantic
8148 SD 8148
4 6 I'M A MAN
Spencer Davis Group-Stone
SX 3702 SXS 3702
5 4 MONKEE HEADQUARTERS
The Monkees-Colgems
COM 103 COS 103
6 3 SURREALISTIC PILLOW
Jefferson Airplane-Rca Victor
LPM 3766 LSP 3766
7 5 GIMME SOME LOVIN'
Spencer Davis Group-Stone
SX 3701 SXS 3701
8 14 THE DOORS
The Doors-Elektra
EK 4007 EKS 74007
9 9 GREATEST HITS
Paul Revere/Raiders-Columbia
KCL 2662 KCS 9462
10 8 GREATEST HITS
Bob Dylan-Columbia
KCL 2663 KCS 9463
11 10 SOUNDS LIKE
Herb Alpert/Tijuana Brass-A&M
LP 124 SP 4124
12 12 ABSOLUTELY FREE
Mothers of Invention-Verve

THE RPM 100
CANADA'S ONLY OFFICIAL 100 SINGLE SURVEY

1 4 8 SAN FRANCISCAN NIGHTS
Eric Burdon-MGM-13769-M
2 6 16 APPLES PEACHES PUMPKIN PIE
Jay/Techniques-Smash-2086-M
3 1 5 ODE TO BILLIE JOE
Bobbie Gentry-Capitol-5950-F
4 17 26 THERE IS A MOUNTAIN
Donovan-Epic-10212-H
5 11 32 THE LETTER
Box Tops-Mala-565-M
6 15 19 YOU KNOW WHAT I MEAN
Turtles-White Whale-254-M
7 5 1 ALL YOU NEED IS LOVE ◆
Beatles-Capitol-5964-F
8 16 17 THE BOAT THAT I ROW ◆
Lulu-Epic-10187-H
9 2 3 COME BACK WHEN YOU GROW UP
Bobby Vee-Liberty-55964-K
10 3 7 REFLECTIONS
Diana Ross/Supremes-Motown-1111-L
11 7 11 YOU'RE MY EVERYTHING
Temptations-Gordy-7063-L
12 21 21 FUNKY BROADWAY
Wilson Pickett-Atlantic-2430-M
13 13 18 BROWN EYED GIRL
Van Morrison-Bang-545-C
14 19 33 THINGS I SHOULD HAVE SAID
Grass Roots-Dunhill-4094-N
15 18 28 I HAD A DREAM
Revere/Raiders-Columbia-44227-H
16 29 43 TWELVE THIRTY
Mamas & Papas-Dunhill-4099-N
17 26 22 GROOVIN'
Booker T/MGs-Stax-224-M
18 8 2 GIRL LIKE YOU
Young Rascals-Atlantic-2424-M
19 9 13 EVERY LITTLE BIT HURTS
Spencer Davis Group-Stone-708-G
20 31 63 BALLAD OF YOU & ME & POONEIL
Jefferson Airplane-Rca Victor-9297-N
21 10 4 PAPER SUN
Traffic-Island-CB-1302-G
22 36 57 LOVE BUG LEAVE MY HEART
Martha/Vandellas-Gordy-7062-L
23 40 46 MAKING EVERY MINUTE COUNT
Spanky/Our Gang-Mercury-72714-K
24 12 6 THANK THE LORD FOR THE
Neil Diamond-Bang-547-C
25 23 23 (I Wanna) TESTIFY
Parliaments-Revilot-207-G
26 25 31 HIGHER AND HIGHER

35 48 50 ANYTHING GOES
Harpers Bizarre-WB-7063-J
36 35 34 HAPPY
Blades of Grass-Jubilee-5582-M
37 56 58 KNOCK ON WOOD
Otis & Carla-Stax-228-M
38 44 45 IT'S THE LITTLE THINGS
Sonny & Cher-Atco-6507-M
39 46 71 THERE'S ALWAYS ME ◆
Elvis Presley-Rca Victor-9287-N
40 42 52 I FEEL GOOD I FEEL BAD
Lewis/Clarke-Colgems-1006-N
41 64 73 NEVER MY LOVE
Association-WB-7074-J
42 41 41 CORNFLAKES & ICE CREAM
Lords of London-Apex-77054-J
43 45 61 SUNNY GOODGE STREET
Tom Northcott-New Syndrome-18-G
44 51 69 BRING IT DOWN FRONT
Jon/Lee Group-Sparton-1617-O
45 72 88 I MAKE A FOOL OF MYSELF
Frankie Valli-Philips-40484-K
46 66 79 I DIG ROCK & ROLL MUSIC
Peter Paul & Mary-WB-7067-J
47 60 ---- LITTLE OLE MAN
Bill Cosby-WB-7072-J
48 37 37 COME BACK GIRL
Jackie Edwards-Stone-709-G
49 58 92 CATCH THE LOVE PARADE
Staccatos-Capitol-72497-F
50 49 49 JILL
Gary Lewis-Liberty-55985-K
51 50 54 ZIP CODE
Five Americans-Abnak-123-J
52 62 83 IN THE HEAT OF THE NIGHT
Ray Charles-Sparton-1623-O
53 57 64 YOU'VE GOT TO PAY THE PRICE
Al Kent-London-127-K
54 61 82 MEMPHIS SOUL STEW
King Curtis-Atco-6511-M
55 55 66 LAURA WHAT'S HE GOT.....
Frankie Laine-Sparton-1622-O
Brook Benton-Reprise-0611-J
56 69 96 THE CAT IN THE WINDOW
Petula Clark-WB-7073-J
57 75 93 DANDELION ◆
Rolling Stones-London-905-K
58 77 94 HOW CAN I BE SURE

67 70 ---- THE LOOK OF LOVE
Dusty Springfield-Philips-40465-K
68 74 90 YOU CAN'T DO THAT
Nilsson-Rca Victor-9298-N
69 78 ---- FISHERWOMAN
Collectors-New Syndrome-19-G
70 71 77 LITTLE BIT HURT
Julian Covey-Stone-710-G
71 79 ---- DEATH OF A CLOWN
Dave Davies-Pye-842-C
72 94 ---- QUANDO QUANDO
Bobby Curtola-Tartan-1036-C
73 95 ---- YOUR PRECIOUS LOVE
Gaye/Terrell-Tamla-54156-L
74 81 100 IT MUST BE HIM
Vikki Carr-Liberty-55986-K
75 83 ---- HEY BABY
Buckinghams-Columbia-44254-H
76 91 ---- WHAT NOW MY LOVE
Mitch Ryder-Dynovoice-901-M
77 92 ---- SUNSHINE GAMES
Music Explosion-Laurie-3400-M
78 99 ---- HOLE IN MY SHOE
Traffic-Island-CB1305-G
79 86 ---- SOUL MAN
Sam & Dave-Stax-231-M
80 82 89 KNUCKLEHEAD
Bar Kays-Volt-148-M
81 93 99 I GOT WHAT I WANTED
The Rainvilles-Red Leaf-634-G
82 ---- ---- YOU KEEP RUNNING AWAY
Four Tops-Motown-1113-L
83 ---- ---- GET ON UP
Esquires-Bunky-7750-G
84 84 91 I CAN'T STAY AWAY FROM YOU
Impressions-Sparton-1624-O
85 87 ---- FOR WHAT IT'S WORTH
Staple Singers-Epic-10220-H
86 96 ---- YOU'VE MADE ME SO VERY HAPPY
Brenda Holloway-Tamla-54155-L
87 88 97 OUR SONG
Jack Jones-Kapp-847-L
88 90 98 IT'S GOT TO BE MELLOW
Leon Haywood-Decca-32164-J
89 ---- ---- GASLIGHT
Ugly Ducklings-Yorkville-45013-D
90 ---- ---- LET IT OUT
Hombres-Verve/Forecast-5058-G
91 ---- ---- THE LAST WALTZ
Engelbert Humperdinck-Parrot-40019-K
92 ---- ---- IF THIS IS LOVE

September 23, 1967

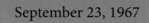

Capitol of Canada sales figures for 1967 show the remarkable success of *Sgt. Pepper*, even in comparison to other releases by The Beatles. Its sales of 145,776 units was significantly higher than the sales posted by the *Magical Mystery Tour* LP (98,463) and the 1967 singles "Strawberry Fields Forever" (91,978), "All You Need Is Love" (82,624) and "Hello Goodbye" (84,351).

And now, as promised, the story of my first significant *Pepper* experience. My initial physical encounter with the album was in August 1967 during a trip to Montreal with my family to visit Expo '67. We were staying with relatives who were visiting "the East" from Victoria, British Columbia. Friends of theirs had offered them their nice old home in Mount Royal and we all stayed there. My cousin Alastair and I shared a room on the third floor. He was almost two years older than I was, but we were both Beatles fans. After a couple of days wandering around the cool country pavilions of Expo '67, Alastair checked out one of the big record shops on St. Catherine Street on his way back to the house. As I recall, it was a record store called The Record Cave, which was run by a jazz music fan named Dave Silver.

When Alastair brought his mono copy of the new album up to the room that evening he told me that he had checked the house and that there was no record player to be found. I thought that was pretty strange. How could you live without a record player? For the next hour or so we both sat on the floor of our room with the colourful new Beatles album cover and took turns reading song lyrics printed on the back cover. We looked at the green cut-out sheet that was under the loose plastic wrap. The bright yellow portrait on the inside of the jacket was new and breath-taking; each Beatle in his own unique and colourful Pepper suit. And that badge on Paul's arm looked vaguely familiar. Why was that? But the best part for me was spending time trying to identify all the people on the front cover. We had fun doing that. Alastair was older so was able to tell me who certain people were. Then we talked about what Beatle idea this whole new package was meant to convey. Perhaps the wax figures of The Beatles juxtaposed beside the "real" Beatles was making a statement about idolatry? Just down the street in Montreal, there were also four wax Beatles at the Tussauds museum. Weird. We had both heard rumors about the drug references in songs like "Lucy In The Sky With Diamonds" and perhaps we felt that there was something a little bit dangerous about this new

Beatles album. And we thought that our parents might be upset if they knew that a copy of this new "drug LP" had been purchased. I recall that it was something that Alastair had to keep hidden away from his parents for a while. Or was I only thinking that? Anyway, that mono *Sgt. Pepper* LP went right into my cousin's suitcase and straight back to Victoria. When I visited him years later, we talked about that time and he told me that he still had the same LP.

My very first encounter with the stereophonic impact of *Sgt. Pepper* occurred while baby-sitting for a couple across the street from my house at 8 Algonquin Drive in Lucerne (now Aylmer), Quebec. The parents had just purchased a brand new Dynaco/Dual component stereo player with Koss headphones. They told me that I could listen to the records on the new system after their daughter was asleep! The couple had also purchased a Canadian stereo copy of *Sgt. Pepper* so I eagerly placed it on the turntable as soon as the little girl fell asleep. I was absolutely amazed that an LP listened to in between two plastic foam edged ear pads could take you to a stunning new world of listening. It was, in short, a mind-expanded experience for me after listening to mono and stereo records in an open space. That inward, aural experience was also heightened by being able to read the lyrics to the songs and admire the colourful gatefold jacket while listening to the music come swirling through the headphones from left to right and all around. Within a few weeks, I had saved the money and purchased a copy of the stereo album.

Fifty years later, I still recall the effect *Sgt. Pepper's Lonely Hearts Club Band* had on me and my fellow Canadian Beatles fans. The visual impact of the special gatefold sleeve was, in a word, stunning! No album cover in the history of pop music had the impact of this gatefold cover. We wondered: why were there various people and characters like Dylan and Stuart Sutcliffe included on the front cover; why were the Beatles looking so serious; were those really marijuana plants in the garden; and why was Paul sporting an Ontario Provincial Police arm badge on the inside cover? The placement of the real costume-wearing Beatles beside their own waxwork figures was a clever juxtaposition. The Beatles were leaving their own initial "mop top" fame far behind! The Beatles had created a new place for fans to visit and return to – perhaps a new kind of Cavern Club for fans to enjoy on demand now that The Beatles were no longer touring.

It was a remarkable time. Canadians celebrated their nation turning 100 years old exactly one month after *Sgt. Pepper* was released. Expo '67 showcased the country for six months, drawing over 50 million visitors at a time when Canada's population was only 20 million. These events made the Summer of Love all the more special. In Canada, the summer of 1967 became a rite of passage for the legions of Canadian youths under the age of 21, with many armed with a copy of The Beatles new *Sgt. Pepper* album. Those who experienced that remarkable package and vinyl album were shown a sneak peek at a new, more reflective, and yet more complex form of both visual and aural communication courtesy of The Beatles and Sgt. Pepper's Lonely Hearts Club Band.

The Communal Sgt. Pepper

by Al Sussman

It was Saturday morning, June 3, 1967. The demands of junior year high school and my duties with Maywood, NJ's Teen Center had prevented me from getting to a record store on Friday, but here I was at nearby Hackensack's Relic Rack to get the most eagerly-awaited album in pop music history, The Beatles' *Sgt. Pepper's Lonely Hearts Club Band*.

I practically sprinted into the store that Saturday morning and immediately saw the album in a prominent spot with the week's other new releases. I picked it up, gazed at the amazing cover, dispensed with my normal habit of browsing for new singles, paid my $2.98 for the mono LP. And practically sprinted home.

In my mind's eye, I can still recall getting home, peeling off the shrink-wrap, and getting my first look at the album. The cover, with both the new-look Beatles in band uniforms and wax figures of the "four jolly moptops" and this assemblage of faces, many familiar (Bob Dylan, Stan Laurel, Stuart Sutcliffe) and some not, the doll with a sweatshirt reading "Welcome The Rolling Stones," the soon-to-be-iconic Sgt. Pepper drum head, the gathering alongside what looked like a grave with "BEATLES" spelled out in flowers. Opening up the album and seeing the close-up of the mustachioed Beatles in their band uniforms and with a certain glint to their eyes that I had never noticed before. Taking out the record, housed in a paisley-themed sleeve and a sheet of Sgt. Pepper cut-outs that would never be cut out, and seeing the familiar rainbow-bordered Capitol Records LP label, about the only link to the past in the entire package. Putting the record on my mono portable record player, putting the tone arm on to start playing, and sitting down with the album cover. On the back cover, the lyrics to all the songs were printed, something unprecedented for an LP by a rock 'n' roll act. Hearing the murmuring sound effect of the audience and then the first notes...

I had actually heard the entire album the previous Monday evening when Murray The K played it on New York's first FM rock radio station, WOR-FM. He tracked the entire album twice that night, with comments and/or commercials between songs, so while I didn't hear it in total context, I had heard the songs. But, in listening to the record itself, it dawned on me that I wasn't the only one having this experience.

I realized that, over that weekend, millions of Beatles fans, not just in America and the U.K., but all over the world, were having the same experience. They were studying the album cover, reading the lyrics and listening to the vinyl record with the same curiosity and intensity as I was. I knew they were. It had been ten months since the last Beatles LP, *Revolver,* with only the exquisite single of "Penny Lane" and "Strawberry Fields Forever" in between, an unprecedented gap between new Beatles albums. This had made the wait for *Sgt. Pepper* all the more excruciating for fans and, on this one weekend, we were sharing in a communal musical Event.

How did I know this? I could feel it; there was no other way. This was 1967. There was no Internet, no cell phones, no texting, no social media, no fan conventions. The rock press that was literally in its infancy. There weren't even any networks of fans, other than small local groups of (mostly female) fans who had formed fan clubs over the previous three years, some of whom would usher in the era of fanzines in the '70s. But, whether alone or in groups, that weekend became a very communal experience for Beatles fans of all ages throughout the world. Getting to know this monumental, ground-breaking record and the package around it was somehow different than the introductory process for any previous Beatles album. And I, like millions of others, knew I was not alone.

A year and a half later, we would have much the same experience with The Beatles' *White Album*, if only because of that album's sheer volume and musical variety. But the first weekend in June 1967 has a unique place in the memories of Beatles fans all over the world, the weekend that we first experienced the most important album in pop music history. And we experienced it together.

Twenty years later, when I sat down for my first listen to the newly-released *Sgt. Pepper* compact disc, I flashed on the memory of that morning as I opened the cardboard long box, slid out the plastic jewel case, flipped it open, removed the shiny compact disc, placed it into my CD player, put on a pair of headphones and listened, gape-mouthed, at the brilliant (for that time) transformation of this immortal album into the digital world. Once again, I knew millions of other Beatles fans were doing the exact same thing. And I know I'll have the same sensation in late May and early June of 2017, when I listen to the stereo remix and 5.1 version of *Sgt. Pepper* over and over again. Only this time, there will be proof of the communal *Sgt. Pepper* experience all over the Internet and social media.

The World of Sgt. Pepper
Pop Music Came to a Crossroads in 1967

By Al Sussman

(originally published in
Beatlefan #106, May 1997)

"For, like, a couple of weeks in the middle of 1967, summer, it was perfect."
— Paul Kantner of Jefferson Airplane

It was a crossroads moment in the development of the '60s youth pop culture. The moment when rock 'n' roll, branded by many adults as silly teenage music for better than a decade, began to be taken seriously as a legitimate musical form, thanks in no small part to the release of one record album. The moment when an alternative music and lifestyle that had been taking shape for close to two years in one of America's greatest cities emerged on a national scale and signaled a new direction for many in the baby boom generation. And the moment when the pop-rock audience began the splintering-off process that would lead to the musically segregated pop landscape of the '90s. They called it the Summer of Love.

As had been the case for much of the previous three and a half years, it started with The Beatles. On June 2, rock music's most popular and influential group released its first new album in nearly 10 months, an eternity between albums back then. *Sgt. Pepper's Lonely Hearts Club Band* was different from virtually any other mainstream rock album. It didn't include a hit single. It appeared to be centered on a theme—a show by this mythical band. The music was rich and diverse, stylistically ranging from the kind of mainstream pop-rock of which The Beatles were masters to a '30s-style ditty to a track with an East Indian motif to a trio of John Lennon tunes that could only be described with a new addition to the pop lexicon: psychedelic.

The album was lavishly packaged, complete with a gatefold picture of the costumed and newly mustachioed Beatles. The back cover included the lyrics, an unheard-of extravagance. The front cover, with its seeming cast of thousands and portrayal of the old and new Beatles, would be a topic of conversation and speculation for decades to come.

Sgt. Pepper took the pop world by storm. Released in America on the first Friday in June, it seemed that any young person with access to a turntable was playing it, over and over, that weekend. And it seemed to be everywhere on the radio, both on Top 40 stations that had leaped on each new Beatles release since they first exploded in the U.S., and also on the new breed of cooled-out FM rock stations that were just beginning to spring up around the country and were run by the first generation that had grown into adolescence with rock 'n' roll.

Unlike today's computerized pop charts that create instant No. 1 records, in 1967, even the hottest new releases took their due course up the charts so *Sgt. Pepper* didn't reach the top of the U.S. LP charts until the end of June. Meanwhile, highbrow music critics, some of whom had glimpsed The Beatles' music maturation over the past two years, were falling all over themselves in rapture over *Sgt. Pepper*. The music industry, seeing the success of such non-singles-oriented releases as *Sgt. Pepper* and The Monkees' *Headquarters* LP, began to shift the industry's focus away from the single and toward the potentially more lucrative LP.

Meanwhile, 6,000 miles away from the city where *Sgt. Pepper* was created, in the city where The Beatles had given their last concert the previous August, a new music scene that had begun to take shape around the same time that The Beatles made their creative turn with "Yesterday" was just now being discovered by the national media. San Francisco long had been a welcome port in the storm for people with a nonconformist point of view—sexually, politically or musically—and a new 'Frisco music scene began to emerge in the city's Haight-Ashbury section (sort of the West Coast equivalent of Greenwich Village's St. Mark's Place). With its roots steeped in blues, folk and bluegrass, plus a dash of rock 'n' roll, this new San Francisco sound was born in the city's ballrooms, clubs and theaters, much like the scene that gave birth to the Mersey sound.

But, while the British revolution was almost entirely music-based, the Bay Area scene took on some of the Bohemian aspects of the Greenwich Village folkies and beats. Many of the bands lived together in seedy crash pads in the Haight. Open sexuality and free love were the norm, not the exception, and there was much experimentation with drugs, both the natural kind like marijuana and chemically-derived hallucinogens like LSD. What emerged was a colorful scene that gave rock 'n' roll some of its most unforgettable characters—Janis Joplin, Jerry Garcia, Grace Slick, and the scene's bombastic den father/big brother, Bill Graham, plus the magazine that would become, for better or worse, the pop culture bible of the next 30 years—Rolling Stone.

While the San Francisco music scene began to take shape in the latter months of 1965 and gained momentum during '66 (the colorful promotional poster for The Beatles' concert at Candlestick Park was a mild taste of the wildly imaginative posters that, by that time, were cropping up all over the city), the story of the scene in the Haight didn't reach the mainstream media outside the Bay Area until the spring of '67, largely because of the success of one band. The Charlatans and The Great Society never made it out of 'Frisco, and Big Brother and The Holding Company, Quicksilver Messenger Service and a band that had started out as a folk-blues group called The Warlocks and gradually morphed into those psychedelic pied pipers, The Grateful Dead, had to wait for their moments in the sun. Jefferson Airplane was the first to bring the sound of the Haight to the masses.

The Airplane had been the first of the 'Frisco bands to be signed by a major label (RCA) and had released a debut album, *Jefferson Airplane Takes Off,* in 1966 with the group's original lineup, including female lead vocalist Signe Anderson. Soon after, Anderson left the band to become a mother and founding member Paul Kantner replaced her with Great Society lead singer Grace Slick, whose style blended perfectly with Airplane male lead Marty Balin. Slick brought with her two original songs that would become the centerpieces of the Airplane's second album. In fact, "Somebody To Love" (then called "Someone To Love") had been recorded by The Great Society and released as a single during '66, but the Airplane's version, with the first wave of "San Francisco sound" publicity behind it, steadily moved up the charts in the spring of '67, hitting the Top Five by the middle of June.

The follow-up, the Lewis Carroll-derived "White Rabbit" (which was widely interpreted as being about tripping on acid), made the Top 10 by the end of July. The LP, *Surrealistic Pillow*, with such chestnuts as Balin's beautiful ballad "Today" and Jorma Kaukonen and Jack Casady's instrumental showpiece "Embryonic Journey" joining the two hit singles, was, arguably, the great American album of the Summer of Love, spending over a year on the LP chart, peaking at No. 3, trailing only *Sgt. Pepper* and *Headquarters*.

What first attracted the national media to the "hippie scene" in San Francisco was the mass gatherings in Golden Gate Park in the early months of '67. Called "be-ins," they attracted thousands of colorfully attired neo-Bohemians or "hippies," as they liked to be called, in flowing robes and with painted faces and flowers in their hair, dancing and prancing to the music of the Bay Area bands, and participating in the other aspects of this communal scene. Young people in other parts of the country saw these scenes on TV news, right alongside the scenes of carnage coming out of the war in Vietnam, and decided to go join the fun.

The Bay Area scene also struck a nerve with a number of transplanted Village folkies who were now part of the L.A. music scene, particularly John Phillips, the leader of the increasingly popular The Mamas and The Papas. Phillips envisioned a music festival, similar to the folk and jazz festivals that had become a summer staple throughout the country, but encompassing many different musical styles and incorporating the happy, communal spirit of the be-ins. Phillips called on a number of his musician friends and colleagues, including Paul McCartney, and thus was born the first (and only) Monterey International Pop Festival. Phillips also penned and produced an anthem dedicated to the San Francisco scene. "San Francisco (Be Sure To Wear Flowers In Your Hair)" was recorded by Scott McKenzie, Phillips' old bandmate from their early '60s folk group, The Journeymen. The song was a top five single by the beginning of July and became one of the two great anthems of the Summer of Love. As for The Beatles, they turned down an invitation to perform at the festival (having given up concert performances), but contributed a poster with the message "Peace to Monterey from Sgt. Pepper's Lonely Hearts Club Band." The colorful poster, which contained art by John and Paul, was reprinted in the official program for the festival.

The Monterey festival was held the weekend of June 16-18, two weeks after the release of *Sgt. Pepper*, and was a total aesthetic and artistic success, the first mass gathering of rock fans that didn't include thousands of screaming teenage girls. It was a coming-out party for a slightly older, definitely more relaxed rock audience, more interested in listening to the music than screaming for Paul or Mick or Davy. And it was the coming-out party for a number of acts not previously seen by a large American audience: sitar virtuoso Ravi Shankar; South African expatriate and jazz trumpeter Hugh Masekela; the king of soul, Otis Redding; San Francisco's Big Brother and The Holding Company and their blues-shouting lead singer, Janis Joplin; The Who, just beginning to make major headway in America; and a literally incendiary performance by a Seattle-born black man who had to go to England to find the first taste of success and who would do things with (and to) a guitar never before seen, Jimi Hendrix. The guitarist was added to the lineup at the recommendation of Paul McCartney, who had seen him perform in London.

A number of pop stars who weren't performing at the festival introduced acts or just roamed the festival grounds, feeling the good vibrations in the air, among them Brian Jones of The Rolling Stones and Micky Dolenz and Peter Tork of The Monkees, who invited Hendrix to appear as an opening act on their upcoming American tour. Jimi, to his later dismay, accepted, setting himself up for an up-close look at rock's first generation gap, playing psychedelic adult-themed songs in front of young girls (many with their moms) waiting to scream for their boy band heroes.

Many of the fans who attended the Monterey festival were among the teenagers whose musical rite of passage was the British Invasion of 1964 and the American rock renaissance of '65. But, someone who was 14 when "I Want to Hold Your Hand" exploded on the U.S. scene, and was pushing 18 by the middle of 1967, old enough to move on to college or descend into the abyss in Vietnam—and old enough to have more adventurous musical tastes. Many followed The Beatles and their contemporaries down their new musical paths. Many also had outgrown the narrow playlists and screaming DJs of Top 40 radio and were listening more and more to the free-form FM rock stations, where personalities like Tom Donahue and Rosko and Top 40 expatriates like Murray the K and B. Mitchell Reed were exposing their listeners to a wide variety of rock, with no yelling and no Clearasil commercials.

However, many also had younger brothers and sisters who were not at all happy with the "weird music" coming out of London, L.A. and San Francisco. They liked the same kind of catchy pop tunes with simple, intelligible lyrics to which their older siblings had grown up listening. The boys preferred Paul Revere and The Raiders and The Young Rascals to the increasingly complex music of The Beatles and The Byrds. The girls read 16 Magazine and Tiger Beat (with its Monkees Spectacular offshoot) and went to shows and screamed for Davy Jones and Mark Lindsay, just like their older sisters had screamed for Paul and Ringo.

But those older siblings now looked with disdain on the younger teens and the "bubble gum" music they had adopted. Other than the East Coast doo-woppers—who, to this day, have never forgiven The Beatles for ending the hit-making careers of the Duprees and Dion—it was the first time that a generation gap had developed within the rock fandom, and that gap would get wider as years went by.

Of course, we're talking about an era when even the music on restricted-playlist Top 40 stations was far more diverse than you would hear on contemporary hit stations today. Listening to a typical station in June 1967, you could hear Petula Clark's "Don't Sleep In The Subway," Jefferson Airplane's "Somebody To Love," a track from *Sgt. Pepper*, The Buckinghams' "Mercy Mercy Mercy," "Jackson" by Nancy Sinatra and Lee Hazlewood ... well, you get the idea. On one of the new FM rock stations, you could hear those same hits, plus, perhaps, Sagittarius' "My World Fell Down" or a whole side of *Freak Out* by Frank Zappa and The Mothers of Invention.

Or, you could hear the first hit single broken by FM rock radio. Back in the summer of 1966, Verve Records had released a single by singer-songwriter Janis Ian called "Society's Child," a song about interracial dating and the stigma attached to it in that era. Not surprisingly, Top 40 radio wouldn't touch it, but FM stations like WOR-FM in New York played it and received good feedback, so they kept playing it and, in spring of '67, Verve reissued "Society's Child." Now AM stations, threatened by the sudden emergence of the FM upstarts, began playing it and, by summertime, Ian's song was a legitimate hit, cracking the Top 15 by mid-July.

On Sunday, June 25, the group that had provided the Summer of Love its soundtrack gave us its second great anthem. Representing Britain on a global satellite TV spectacular called Our World were The Beatles, performing a new Lennon song called "All You Need Is Love," which in later years would be viewed as quaint and naïve, but which was perfect for the utopian hopes running rampant in the summer of '67. Released in the U.S. on July 17, 10 days after its British release, "All You Need Is Love" reached the top of the pops in mid-August, The Beatles' 14th American No. 1 single in about three and a half years.

Mick Jagger and Keith Richards of The Rolling Stones needed more than just love a few days after appearing in The Beatles' "All You Need Is Love" telecast. On June 29, having been busted for possession of grass back in February, Richards was sentenced to a year in jail, with a fine of £500. Jagger was convicted of possession of pep pills, fined £300 and sentenced to three months in jail. Two days later, the staid and stodgy London Times ran an editorial charging that Jagger had been given an excessive sentence just because he was a pop star. The pop world also rose to Jagger and Richards' defense. The Who recorded a single with a pair of Stones songs, "The Last Time" and "Under My Thumb," as a tribute and promised to keep recording Stones songs as long as Mick and Keith were in jail. The weight of public pressure, though, caused their quick release and, on July 31, an appeals court tossed out Richards' conviction and reduced Jagger's sentence to probation.

Six days earlier, a full-page ad ran in the Times calling for the legalization of pot. It signed by all four Beatles, Brian Epstein and numerous other British pop luminaries.

Upon their release, Jagger and Richards went right into the studio with the other Stones and recorded their own sardonic take on the Summer of Love, "We Love You," with backing vocals provided by Lennon and McCartney. Released in August, "We Love You" was the A-side in Britain, but in America, where less was known about the whole episode, the more pop-oriented "Dandelion" was deemed the plug side. It was the first Stones U.S. A-side to fail to reach the Top 10 since "Heart of Stone" better than two a half years earlier.

Even amid this somewhat sobering episode, the spirit of flower power was very much in evidence in Swinging London in the summer of '67. Probably the best-remembered record of that summer in Britain was a melody based on the Bach cantata "Sleepers Awake" performed by the group whose Latin name meant "beyond these things"— Procol Harum, centered around the image-laden work of lyricist Keith Reid and soulful vocals and hypnotic keyboard work of Gary Brooker. "A Whiter Shade of Pale" was a multi-week No. 1 in the U.K. and soon would reach the U.S. top five. The musical darlings of the London avant-garde underground, Pink Floyd, had their first British top 10 single with "See Emily Play," followed by the first album of a long, influential career, *Piper At The Gates Of Dawn*.

Traffic, a new group formed by Steve Winwood, the wunderkind keyboardist-singer of The Spencer Davis Group, made the U.K. top five with its first single, "Paper Sun." Jimi Hendrix had his third British Top 10 single with "The Wind Cries Mary." The Kinks got to No. 2 with one of Ray Davies' greatest songs, "Waterloo Sunset." At the tail end of the summer came two English tips of the hat to San Francisco, Eric Burdon and the Animals' "San Franciscan Nights" (which Burdon inexplicably referred to as "warm") and the Flowerpot Men's "Let's Go to San Francisco."

By midsummer, thousands of young people had done just that, in search of the hippie paradise that had been portrayed in the media. Unfortunately, many came with little or no money, no place to stay and quickly got caught up in the drug vortex that was the flip side of the hippies' light-hearted experimentation. By the time George and Pattie Harrison visited Haight-Ashbury on Aug. 7, the district was awash in panhandlers, hustlers and derelicts, and the Harrisons were disgusted and quickly left. Within a few weeks, the real hippies would pronounce the Summer of Love dead and stage a mock funeral through the streets of the Haight.

For the millions of kids who didn't journey to San Francisco, the Summer of Love would live on in their memories as a particularly rich musical time. Soul music was into the third year of a golden era. From Detroit to Memphis to Muscle Shoals to New York, some of the greatest black music of the decade was reaching the public. As *Sgt. Pepper* was being released, the No. 1 single in America was Aretha Franklin's immortal reworking of Otis Redding's "Respect."

The Motown hit machine was in high gear, churning out such classics as Stevie Wonder's "I Was Made To Love Her," Gladys Knight and The Pips' "I Heard It Through The Grapevine," Marvin Gaye and Tammi Terrell's "Ain't No Mountain High Enough," The Four Tops' "7 Rooms Of Gloom" and "I'll Turn To Stone," and The Temptations' "You're My Everything." It was also a transitional period for Motown. Florence Ballard exited The Supremes, and the group's first single without her, "Reflections," had a near psychedelic feel and just missed becoming their fifth straight No. 1 single. Diana Ross' name was placed in front of the group's, as was Smokey Robinson's with The Miracles.

It was also the soulful summer of Wilson Pickett's "Funky Broadway," James Brown's "Cold Sweat," The Bar-Kays' "Soul Finger," King Curtis' "Memphis Soul Stew," Jackie Wilson's return to hit-making status with "Higher And Higher."

Even with all the flower power and psychedelia, there was still plenty of room on the charts and both sides of the radio dial for more conventional pop groups and hit records. The Association had entered the pop consciousness with a bang in 1966 with "Along Comes Mary" and "Cherish." In '67, they moved to Warner Bros. Records and recorded one of their finest LPs, *Insight Out*. The album included "Windy" (written by Ruthann Friedman about her Haight-Ashbury hippie lover), which spent four weeks in July at No. 1; "Never My Love," which was released as a single in late summer and just missed hitting the top of the pops in October; and "Requiem For The Masses," a powerful take on the costs of war, which gained the clean-cut band some FM airplay and credibility.

The Young Rascals, who had become one of the more popular American bands (particularly on the East Coast, where they were huge) thanks to their blue-eyed soul garage band sound, were in a transitional phase of their development. The Little Lord Fauntleroy outfits had given way to colorful prints and love beads, and "Groovin,'" which spent four weeks at No. 1 as spring turned to summer, had a looser, jazzier groove than their earlier high-energy hits. *Groovin'*, their third album, ushered in more changes, including soulful horns in "A Girl Like You" and accordion on Eddie Brigati's showcase, "How Can I Be Sure," both of which became Top 10 singles by early fall, plus even more adventurous album tracks, which gave The Rascals credibility with the FM audience.

In April, Murray the K, on his show on WOR-FM in New York, had played two songs he called "English Surprise 1 & 2," which sounded so much like The Beatles that many were sure they had to be tracks from the eagerly awaited new album. In reality, they were tracks leaked to Murray by Nat Weiss, the American lawyer for Brian Epstein's NEMS Enterprises, which had recently entered into a partnership with Robert Stigwood. One of the acts managed by Stigwood was a group fronted by three English brothers who had grown up in Australia and enjoyed some success there. They returned to England in early '67 and recorded their first worldwide-released LP, which was issued at midsummer, after the success of one of the songs Murray had debuted back in April. "New York Mining Disaster 1941" made the U.S. Top 20 and introduced the American audience to The Bee Gees. A second single, "To Love Somebody," did nearly as well and became a mini-standard. The LP, *Bee Gees 1st*, was an absolute delight. Indeed, it was like having another new Beatles album, complete with inventive arrangements, catchy melodies and gorgeous harmonies. And, frankly, it has aged far better than The Bee Gees' more celebrated later work.

Missing from the pop scene for much of the year had been the most successful American band of the decade. Ever since the massive success of "Good Vibrations," the rock world had been waiting for a new album from The Beach Boys and the next chapter in the creative evolution of Brian Wilson. All winter and into the spring, even as the first reports about the *Sgt. Pepper* sessions were surfacing, reports were filtering out of L.A. about the amazing sessions for a new Beach Boys project called *Smile*. The album originally was set for release in early '67, but a series of postponements was followed by the news that Brian had abandoned *Smile* and was starting the next Beach Boys album all over. It took until July for a new single to be released, the harmony workout "Heroes And Villains," one of the Brian Wilson-Van Dyke Parks collaborations from *Smile*. With the summer slipping away and no new album ready, Capitol released a second *Best Of The Beach Boys* collection (the label had issued the first volume the previous summer to make up for the sales disappointment of *Pet Sounds)*. Finally, in late August, the new album, *Smiley Smile*, appeared. It had some elements of the *Smile* project and some newer songs, but, while the new mellower Beach Boys sound gained them some FM airplay, *Smiley Smile* was widely viewed as a real disappointment, and it became the first album of new Beach Boys material to fail to reach at least the Top 40.

Another, younger L.A. group fared much better that summer. The Doors had built the same kind of solid following in the clubs of Sunset Strip during 1966 that The Byrds had enjoyed in early '65. Late in the year, they were signed by folk-and-blues-based Elektra Records and their first album, *The Doors*, was issued that winter. Even with some L.A. and New York FM airplay, nothing much happened until the label took one of the LP's highlight tracks, "Light My Fire," edited out almost the entire instrumental midsection, sped it up a bit, and released it as a single. By the beginning of August, "Light My Fire" was the No. 1 single in the U.S., and FM began giving heavy exposure to the 6-minute-plus album version and the rest of the stark, atmospheric LP, which by late summer trailed only *Sgt. Pepper* on the album chart on its way to becoming one of rock's all-time classic albums.

By the time "Light My Fire" hit the top of the charts, the first album by the sensation of June's Monterey Pop Festival, The Jimi Hendrix Experience, had been released. *Are You Experienced?* quickly became, along with *Sgt. Pepper* and the first Doors LP, among the most-played albums of the moment on FM rock stations and college stations. To say that this was a new sound is indeed an understatement. It seemed that no one had ever gotten the sounds out of an electric guitar that Hendrix could. Teenagers in garage bands were falling all over themselves trying to learn "Purple Haze," "Foxy Lady" and "Fire," and soon debates over the merits of Hendrix vs. Cream's Eric Clapton would take on some of the same fervor that baseball fans of that era showed when debating who was better, Mickey Mantle or Willie Mays.

Hendrix had been a part, albeit briefly, of the summer's biggest rock tour. With no August Beatles tour for the first time since their initial big splash in America, The Monkees crisscrossed the continent for much of the summer, playing to the same type of sellout crowds of screaming girls that The Beatles had performed to the three previous summers. But, the crowds at Monkees concerts were, on average, younger than those for Beatles shows, heavily weighted toward pre- or barely pubescent girls, often with a parent or guardian of some kind in tow. The scenes at the concerts didn't have the frightening air of Beatlemania at fever pitch but, as Hendrix discovered, it was a far cry from the cool "love crowd" at Monterey.

Meanwhile, The Monkees' third LP (and the first on which the group had artistic control), *Headquarters,* spent most of the summer trailing only *Sgt. Pepper* on the album chart. Their fourth single, "Pleasant Valley Sunday," hit the singles list in late July and, a month later, trailed only "All You Need Is Love"—and another song that became the summer's final (and most unusual and talked about) No. 1 hit.

On July 10, a singer-songwriter named Roberta Lee Street, who was professionally known as Bobbie Gentry, recorded a song based on her upbringing in Chickasaw County, Mississippi. It told the story of how the suicide of a boy affected a local farming family, particularly the song's narrator, who appeared to have had a relationship of some kind with the boy. Indeed, at one point, there was a reference to the girl and boy being seen throwing something off the Tallahatchie Bridge sometime before the boy jumped off the same bridge. (This was to be the subject of conjecture for years to come, culminating in a 1976 Robbie Benson-Glynnis O'Connor movie based on the story.) Gentry's record, a languid, four-minute-plus country ballad titled "Ode To Billie Joe," debuted on the national singles chart the first week of August. Three weeks later, with the song becoming a national obsession, it was No. 1, and had reached saturation airplay on Top 40 radio. It ended up spending four weeks at the top of the chart, and was the only major pop hit of Gentry's career, though she cracked the Top 40 three more times over the next three years.

A number of other acts made their big-time breakthrough in the summer of 1967 and had longer-lasting careers than did Bobbie Gentry. There were The Fifth Dimension, with Jimmy Webb's "Up, Up, And Away"; Glen Campbell, with John Hartford's "Gentle On My Mind"; Spanky and Our Gang, with "Sunday Will Never Be The Same" (co-written by future baseball balladeer Terry Cashman); The Grass Roots, with "Let's Live For Today"; Van Morrison's solo breakthrough with "Brown Eyed Girl"; and The Box Tops, with one of the year's biggest hits, "The Letter."

Then there were a couple of acts who had one brief moment in the pop spotlight before fading back into obscurity, leaving only a memorable song—"Little Bit O' Soul" by The Music Explosion and "Come On Down To My Boat" by Every Mother's Son.

There also was "Mercy Mercy Mercy" by The Buckinghams, who had five major hit singles in 1967 and never had another one after that year, and "Silence Is Golden" by The Tremeloes, who had three hits in '67 but never made it big again.

Other hits heard that summer included Engelbert Humperdinck's version of "Release Me (And Let Me Love Again)"; The Happenings' reworkings of "I Got Rhythm" and "My Mammy," The Turtles' "She'd Rather Be With Me" and "You Know What I Mean," The Hollies' "Carrie Anne" and "Pay You Back With Interest," The Four Seasons' "C'mon Marianne," and their lead singer Frankie Valli's classic "Can't Take My Eyes Off You." Also: Petula Clark's "Don't Sleep In The Subway," Nancy Sinatra's theme from the latest James Bond flick, "You Only Live Twice," Neil Diamond's "I Thank The Lord For The Night Time," Simon and Garfunkel's "Fakin' It," Tommy James and The Shondells' "Mirage" and "Gettin' Together," and Paul Revere and The Raiders' "Him Or Me—What's It Gonna Be" and "I Had A Dream."

We also listened to Donovan's "There Is A Mountain," Johnny Rivers' cover of Smokey Robinson's "The Tracks Of My Tears," Peter, Paul and Mary's take on the current pop scene, "I Dig Rock And Roll Music," Jay and The Techniques' "Apple Peaches Pumpkin Pie," and The Mamas and The Papas' next to last single before their first breakup, "Twelve-Thirty (Young Girls Are Coming To The Canyon)."

Among veteran acts, Bobby Vee returned with "Come Back When You Grow Up" and The Everly Brothers were back briefly, barely cracking the Top 40 with "Bowling Green." Meanwhile, Elvis Presley may have reached the low point of his professional career with the wretched "Long Legged Girls (With The Short Dress On)" from the equally awful film "Double Trouble." But, the King would begin the journey back to respectability with his next single, "Big Boss Man."

On the FM side, there was The Byrds' "Lady Friend," Buffalo Springfield's "'Bluebird," The Who's "Picture Of Lily," Country Joe and The Fish's "Not So Sweet Martha Lorraine," and two future pop hits—Vanilla Fudge's slow-motion cover of The Supremes' "You Keep Me Hangin' On," which would become a Top 10 single during the troubled summer of 1968, almost exactly a year after its first release; and The Youngbloods' version of "Get Together," which would become a top five hit and part of the soundtrack for the fairy-tale summer of '69 after the National Council of Christians and Jews began using it to promote brotherhood.

And it was in the summer of '67 that the cultural establishment finally began to take the youth pop culture seriously. CBS-TV, which had run documentaries about Phil Spector and Motown over the past couple of years, broadcast a program on rock's new sound, hosted by Leonard Bernstein and featuring, among others, Brian Wilson performing "Surf's Up," one of his songs from the shelved *Smile* project, and Janis Ian performing "Society's Child."

Come September, Time magazine—in those days a publication not easily disposed toward putting pop stars on its cover—did just that with an op-art caricature of The Beatles and a lengthy, laudatory feature article inside.

But, in the meantime, on Aug. 25, The Beatles, still searching for The Word or the key to enlightenment, were joined by assorted denizens of the British pop scene in boarding a train for Bangor, Wales, for a weekend of exploring the world of Maharishi Mahesh Yogi and transcendental meditation. The weekend suddenly was interrupted on Sunday, Aug. 27, with the news that Beatles manager Brian Epstein had been found dead at his home outside London. In retrospect, it was Epstein's death, not the Haight-Ashbury hippie funeral, that brought the curtain down on the Summer of Love. With Epstein no longer around to keep their affairs in order, The Beatles' "love is all you need" philosophy soon would prove as naive and short-sighted as the thousands of young people who had journeyed to San Francisco that summer.

Of course, the Summer of Love was really just a beginning—the first flowering of a new, more musically diverse segment of the rock world, the birth of a new, more studious and analytical pop media, and the first real stirrings of youth culture for a generation that would have to go through major growing pains and gain much life experience before they could lead the world toward that bridge to the 21st century.

Tributes to the man who revolutionised British pop by giving the world the Beatles . . .

BRIAN EPSTEIN

HE was 26 when he was asked for a record called "My Bonnie" by the Beatles by a Liverpool teen-ager. He was running the record department of his father's store. He hadn't the record, but he thought he'd have a look at the group. He saw a future in their happy, energetic sound—AND HE DID SOMETHING ABOUT IT. He gave it to the world and became world famous himself as the man who managed the Beatles—Brian Epstein.

Right up until his untimely, sad death at the age of 32, he was planning new enterprises for his Beatles and other artists, like Cilla Black. His great strength was his faith in their entertaining ability and the way he guarded this by never selling it cheaply.

In the beginning he spent money promoting the Beatles when they were almost unknown. He toured London with their tapes. Record companies turned them down. EMI put George Martin on to the Beatles. George was with Parlophone, till then a label concerned with comedy records. But the Beatles changed all that.

Brian Epstein had several tempting offers to sell his contract with the Beatles. But the Beatles didn't want him to, so he

ANDY GRAY

didn't want to either. As one of the Beatles said on hearing of his death: "He was one of us."

The fifth Beatle did more for British show business than any manager, agent or impresario has ever done—he tore down "closed shop" signs in America and allowed many, many recording stars to win fame there and, in consequence, all over the world. Show business owes a great deal to Brian Epstein.

Elvis : Deepest condolences on loss of a good friend to you and all of us.

Cilla :
The news is so awful I scarcely know what to say. He was so much more than a manager to me. He was a close friend and adviser.

Gerry:
There will never be another manager like Brian. When I heard the news I was completely shattered. I knew Brian about ten years and he was my manager for five.

John :
I can't find words to pay tribute to him. It is just that he was lovable and it is those lovable things we think about now.

Paul :
This is a great shock. I am terribly upset.

George :
He dedicated so much of his life to the Beatles. We liked and loved him. He was one of us. There is no such thing as death. It is a comfort to us all to know that he is okay.

Ringo :
We loved Brian. He was a generous man. We owe so much to him. We have come a long way with Brian along the same road.

The personality I knew

Norrie Drummond

THE last time I met Brian Epstein was just over a week ago. We had dinner together in a small Italian restaurant in Soho. He was in excellent spirits and, as always, he was planning great things for the future.

He talked enthusiastically about the Beatles' big television show, and of the plans he had for Cilla Black.

He was much happier than he had been for some time. "I'm delighted with the way things are going now," he told me. "In fact, everything's grooving along so nicely."

He talked about his visit to America which he was to have made next weekend. In the past year he had turned down many offers to appear on TV, but had accepted this one invitation to host his own spectacular in the States "because I have a lot of say in the show."

Brian Epstein knew hundreds of people, but had very few close friends. Those he trusted and confided in amounted to no more than about half a dozen — the Beatles, Peter Brown, his right-hand man, Robert Stigwood, joint managing-director of NEMS, his younger brother Clive.

He was one of the most complex men I have ever met, a man of extremes—with him there were never half measures. He was either deliriously happy or miserably depressed ; he either liked or disliked a person.

He was also one of the most honest men I've ever met. He always kept his word and was tremendously loyal to the people whom he admired or respected.

Naturally he made enemies with other agents and promoters, largely because he always wanted the best for his artists. But he never held grudges against any of those he had quarrelled with in the past.

When I first met Brian Epstein during the Beatles' first major concert tour of Britain he dressed rather like a young advertising executive, giving the impression of being slightly above the pop business. He appeared aloof and silent. But this I later discovered was only a shield for the shyness

Continued on page 9

The BEATLES were in Bangor, Wales, on a meditation course conducted by their new hero, Indian mystic MAHARISHI MAHESH YOGI (right), who told them to have happy thoughts of Brian and they would reach him.

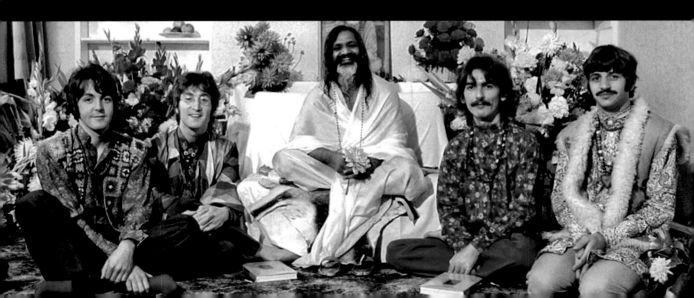

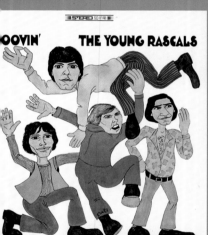

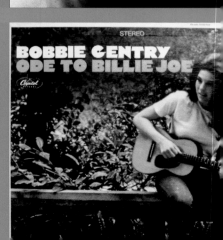

Call his wife in
Influences on and of Sgt. Pepper

by Frank Daniels

Truly it may be said that when someone listens to the *Sgt. Pepper's Lonely Hearts Club Band* album, rarely is it of no effect. Far more likely, people react either with admiration or rejection; there is very little middle ground. Should you walk into a room containing a round-table discussion by twenty music critics, I suggest that you state clearly and loudly, "*Sgt. Pepper* is the most influential rock album of all time." I predict that you will spend the next thirty minutes hearing impassioned arguments from both sides of the issue.

The fact of the matter is likely to be found in the unspoken center of the debate. *Sgt. Pepper* was influenced by many other artists, and in turn, it influenced many. The album was a clear snapshot of the time in which it was made: indicating the state that The Beatles and popular music were in, the directions from which it had come, and the directions toward which it was about to go.

When The Beatles arrived at the point where they were ready to record material for *Sgt. Pepper*, their influences were spread far and wide. They had been reading Lewis Carroll's *Through The Looking Glass* – a fact that is quite evident by references to it in "Lucy In The Sky With Diamonds" and "Getting Better."

Everyday news stories and ordinary events became creative catalysts for "She's Leaving Home" (Melanie Coe runs away from home), "Good Morning, Good Morning" (Cornelius the Rooster – a commercial for Corn Flakes) and "A Day In The Life" (stories ripped from the headlines). Paul's delight over the American use of the expression "meter *maid*" to refer to traffic wardens inspired "Lovely Rita."

Even the concept's framework derived itself from the band names that American hippies were using, including some that became quite well-known: Captain Beefheart and His Magic Band; Lothar and the Hand People; Big Brother and The Holding Company. When Paul conceived of an alter-ego for the Beatles, these sorts of names sprung to mind, and *Sgt. Pepper's Lonely Hearts Club Band* was born.

In more recent years, Mr. McCartney has also recalled reading an article stating that Elvis Presley was sending his solid-gold Cadillac out "on tour" late in 1966. At the time, the King himself had not toured in years, and the Beatles had just decided to stop touring. Paul joked about sending the band's next album out on tour like Elvis' car. Of course this gave rise to pretending to be someone other than the Beatles and letting the LP substitute for touring.

Musically, The Beatles were listening to anyone and every sound that they found to be new or exciting. Paul and Ringo attended a performance by Jimi Hendrix at the Bag o' Nails club – at which Jimi was by that time a regular. They were as impressed by him as he was by them, and that mutual influence took both of them in new directions. In the Fabs' case this happened just in time for *Pepper*.

The Mothers' first album, *Freak Out!*, had demonstrated new ways in which one might use traditional instruments. The Beatles picked up on what Frank Zappa was doing, and they took his experimentation in other directions. One astonishing feat that the Beatles almost always accomplished was this: they had the ability to push the experimental envelope while at the same time creating a popular record. While The Mothers' album was powerful enough to be on the album chart for nearly half of 1967, it usually hovered in the bottom half. When The Beatles wanted to, they created experimental records that sounded like hits. Such was the case with *Sgt. Pepper*.

In addition to being influenced by the San Francisco sound, it happened that Pink Floyd were recording *A Piper At The Gates Of Dawn* in the same building at the same time as when The Beatles were creating *Pepper*. If you play both albums back to back, you'll hear that they both seem to be – at times – fruit from the same creative trees. The two bands influenced and perhaps challenged one another.

Exciting unusual sounds included not only bands but instruments as well. A tambura crops up in "Lucy In The Sky" and in "Getting Better," and "Within You, Without You" sounds like a mini-raga. Sheila Bromberg's harp ("She's Leaving Home"), French horns (on the title track) and saxophones and trombones ("Good Morning, Good Morning") add to the overall feel that this is indeed not a Beatles album but is, in fact, a concert by a rocked-out 1930's band named for a mythical sergeant. Jim McCartney was certainly proud! Of course the effect created by the quadruple-tracked pops orchestra on "A Day In The Life" was insane, impossible, and breathtaking at the same time.

Robert Fripp, of King Crimson, told Jason Gross in 1997, "When I was 20, I worked at a hotel in a dance orchestra, playing weddings, bar-mitzvahs, dancing, cabaret. I drove home and I was also at college at the time. Then I put on the radio (Radio Luxembourg) and I heard this music. It was terrifying. I had no idea what it was. Then it kept going. Then there was this enormous whine note of strings. Then there was this colossal piano chord. I discovered later that I'd come in half-way through *Sgt. Pepper*, played continuously. My life was never the same again."

Activist Abbie Hoffman said in a 1987 interview, "There's two events outside of my inner family circle that I remember in life, and one was Kennedy's assassination – John Kennedy – and the other was where I was when I heard *Sgt. Pepper's Lonely Hearts Club Band*." The album was somehow that big. Influenced by everything and everybody, the album went on to influence everything and everybody.

Peter Frampton commented in 1978, "There's a place in England called Petticoat Lane, and... they always used to get the heavy albums like a week before. So I went down there and got it, and I went back home. I didn't come out of my room for about three days. I just played it nonstop...*Sgt. Pepper's* was the best thing I'd ever heard in my life."

Roger Waters told Howard Stern (January 18, 2012): "I remember when [*Pepper*] came out pulling the Zephyr 4 over into a lay-by and listening to the whole thing, and just sitting there with my mouth hanging open, going 'wow, this is so complete and accomplished, and whatever.' But it also was more than that: it had a ton of ideas and a ton of narrative in it. And I feel more than any other record it was the record that gave me and my generation permission

to branch out and do whatever we wanted. Well, if they can do it we can do it. We don't need Tin Pan Alley any more. We can write our own stuff….It changed everything…. They had instigated their own revolution. They had transcended all the nonsense of Shea Stadium."

Several in the prog-rock movement have praised *Pepper*, prompting authors of books on the history of the movement to include *Sgt. Pepper* as an antecedent.

Steve Howe (of Yes) reported, "Jon and I had a vision for [*Close to the Edge*]. After 'Roundabout,' we saw that we'd only touched the tip of the iceberg. Could we do something bigger than that? We were thinking classical, orchestral. We were thinking outside the limits of a band. Mind you, The Beatles had done that with '*Sgt. Pepper*' and all the records with George Martin. So we were trying to seize the opportunity to stand out" (interview with Music Aficionado, 2016). Later musicians like Brandon Boyd of Incubus, have also celebrated the album: "I heard *Sgt. Pepper's* and that was actually one of the first times I felt that magical feeling of music really kick in. I was magically, mystically inspired artistically and musically by The Beatles."

Not all of the response was positive. Some musicians have heard the record and thought it to be so excessive that they deliberately moved in the opposite direction – toward what they considered to be a purer sound. Today, Beatles critics debate with Beatles fans that *Pepper* isn't really a "concept album" – at the same time claiming that others did it better or first. It is true that there were conceptual collections of new songs necessarily appearing in a certain order as early as the start of the 1950's. Yet in the sense that commentators defined that term in the late 1960's, *Pepper* was the first of its kind. What the debate demonstrates is that the album has touched far more than simply "Beatles fans." Even if someone is adamant in thinking that *Pepper* was not the first concept album, they are still talking about the record as a sort of benchmark. It has impacted not merely its own generation but all generations since June 1967.

This impact spread so widely that people began to refer to a crowning achievement as "a *Sgt. Pepper* album." Consider these comments from musicians:

Brian May (of Queen), "It worked brilliantly. We had time to write. I think we knew we had something special. We said, 'This can be our *Sgt. Pepper*. Or whatever.'" (about *A Night at the Opera*, interview with Q magazine, 03/1991)

Kevin "Noodles" Wasserman (of The Offspring), "*Smash* was our third record. And it was just another record. It wasn't like all of a sudden we were doing our *Sgt. Pepper's*. Though some of the songs seemed a little different, certainly." (interview with Rolling Stone, 2014)

Looking ahead to their new LP, Dogdy heralded, "It's released in January next year and it's called *Stand Upright In A Cool Place*. It's the best stuff we've done, it's our *Sgt. Pepper*." (interview with 247 Magazine, 2011)

Even greats like Ozzy Osbourne have pointed to *Pepper* as being a crest...a pinnacle. "I ask this question, 'What's my best record, and what's my worst record?' I always say I haven't made my *Sgt. Pepper*, meaning the pinnacle of the greatest band ever. For The Beatles, it was *Sgt. Pepper's Lonely Hearts Club Band***,** and if I say any one of the past albums is my *Sgt. Pepper*, that means that every other one is on a downer. I'm a perfectionist, and I strive for that one album." (interview with Lior Phillips, 2014)

Tommy James observed the influences that the album had on music. "I was such a Beatle fan. All of us were in one way or another following The Beatles, and that's what the '60s were all about. If you were a musician in the '60s, you listened very carefully to everything The Beatles were doing, including what studio they were in, how they were miking the drums and so forth... You know, what they did with the *Sgt. Pepper* album just from inside the industry is they changed the whole nature of the industry. Literally, we went from singles to albums that fast because as soon as the record companies saw the incredible money that could be made from really having a monster album, suddenly it went from singles to albums." (interview with Jennifer Dodge, 2014)

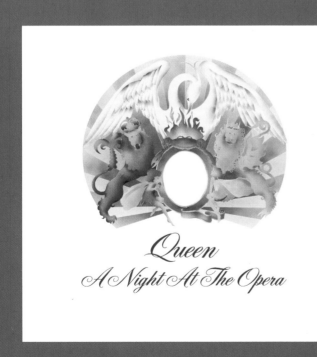

How widely did that influence spread? *Tropicália: ou Panis et Circencis* by various Brazilian artists, was a musical statement in 1968 making experimental art out of popular music. It was strongly influenced by *Pepper* and remains as one of the important records in the modern history of Brazilian music.

Remarking on how the album shaped her background in music, the "notorious" Tori Amos said, "I listened to The Beatles all the time. … My mother had LOADS of records from the '30s, '40s, and '50s. …. So I had access to things like Fats Waller and Nat King Cole, George Gershwin, and Judy Garland. But I remember hearing *Sgt. Pepper* and just going, "I want to be in that band!" So when my father said me, "What kind of musician do you want to be when you grow up? Do you want to play Bach or Beethoven?" And I went over to the record collection, pulled out *Sgt. Pepper* and said, "I want to do this!"" (interview with Creem, March 1994)

So we see that *Sgt. Pepper* was part of a great transition in music—of which The Beatles were a large part. Artists at the time competed and collaborated with one another, sometimes unintentionally. They responded and reacted to what one another were doing, with each artist adding their own unique spin to the culture. From *Rubber Soul*, The Beach Boys went to *Pet Sounds*, and *Pet Sounds* led to *Pepper*. Such transitions weren't always linear. The Rolling Stones' first British LP did not mention the group's name on the front cover because it would be unnecessary to their fans. *Rubber Soul* and *Revolver* went further with that concept, and *Sgt. Pepper* made the group's name part of the cover photograph. The Stones' next album, *Their Satanic Majesties' Request* was, like *Sgt. Pepper's Lonely Hearts Club Band*, an album that paid great attention to production. It would not be accurate, though, to say that these groups were "copying" one another. Rather as we have seen, the artists and their records became inspirations for one another, and the records sometimes became popular enough that collectively they influenced the genre itself.

We see this even in small places. The inner sleeve to Captain Beefheart's first album, *Safe As Milk*, shows a picture of the *Sgt. Pepper* album cover. Photographs of John Lennon from 1967 show (in the background) the promotional bumper sticker for *Safe As Milk*. These photos gave rise to rumors. Did John like Beefheart? Were they going to create an album for Zapple in 1969? What was Beefheart trying to say with his 1968 song, "Beatle Bones And Smokin' Stones?" The relationship was clearly more complex than "one influenced the other."

For certain, whenever The Beatles come up in conversation, not too much time passes before someone mentions *Sgt. Pepper*. They hate it. They love it. It was the best. It was overrated. It was too much. There should have been more. Did Brian Epstein really suggest that they replace the expensive cover with a brown paper bag? It has been fifty years, and we still talk about it.

Sgt. Pepper's Lonely Hearts Club Band topped the album charts without any singles. Perhaps this was because the album touched people in magical and mysterious ways. It was influenced by everything that The Beatles could see and hear, and the record wound up generating enormous influence. Whether you love it or hate it, there has never been anything else like it.

PENNY LANE

STRAWBERRY FIELDS FOREVER

E.M.I. RECORDS · HAYES · MIDDLESEX · ENGLAND
(The Gramophone Company Ltd.)
Made and Printed in Great Britain

FAN RECOLLECTIONS

KAREN, MARY AND KRIS

In June of 1967, I was 17 years old, a high school junior, looking forward to becoming a senior. But that was nothing compared to the biggest event of the summer when The Beatles released *Sgt. Pepper*! By that time, it seemed like forever since their last U.S. tour in the summer of '66. Every summer was magic because "THEY" would be here on American soil. We would get to hear the tour reports on our local radio stations from those privileged DJs who got to go along for the ride. But there would be no 1967 tour.

We saw them change in February 1967. Films of "Penny Lane" and "Strawberry Fields Forever," shown on Hollywood Palace, introduced us to the incredible visual of that change...from mop tops to mustaches, they evolved from "the lads" and "the boys" to men.

The music was captivating. We loved them, so we grew and changed with them. If it made them happy, it made us happy.

That spring, I had just made some new friends. We met over Beatle magazines at the neighborhood drug store and are friends to this day. In mid-April, we were all going crazy over a sneak preview of a new Beatles song on KYW radio's Jerry G show. Somehow, a low fidelity copy of the recording (which we later learned was titled "A Day In The Life") snuck out. The song was voted the number one song every night during the station's top ten countdown. We waited on pins and needles each night to hear it again!

Then came the day *Sgt. Pepper* was released! We raced to the local record store to get our copies. What a treasure to hold in our hands, to experience that amazing cover, which opened up to show that marvelous photo of them! We were so proud of our precious new Beatles album that we had our picture taken with the open gatefold cover on the steps to my house in Cleveland, Ohio. (That's me on the right.)

What did this album mean to young girls who had fallen in love with those four lads three years earlier, who had obsessed over every picture and every teen magazine article, who loved their Liverpool accents and who loved how great their friendship was with each other?

We loved the "goodies" inside the cover jacket! We loved reading the lyrics to the songs! We loved the idea of the "concept" album, with all those cool segues and crossfades. And when we finally got to hear a proper recording of "A Day In The Life," we realized how truly unique it was, combining John's song with Paul's,

and the "big build up" at the end with the loooong chord closing out the album.

Even though George Harrison played sitar on "Norwegian Wood" and "Love You To," "Within You Without You" was the first song he had that sounded "fully Indian." I LOVED the guitar part on "Fixing a Hole." There was Paul's unique "old style music hall" sound on "When I'm 64" and the "circus sounds" on John's "Mr. Kite!" To us, "She's Leaving Home" hit home. We just knew it had to be a true story. Every song on the album was magnificent and unique. We didn't listen to anything else for weeks.

Can it really be 50 years ago? Those songs still sound as wonderful today as they did then, and listening to *Sgt. Pepper* takes you back into a time when there was a real sense of hope that things would change for the better. And leading the way...who else? Our Fabs!

Kris Spackman Tash

What did *Sgt. Pepper's Peppers Lonely Hearts Club Band* mean to us in 1967? Everything! I have such vivid memories of walking to the nearest record store (at Cedar Center) on the long-awaited day of Friday, June 2, to buy my copy of the new Beatles album, walking home gazing at the amazing colorful cover and then listening to the album for the first time! We spent the entire summer listening to the album, talking about the songs and about the guys' new look (mustaches!) and colorful clothes. At 15, I was still too young to work (other than babysit). I had such a great group of girlfriends and fellow Beatles fans to hang out with: Kris, Mary, Marla, Nancy, Maureen, Debbie and Leslie. (That's me on the left with Mary and Kris). I remember the summer of '67 as one of the best of my youth.

Karen Rothman

Growing up in rural Maine, my brothers and I had to wait a few weeks to get a copy of *Sgt. Pepper* until we could go to a city record store as it was not available in our local hardware store (which fortunately did sell 45s). We loved the gatefold sleeve, the inserts and the lyrics on the cover. And of course, whenever our father wasn't around, we played the hell out of it. One day he came home earlier than expected while "When I'm Sixty-Four" was flowing from the speakers. He actually inquired what the song was and was surprised when told it was The Beatles. Later, if I was playing records, he would ask to hear it again. I'll be Sixty-Four next year and will play that song with gusto and imagine my now deceased dad joining in.

Gary L. Anderson

I was visiting relatives in the summer of 1967 when *Sgt. Pepper* was released. A teenage cousin, who was six years older then me, played the album for me. Its impact on me was like the scene in *The Wizard Of Oz* when the door to Dorothy's house opened in Munchkin Land and the world changed from black & white to glorious vivid color! During that visit, I celebrated a birthday, and my father asked me what I wanted. I said "The Beatles' *Sgt. Pepper* album." Although he was not a Beatles fan, he bought it for me. I still have it.

Jeff Mooney, Atlanta, GA

I was the ripe old age of 14 in the summer of 1967 when I was spending my vacation with my grandmother and uncle on the family farm in northern Alberta, Canada. One afternoon we took a drive to the nearby town and lo and behold there in a shop window was *Sgt. Pepper*! This was a very small town and they didn't have a proper record store, but this particular shop had the new Beatles LP displayed in its window. My grand-ma bought it for me that day! I took in back to the farm and played it on my uncle's stereo system. Having heard all of their albums up to that time, I remember being awestruck at how different it was. Sure you had the guitars and such but there sure were some unusual sounds on that LP. It was all so different. The artwork, which had so taken me in at first glance, was so cool. I spent countless hours studying it. The words to the songs were printed on the back! Reading the printed lyrics along with the music was something unique for me. My copy was played to death, but I still proudly have it in my collection to this day.

Richard Zahn

I am a second generation Beatles fan and the first Beatles album I ever owned was *Sgt. Pepper*. In 1988, I was watching television with my mom, when a new show called The Wonder Years came on. It was about a boy growing up in the 1960's and the theme song was "With A Little Help From My Friends" sung by Joe Cocker. I said to my mom that I liked the song and asked her if she had heard it before. She said, "Yes, but the original by The Beatles is much better." The next day, I was at my friend's house for a sleepover and mentioned something about the show to my friend's mom. Through this conversation, she told me all about her love for The Beatles and seeing them in concert at Busch Stadium in 1966. I was interested and went out to the mall and looked at the Beatles cassette tapes. I spent my babysitting money on *Sgt. Pepper* because I wanted to hear what the "real" version of "With A Little Help" sounded like. Needless to say, I was blown away by the entire album and I listened to it over and over again on the cassette deck in my bedroom. A Beatlemaniac was born!

Sara Schmidt

I was in 6th grade when *Sgt. Pepper* was released. By then, many kids had switched to The Monkees. My older sister brought the album home and we gave it a listen. The first song was okay and the Ringo song was fun, but then it got weird. I found myself longing for my old Beatles. As I grew older, I learned to appreciate *Pepper* more for the historical event that it was, but it is probably still the Beatles album I play the least. I'm not sure if it is because it really isn't a rock and roll album or if there something inside me from 50 years ago that I've never gotten over.

Brian Barros

I was 18 in 1967 and had always been a Beatles fan, buying all their records as they were released, including *Sgt. Pepper*. I remember frequently hearing the album's songs on Radio London.

My friends and I were urban hippies in those days and listening to a lot of psychedelic music from the U.S., so we welcomed *Sgt. Pepper* with opened arms with its metaphors to LSD. My favorite song was "Within You Without You," showcasing George's expertise with the sitar. The cover was amazing! Those military style jackets were all the rage, and the guys wore them so well. Plus there was the added challenge of identifying the personalities featured in the crowd. Discussions about the real meaning of the cover and its symbolism was the topic of conversation for a long, long time.

Linda Marshall

I was just seventeen and living in a rural market town in Berkshire, England in the summer of 1967. As a member of the Beatles Fan Club, I was kept informed of what was going on with the group through The Beatles Book monthly issues. I used to listen to Radio London on my transistor radio. The BBC was old school and stuffy, but it did steal Kenny Everett, a true champion of The Beatles, from Radio London in May 1967.

I bought a mono *Sgt. Pepper* with my own money earned from a Saturday job at a grocery store. I was rather taken aback by the album and can't say I liked it right away. It was a mash up of jokey (sing songs on the bus) stuff like "When I'm Sixty-Four" and "With A Little Help From My Friends," which to me sounded like throwbacks to the 40s and 50s. But it had clever innovative songs that told stories like "Mr. Kite!" and George's Indian influences. *Sgt. Pepper* was jarring as it wasn't all short repetitive bouncy pop sounds that The Beatles had produced before. The cover was out of the Monty Python school and, while different for The Beatles, it was a quirky style popular in the 60s. The words on the back of the cover was a first for me.

Valerie Strand

During the summer of 1967, I was 16 and living in Farnborough, Hampshire, England. Because *Sgt. Pepper* was so different, it confused some fans. There was talk of the songs having been written while members of the group were taking mind-altering drugs and the BBC banning of "A Day In The Life" because of possible drug references. The cover is still one of the best.

Sandra Eagleton Venables, Australia

While I don't have any particular memory of *Sgt. Pepper* when it first came out, I do have a couple of great memories of it a little later on. In 1974, the album was adapted into an off-Broadway play at New York's Beacon Theater and John and I attended opening night. And then there was the time that John had me try on his Sgt. Pepper suit which was much heavier than I expected ... It was certainly a thrill!

May Pang

THE MONTEREY

CAROL DECK REPORTS ON A MAD, MAD WEEKEND OF MONKEES, BEATLES AND THE GROOVIEST GROUPS IN THE WORLD!

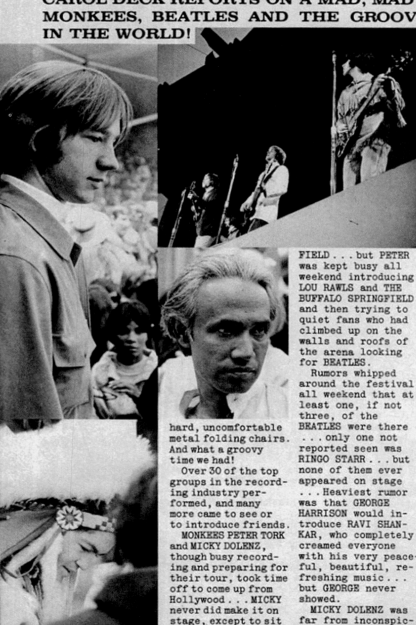

hard, uncomfortable metal folding chairs. And what a groovy time we had!

Over 30 of the top groups in the recording industry performed, and many more came to see or to introduce friends.

MONKEES PETER TORK and MICKY DOLENZ, though busy recording and preparing for their tour, took time off to come up from Hollywood . . . MICKY never did make it on stage, except to sit on the side and watch the BUFFALO SPRING-FIELD . . . but PETER was kept busy all weekend introducing LOU RAWLS and THE BUFFALO SPRINGFIELD and then trying to quiet fans who had climbed up on the walls and roofs of the arena looking for BEATLES.

Rumors whipped around the festival all weekend that at least one, if not three, of the BEATLES were there . . . only one not reported seen was RINGO STARR . . . but none of them ever appeared on stage . . . Heaviest rumor was that GEORGE HARRISON would introduce RAVI SHANKAR, who completely creamed everyone with his very peaceful, beautiful, refreshing music . . . but GEORGE never showed.

MICKY DOLENZ was far from inconspicious in his complete (American) Indian outfit, including feathered headress which flowed down to his heels . . . MICKY told FLIP that he made the entire outfit himself and that the head-dress, despite its size, was really very light and comfortable . . . but he did have to take it off when he went out into the audience to watch the who because people couldn't see over it.

At one point MICKY couldn't find a seat and decided to sit on the ground in an aisle but told he would have to clear the aisle, so he returned backstage where he spent most of the festival.

Another who made no attempt to remain unnoticed was Rolling Stone BRIAN JONES, who strolled about during the entire festival in floor length (India) Indian beige robes . . . Brian looked very pale and his hair seems to be a lighter shade of blond . . . he could definitely use a little of the good California sunshine . . . unfortunately he didn't get any in Monterey where it was cold and overcast the entire weekend and even rained once while OTIS REDDING was on stage.

Photographers at the festival didn't

FLIP

From about 1963 or 64 on, for me and my crowd, The Beatles were the go-to group, the gold standard. Other groups and individual artists might be very good, even have strokes of genius, but still not come close to The Beatles.

I was living in Hollywood on the day *Sgt. Pepper* came out, and I drove up to David Crosby's place in Beverly Glen, maybe 3½ miles from Laurel Canyon as the crow flies. David had the good sound system and a copy of the album. My system wasn't as good as David's, so I called him. He said, "well, I won't be there, but you're welcome to come and listen." On the way there, I heard "Fixing A Hole" on the radio, and recognized the voice and style, but didn't know it was on the album. I enjoyed a lot the rhythm and production of the song, and I was delighted to hear it on *Pepper*.

So, I sat down and listened. Finally, when the last, grand orchestral hit had died away, I continued sitting there in front of the speakers, awestruck.

Later, I heard that the notion of a "concept" album was not part of the original plan, that it was only after much of it had been recorded that The Beatles themselves said like "hey, this is a concept album." Personally, my thought on that matter is: who cares? It hangs together rather well for a concept album, just a few cuts leaking out, but as a whole record, it was The Beatles at their peak, and The Beatles at their peak was the peak of pop music then and for years afterwards. Overall, no one else has come close. Truly one of those once-in-a-generation miracles. Maybe once in a century. Smile.

Peter Tork

The first time I heard *Sgt. Pepper* I was at Micky Dolenz's house in Laurel Canyon, Hollywood. Micky had an advance press copy. We would listen to *Sgt. Pepper* while watching Disney's *Alice In Wonderland*, night after night. *Sgt. Pepper* was our soundtrack for the movie. A group of us traveled to the Monterey Pop Festival June 16th and that recording was "the happening" of 1967, along with all of the great performances in Monterey. It remains my favorite Beatles album today because it was a journey in itself. When I hear any of the *Sgt. Pepper* tracks, I go back in time to a special place where memories are filled with music, laughter and mystique. The album is pure musical genius.

Kay Zar Crow, Helicopter Girl who buzzed The Beatles in 1965, Benedict Canyon house

I was an 8-year-old kid actor in Hollywood getting ready to start a new series for NBC, with three older siblings, two of whom had a band called The Uncut Version. My eldest sister was turning 15 the weekend of the Monterey Pop Festival and our parents took the whole family. I remember getting the word LOVE painted on my face and I wishing we could go to San Francisco with flowers in our hair. We saw Janis, Ravi, Mamas & Papas, Laura Nyro...but not Hendrix. I was starting a job on Monday. There was a tent with a record player inside of it, incense flowing out through the opening. On the turntable was the most glorious, strange and beautiful sound I ever heard: "Lucy In The Sky With Diamonds." The Beatles didn't look like The Beatles anymore, but reminded me more of figures from the Civil War. They didn't really sound like The Beatles either. They had found a secret formula to expand their minds and they took us all with them for a while. They were a great unifying force. That summer, *Sgt Pepper* meant more to me than anything on TV.

Ted Quinn

I had my 14th birthday shortly after *Sgt. Pepper* was released. My sister got her copy of the album the day it was released. She brought it home, disappointed that "Strawberry Fields" and "Penny Lane" were not on the LP. Her disappointment disappeared as each song filled the house with such a new and fantastic sound that was a big change from previous releases by our boys from Liverpool. Although my sister allowed me to listen to her Beatles records with her or on my own just about any time I wanted, I needed to add *Sgt. Pepper* to my limited collection of Fab Four records. After cutting enough lawns to pay for the album, I had my mother drive me to K-mart to obtain my treasured booty. After returning from the store, I plunked the LP on her turntable and set the tone arm down. As it started to play, my sister asked me why I had bought a record she already had and that I could borrow any time. I told her that I just had to have my own *Sgt. Pepper* album. My mom just shook her head.

Dan Tomaszewski

I became a full-fledged Beatles fan in 1972 at age eleven when my brother bought a copy of *Sgt. Pepper* on the lime green Capitol label. Once that wore out, he replaced it with a copy on the Apple label. I finally got my own copy in 1980 on the purple label. For English class, I wrote an essay about the album and got an A! Fifteen years later, I went to a used record store in Portland, Oregon. There was a near-mint copy of the album in mono with everything intact priced at $200, which was more than I was planning to spend. I went to a yard sale less than a mile away and found five mono copies of the album, all in varying conditions, but with the custom inner sleeve and the insert. I asked the man in charge, "How much would you take for one of these albums?" He said, "a buck each." Without hesitation,

I quickly purchased them all and still have them. Of course, I enjoy listening to both the mono and stereo versions of this album. It Was 50 Years Ago Today!

Timothy Swan

In 1973, at the age of 10, I bought an Apple reissue of *Sgt. Pepper* for $4.57. Our original mono pressing was worn out and needed replacing. This was my first time hearing the stereo mix and it was a lot of fun turning the balance switch from side to side so I could hear the separate channels with all the different sounds on each speaker. The album still blows me away as it's just as beautiful to listen to as it is to look at. It still sounds fresh and exciting. It feels like much more than just a great album, it really feels like I'm attending a performance that leaves me in a daze after that brilliant piano chord at the end. It certainly makes good on its guarantees of a smile and a splendid time.

Farrell McNulty

I had just finished my junior year in high school when *Sgt. Pepper* was released. I bought the album within days of its release. I thought it was fantastic, but was a little disappointed it did not include "Penny Lane" and "Strawberry Fields Forever." Everyone had transistor radios and listened to Top 40 AM radio. The local stations only played Top 40 singles, not album tracks. However, *Sgt. Pepper* was so influential that AM stations played several songs from album. That fall, my art teacher devoted an entire class to *Sgt. Pepper*, where we listened to the entire album and then discussed the lyrics and the artwork. I placed a quote from "Within You, Without You" next to my photo in the school's yearbook. It is still one of my favorite Beatles songs, along with the atmospheric "A Day In The Life."

David Rauh

The summer of 1967 was big—the Summer of Love. I was 18, living in Long Island, just outta high school, cut loose and fancy free. I was in a band, The Hassles, a white soul band. The big local bands at the time were The Young Rascals and Vanilla Fudge. There were plenty of clubs, I was playing constantly.

The first time I heard *Sgt. Pepper* was at an ex-girlfriend's place. It was also the first time I smoked pot. They handed me a joint and said, "You gotta try this." I'd never done drugs, didn't even drink. It wasn't my thing. Still isn't. But I smoked a joint and then they gave me these big Koss headphones and played *Sgt. Pepper* on a Garrard turntable. I went into another universe, a whole other world. I couldn't believe what I was hearing. I didn't know if it was the pot I had smoked or The Beatles!

And then I bought the album. It wasn't the pot; it was The Beatles. They had actually transported me into another world. The intro, they took on a different persona, that mythical band. It got me right off the bat. The sonic effects were incredible. Their use of instruments was amazing. The production so rich and so new, the genius of George Martin. The words were so surrealistic. So many English references, so colorful. So new to kids in America. "Blackburn, Lancashire." "The House of Lords." A texture unto themselves. My favorite song was "A Day In The Life." It was a sonic adventure.

Many years later, there have been these negative revisionist reviews. They're absurd. You can't revise what it was then. This was 1967. What they did was so revolutionary, so new, so daring, so genius.

I was precisely the right age—in the heart of that generation—to hear that album. It hit my mind, my heart and my soul. It is a masterpiece.

Billy Joel

After my sophomore year at Adelphi University, I drove to Montreal to spend a few days at Expo '67. Driving back on Saturday, June 3, 1967, I heard something exciting cutting through the static coming out of the car's AM radio. I yelled out "It's a new Beatles song!" I could hardly hear a thing, but knew it was them! The song was "Lovely Rita." I didn't know a new Beatles album had been released the day before.

I got back home Saturday evening after all stores were closed. On Sunday morning, the only store open was Two Guys in Harrison. I was there at 10:00 sharp as the doors opened. I ran to the record department and there it was, in its own display – with a cover totally unique in every way. I grabbed a mono copy (it was a buck cheaper), drove home and immediately played the record. My older brother, Howard, listened with me. As it went from track to track, what was unfolding was breathtaking. Side One ended in that calliope dance of sounds I never heard. Side Two began with a track that was so foreign to my ears, I couldn't initially relate to it, although I later came around. The magic continued till the reprise into that final song. Was the entire album of newness personified, just a buildup to the final song? My instinct told me this was historic. Howard had his own perspective, asking "Why did they have to put that last song in there after the reprise. It's filler."

I spent the entire summer listening to *Sgt. Pepper*, digesting its so many layers. *Sgt. Pepper* is the most famous, most important, and to many the greatest album of all time, by anyone. If it wasn't for three or four other Beatles albums, it would be my favorite. The Beatles always had to go out and outdo themselves EVERY TIME! For that reason, it is too difficult to pick a favorite. But the good news is, I don't have to.

Mark Lapidos
Promoter of The Fest for Beatles Fans

I was 12 years old when *Sgt. Pepper* was released. Expecting another collection of great pop songs, I was ill-prepared for what I heard when the album made its radio debut in Hartford, CT on WDRC. They played the entire album without any interruptions--unheard of in those days. As I was listening, I had mixed feelings, being used to the more poppy Beatles, not the sophisticated sounds I was hearing. For a brief time, I even preferred the more poppy approach of The Monkees. That did not last long. As their fans were maturing, The Beatles artistic talents were as well, dealing with topics we became more interested in as we left childhood. I recall buying *Sgt. Pepper* and being amazed with its ornate cover, wondering who all those people were. As we were getting older, listening to this album assured us of one important thing, we and the world would never be the same again...

John Bezzini

Even though I was born in 1962, my first listen to *Sgt. Pepper* wasn't until 1977. I didn't hear it on a turntable like most, but rather in the back of a very small car on an eight-track tape player with members of my high school cross country team. We were driving from San Diego to Arizona to do some high-altitude training. That trip was the moment I became a huge Beatles fan. Sure I had older siblings that spun the records of the Fab Four all through my growing up years that made up my Rock and Roll DNA, but *Sgt. Pepper* was my game changer. My memories of me sitting in the back seat of the Orton brothers' car on an open two-lane freeway, in the middle of nowhere, listening to "Lucy In The Sky With Diamonds" left an indelible impression. When I came home I wanted to buy every Beatles album the group ever made...and *Sgt. Pepper* was the first.

Chuck Gunderson, Beatles author

In our house, I was the youngest. In the 60s, I didn't have my own records, save for a few Monkees 45s my allowance could afford. I listened to whatever my brother, Seth, had, and he had a lot, including some Beatles albums. He bought *Sgt. Pepper* in 1968, and, at that time, my dad had an old Garrard monophonic turntable. Even hearing the stereo album on our single living room speaker, it was magic – and you could follow along with the lyrics on the back! Perfect for an 8-year-old to read while the record played and live in the fantasy of this imaginary band's amazing world.

A few years later that my dad sprung for a stereo and headphones. I finally got to hear the album, and those which came after, in stereo, and really see the fantastic picture The Beatles and George Martin had painted. I never imagined I would later meet and learn from some of them how such records were made. But even meeting and speaking to Paul, Ringo, Sir George, and Geoff Emerick and studying Mark Lewisohn's book could never bridge the gap into the world they had conjured. Then and now, it lives in its own universe, both in sound and fantasy. Nothing has or will ever top it.

Matt Hurwitz, Beatles historian

I spent my teenage years in Hampshire, Illinois as a member of Beatles Generation 1.5 (those born in the sixties who discovered The Beatles in the seventies). By the time I first heard the full *Sgt. Pepper* album in 1978, I already knew a few of the songs from hearing them on the blue hits album. Upon experiencing *Sgt. Pepper*, those songs became part of an indivisible whole. Never again would I expect "A Day In The Life" to be heard in isolation without the guitar notes softly fading in from the "Sgt. Pepper Reprise." The *Sgt. Pepper* LP was a cohesive piece; the shorter spaces between songs and the segues contributed to that impression. Throughout the rest of middle and high school, this was the one album for which I would clear time after everyone else was asleep, lie on the floor with a pillow and blanket and headphones, and listen to every note in the darkness, only sitting up to flip the record. At the end, I would drift off to the long fading chord of "A Day In The Life" (mercifully, the American album didn't have the run-out groove gibberish). *Sgt. Pepper* made me feel like I'd had the privilege of being allowed to experience something masterful that I could never adequately describe.

Karen Duchaj

During the 60s, I was living in Oakland, New Jersey, and served as president of a branch of the Official Beatles Fan Club. We weren't given much insider information, but Capitol would send us Beatle albums a week or two prior to their official release date. It was always exciting to hear the latest records before anyone else! I was anxious about *Sgt. Pepper*. One year earlier in June 1966, the controversy over the "Butcher Cover" caused fan club members to drop out. After John's comment that The Beatles were more popular than Jesus, people scorned me at school. So I felt particular urgency for the group to re-establish their artistic supremacy with this album. The day the record arrived in mid-May 1967, I invited the remaining club members over to listen. What first struck us all was the album cover art. We put the record on the turntable and listened enraptured for hours while we intently studied the cover trying to identify everyone. I carried the album to school and played it for my English class. For the first time it was the boys who showed interest. Their excitement for the innovative sound was intense. *Sgt Pepper* securely established The Beatles as the musical geniuses we girls knew they were all along.

Debbie Gendler Supnik

My first encounter with *Sgt. Pepper*, back in June 1967, took an unexpected turn. Having just purchased a mono copy from Sears in downtown Chicago, I had headed home to listen. That's when I faced a serious unplanned teenage dilemma. Though scheduled to depart within days for a summer-long foreign travel school trip, I wanted to plug right into uninterrupted listening – to be ready to share my *Pepper* observations with my peers. Instead, at home, my mother wanted to offer parental words of advice before my trip. I had little interest in such matters and wanted to listen to *Sgt. Pepper*. We compromised. Before our talk, I would first listen to *Sgt. Pepper*. As the disc cued up on my portable Zenith stereophonic automatic record changer in the living room, much to my surprise my mom pulled up a comfortable chair to listen with me.

This was to be *Sgt. Pepper's Lonely Hearts Club Band* for a multi-generation audience. Me and my mother. My mom was super cool, not talking over the music as I followed along with the printed lyrics. At the end, we both sat quietly as the last notes of "A Day In The Life" faded. Then, we shared observations. We had both been instantly won over by the old-timey sounds of "When I'm 64" and "Mr. Kite!," and found other memorable moments throughout. She wasn't a big fan of drug references, or of their facial hair, though the latter seemed appropriate as part of the costumes of the album cover. But overall and much to my surprise, she liked the album. This anthem for the Summer of Love, this Youth Culture collection, was just fine with the Older Generation in my household. (OK, my dad had skipped the listening session, instead being outside – dare I say it – doing the garden.)

Yes, I could attribute my mom's openness to her being a super cool mom. After all, later she would surprise me with a Nehru shirt as a gift. But looking back I think there was something more going on. Brian Epstein spoke with pride about the group's new "mature" music that adults could enjoy. It was The Beatles beyond "Yesterday." Most striking in retrospect, though, was such adult acceptance did not in diminish my own affection. The Beatles retained their cutting edge credibility even while being embraced by the mainstream. There would be a great deal of talk about "the generation gap" as that era played out. But *Sgt. Pepper* showed me that pop music from The Beatles was one very real way to bridge that gap.

My parents are long gone. Yet that first listening impression has remained with me after all these years. Hearing those songs for the first time with a respected grownup helped me put one teenage foot into the adult world. Memories of that experience have continued to deliver on the opening song's promised guarantee "to raise a smile." Thinking of my loving mom, it still does.

Walter J. Podrazik, author

My first introduction to the songwriting team of Lennon-McCartney was in high school reading the liner notes of the *Shout At The Devil* album by Mötley Crüe. In the days before the Internet, it took a little reading to figure out who had originally recorded "Helter Skelter." This was how I discovered The Beatles (and simultaneously Vincent Bugliosi). My formative music years being the "hair band" era, the *Sgt. Pepper* album was a conundrum for me. Let's be honest, "Fixing a Hole" or "She's Leaving Home" are not songs that you crank up the volume to rattle the windows, but there was a level of musicianship and song writing that was incomparable to anything I had in my collection. Although *Sgt. Pepper* isn't my favorite Beatles album, it's a testament to *Pepper* that it is my 14-year-old's favorite album!

Dwayne Hicks, West Memphis, Arkansas

June 1967, the month Sgt. Pepper came out, I turned nine years old. LPs were expensive and I'd never bought one before; I can't remember how much time passed before I was able to save the money, but didn't think twice about spending it, because this manifestly beautiful object was something I had to have.

I got it on a Saturday from a local record shop, my dad and big brother with me. Most stores in those days slipped your purchase into a brown-paper bag – I wrote "SGT. PEPPER'S LONELY HEARTS CLUB BAND" in big biro capitals on the bag, unmindful that it would make an impression on the sleeve inside. For years afterwards, if I tilted that wonderful cover at a certain angle, there was my child handwriting etched into it.

To begin with I mostly loved side one. Unbelievably good. I felt the same about side two except for "Within You Without You," which was way too dense for my young mind. Because the vinyl had no visible breaks between tracks, I'd drop the stylus roughly where it ended, resuming with a progressively more scratched "When I'm Sixty-Four." These days I groove often to "Within You Without You" – it's an extraordinary piece of work, I just needed to grow/wise up to realise. Every song on Sgt. Pepper's Lonely Hearts Club Band, every element, every atom and droplet, remains what it always was and will be: an intoxicating, inspiring, magical, uplifting, dazzling, riveting work, an outstanding achievement for the four brilliant young Englishmen.

I cut out the novelties from the card – the moustache, sergeant's stripes and badges – and one day put them all on and encouraged my mother into the garden with our family camera. I look at the small square black-and-white snap now, half a century on, and observe a lad of nine or ten whose Beatles hairstyle will soon recede. Effecting a sergeant-serious study, the boy turns his arms to show the stripes, deeply proud to be in Sgt. Pepper's outfit. He's still me.

Mark Lewisohn
Photo by Jo Lewisohn

MARK LEWISOHN

In 1967 I was growing up in regional Australia and listening to local radio on a small transistor radio. Every Thursday at 8 pm it was Beatles hour and sometime in mid 1967 I heard my first *Sgt. Pepper* track. It was "With A Little Help From My Friends." The next day I took the bus to my local country town and at the small record bar in the electrical appliance store put in my order.

It arrived (a mono copy) and stayed on my 'stereogram' record player every day for weeks. It was the first album that truly captured both my heart and mind and set my life on a path of listening to music and collecting Beatles records – all of which I treasure to this day.

I am nearly "Sixty-Four" and treasure the memory of that time. I try to pass that love on to my children, who I believe do understand at least to some extent. But then again, you had to be there to feel the magic.

Tim Goodacre

I was only seven years old when *Sgt. Pepper* came out, so I have no real memory of what that time was like. I've often fantasized about traveling back to June 1967 to experience what it must have been like for first-generation Beatles fans to suddenly see and hear those new Beatles, and to be surrounded by that music. How peculiar, wild, and exciting it must have been!

However, even as a black child living in an all-black section of Washington, D.C., I have several memories of The Beatles, including seeing them on The Ed Sullivan Show. But *my* musical world consisted of Motown, James Brown, Aretha Franklin, Lou Rawls and others of my parents' favorites, who of course became my favorites, too. My parents were young, hip, and cool!

When I truly began to "discover" The Beatles on my own, they had already broken up. But childhood memories of having heard "I Want to Hold Your Hand," "She Loves You" and other hits led me to seek them out. And what an eye-opening journey that became!

Initially, I was only interested in the early Beatles. The latter-day Beatles looked too weird and freaky for me. But I was being drawn to *Sgt. Pepper* in the album bin at my local record store. How were *these* guys the same as the guys that wrote "A Hard Day's Night"? And crazy song titles like "Lucy In The Sky With Diamonds." I eventually took the plunge and bought the album.

Needless to say, the *Sgt. Pepper* album was one of the strangest but most amazing things I'd ever heard. Oddly enough, it kind of fit right in with the "new" sounds in black music that I was hearing at the time, like Marvin Gaye's *What's Going On* and Stevie Wonder's *Innervisions*. The Beatles' *Sgt. Pepper* taught me that pop music wasn't just silly love songs; it could be about *anything*. The album was (and still is) incredibly inventive, diverse and mesmerizing. I probably played it five times in a row when I first got it.

I know latter-day fans tend to rank *Revolver* or *Rubber Soul* higher than *Sgt. Pepper*. I get that. *Pepper* is certainly more "of a time" than some of the other albums. But for my money, *Sgt. Pepper* still stands as The Beatles' crowning achievement: an audacious, challenging-but-accessible masterpiece that changed the course of popular music. Yep, they did it AGAIN!

And don't get me started on how *risky* it was for the Biggest Band in the World to release what would now be called an art-pop album! The balls on these guys!

Tony Perkins, Anchor, Fox News, WTTG-TV

In June 1967, I was 13 years old and living in Southampton, England. I had been a huge fan of The Beatles since hearing "Please Please Me" in January 1963. I saw them live at the Southampton Gaumont on 6th November 1964.

The anticipation for each new Beatles release was intense. I remember listening to a special BBC Light Programme show hosted by Kenny Everett for the *Sgt Pepper* release, with tracks and interviews.

I did not get my copy of *Sgt. Pepper* until Christmas of that year. Luckily my friend Tony had a copy close to the release date, and a number of friends and I sat in his bedroom listening to the album over and over. I liked most of the tracks, particularly "She's Leaving Home," "Fixing A Hole" and "Lucy In The Sky With Diamonds."

I loved the album cover, and it was great to have the lyrics to enhance the listening pleasure! I recently had a look at my original stereo copy of the album, and was amazed how good the condition is.

The summer of 1967 in England was for me a great time for pop music, led by *Sgt Pepper* and "All You Need is Love." I have fond memories of the glorious weather and that wonderful music.

Andrew Phillips

In June of 1967, I was 11 years old, living in a suburb of Chicago. That summer I was in a baseball camp. Every day, we would practice and play baseball all day long. I dreamed of one day taking the place of Ernie Banks at first base on the Chicago Cubs. After baseball retirement, I wanted to work for The Beatles.

I had not heard much from The Fab Four in a long time, so I was buying Monkees albums and watching their TV show. But it was just not the same. At a time when there was no cable news, Internet, cell phones, or social media, all I could do was wait.

When *Sgt. Pepper* came out on June 2, I was unaware; and since there was no formal single, I didn't hear anything on WLS AM radio. On June 26th, my birthday, I came home from baseball camp to find a strange and colorful album propped up on my record player. It had a little card from my big brother that said, "Happy Birthday Jim. I hope you like this album. Love, Gene."

Who was this group? I had to study the cover for a minute to figure out that it was The Beatles! But their appearance had changed dramatically from mop top youths to mustachioed men. I must have spent an hour scanning the cover trying to identify some of the icons, and figure out what it all meant. I was thrilled to find Laurel and Hardy on there. The wax figure "mop tops" contrasting with the live colorful Beatles really baffled me as a kid. My brother would fill me in later on the symbolism, when he got home from his summer job.

Finally, I un-wrapped the album and put my mono copy of *Sgt. Pepper* on the turntable and jumped onto my bed. I was intrigued with the fun inserts and excited by the printed lyrics, when the anticipatory audience came on before the title track. Suddenly I felt transported into a fantasy world of Sgt. Pepper, Billy Shears, Lucy in the Sky and the celebrated Mr. K. The music was mind blowing and the lyrics were teaching me about philosophies and events years above my maturity level; yet the sound was distinctly The Beatles. Having never taken LSD or any other drugs, I had no idea of the perspective in which these songs had been influenced by The Beatles' changing lifestyle. I just knew that I had to listen to this album repeatedly all summer to figure it out and enjoy the new sounds I would discover each time. It became the album of the Summer of Love... or in my case, the Summer of Baseball and Beatles.

I never got to play first base for the Cubs, but I did get to work for them. And in 1998, I started consulting to George Harrison, and in 2001 for The Beatles' Apple Corps. So, I guess childhood dreams can and do come true... if you keep your eye on the ball.

Jim Berkenstadt, Rock And Roll Detective®

As a first generation fan 11 years old in 1963 in London, Ontario, Canada, my collection of Beatles LPs began with *Beatlemania, With the Beatles*. From that point on, every new release made its way to our home through individual purchases or gifts. Each new 45 and LP release was awaited with great anticipation and came fast and furious in those first years. After *Revolver* this all changed. While we anxiously waited for a new LP, a hint of things to come was revealed with "Penny Lane" and "Strawberry Fields Forever." I purchased a mono copy of *Sgt. Pepper* on its day of release. Upon arriving home, I listened to it through two complete runs. I followed the lyrics on the back cover as the songs played, noted their new facial hair look and attempted to figure out who all those people were on the front cover. But at the end of the day it was still about the music. I loved it. For me the extended wait was worth it. Again, this was something fresh and exciting and confirmed what I always believed—The Beatles were the best!

Mark Alan, Canada

I must admit at first I resisted the new look and sound of The Beatles when they released their first single of 1967. It had been over a half year since the last Beatles record, an eternity in those slow-moving days. By then we had our own Beatles–The Monkees. We could see them each week on TV and they were churning out hit records just like The Beatles used to do.

As a junior high student, I didn't like "Penny Lane" when I first heard it on WABeatleC. My cousin Marlene, who had expanded her mind to hipper elements as a first year college student, demanded that I give the record a serious listen. I got the 45 and listened to both sides with a friend. We must have played "Penny Lane" and "Strawberry Fields Forever" a hundred times that day. I finally got it, so I was somewhat prepared for what would come next.

I wasn't able to buy *Sgt. Pepper* the instant it came out. It took a while before my dad gave me the five bucks I needed to purchase a copy. But as soon as I held it in my hands, I knew it was something special. The cover was remarkable, still unmatched in terms of imagination. The open gatefold photo, the lyrics on the back, the cutout sheet. And the music, it was like a miracle, the way the songs melded together, the sound effects. It was a wonderful trip, very psychedelic. You listened to it as a whole, but each song was a world of its own. Who couldn't identify with taking a walk by the old school or "woke up, fell out of bed"? And the ending chord of "A Day In The Life" was genius.

I'm glad I gave in to my initial resistance of the changing Beatles. They were leading the way, ahead of their time and unafraid. They were my education. And although I didn't know it at the time, their music would, a decade or so later, influence my music in so many ways.

Pat Dinizio, The Smithereens

I was driving back from Daytona and heard the first track of *Sgt. Pepper*. I had to pull over. The Beatles had inspired me to learn to play guitar (left handed was finally cool), and help start a cover band I joined in '65... The Royal Guardsmen. We were very lucky to have a hit record so early ("Snoopy Vs. The Red Baron"). We were getting ready to record "Snoopy's Christmas" when I thought, just when you know The Beatles have peaked in writing, *Sgt Pepper* comes out. Truly a masterpiece to this day. To me, they have lead the way in song and recording techniques for many years.

Barry Winslow

In June 1967, I was 12 years old. I was in my back yard listening to Cousin Brucie on my transistor radio on 77 WABC. There was an excitement in the air about the new Beatles album, *Sgt. Pepper*. Cousin Brucie was trying to explain the album cover and how The Beatles didn't look like they used to: mustaches and bright color suits. The album cover opened up. The words to the songs were on the back of the cover. Etcetera, etcetera, etcetera.

For the life of me I couldn't picture this cover. I hopped on my bike and rode two miles to the nearest record store. As I walked int, I felt like Dorothy when she went from B&W to the world of color in *The Wizard of Oz*! There was an entire wall devoted to *Sgt Pepper*! I looked. I stared. I picked it up and held it in my hands. It was even heavier than other albums. It had the words to the songs on the back of the album. So cool. So different. I bought it, flew home on my bike and spent the beautiful summer day in my basement playing that magic album over and over, learning EVERY word. One of my best Beatle memories! They guaranteed a splendid time for all. They delivered! Big time!

Brian J Moran

I was 7 years old when *Sgt. Pepper* came out. I was a big Beatles fan since I had seen them in 1964 on The Ed Sullivan Show. I had just gotten the "Penny Lane"/ "Strawberry Fields" single two months previously. It was 50 cents with a picture sleeve. I remember being shocked with their recent addition of facial hair. I thought, in my 7-year-old mind, they were wearing fake mustaches, sort of like a costume. My mom and dad were tight with their money back in the 1960's, so back then it was impossible for me to own every Beatle single and album.

In June of 1967, my aunt was going to my local department store in Michigan and asked me if I wanted to go with her. I said yes. When I went to the store, I immediately went right to the records instead of the toys. I was a weird 7 year old. Anyway, I went to the Beatles section and saw *Sgt. Pepper's Lonely Hearts Club Band* for the first time and was very impressed with the cover. I asked my Aunt if she could buy it for me and she said of course. If my Mom would have been with me that day, it would have been a no. I got it home and within a week, I had already taken the the scissors to the cut out sheet. I remember being not too fond of "She's Leaving Home" and "Within You, Without You" for some reason and always skipped those songs. I had the mono album. Years later I noticed some of my friends had the yellow strip on the top of their cover that said "Stereo."

I was so proud to own the album, as it had just come out, that I carried it around like a proud peacock. When a family picture was taken of me and my siblings, I held the open gatefold cover for all to see. That's me on the left. Although the border of the picture says "NOV 67," that is when it was developed. The picture was taken in June. I know this because we people here in Michigan do not wear shorts in November! I'm still proud to be a Beatles fan.

Terry Thompson

I was wrapping up the 8th grade of Immaculate Heart of Mary Catholic School in Towson, Maryland (just north of Baltimore) in June 1967. Since I lived close to the school, I used to walk home for lunch. There was such a pre-release buzz about The Beatles new *Sgt. Pepper* album that I had talked to the Music House and knew exactly what day they would have the album for sale. On that day, I ran home at noon, hopped on my bike, rode the mile plus to the store, rode back to drop the album off back home, and ran back to school before the nuns could whack me with a ruler for showing up after 1:00. The cover was so amazing, I just knew the music would match it. The 2 1/2 hours until I could go home at 3:30 was the longest afternoon in my scholastic life. But by 4:30 and the last note finally faded away, I thought I had died and gone to heaven!

Larry Miller

I was a 12-year-old Army brat in Rio de Janeiro when *Sgt. Pepper* leapt into my arms at the PX. Away from the US marketing hype, this was the first I'd seen it – amazing! At $2.50, I splurged! I spent countless hours holding that cover, hearing music as I'd never heard music before, wondering who those people were, and singing along with – wow – printed lyrics. It was everything. And why did Paul have his back to us?

Summer meant BEACH in Rio, so I packed my magical album with my battery-operated little record player and headed to the end of Ipanema where the American kids hung out. We blasted both sides, running through batteries while dancing in the sand, surfing the waves, getting plenty sunburned. And we sang loud!

Then, tragedy. My brother left my *Sgt. Pepper* by the pool, warped to death by the tropical sun. I thought I would die. The PX had sold out, of course, so I had to wait and then spend another $2.50 when it arrived. The new record went into my well-loved original cover and, once again, all was right with the world.

I broke the bank for that album, but what I got in return! Memories of those innocent days – forging independence in dazzling Rio, Coppertone tan and popsicles, crazy friends in puberty – swirled together and forever entwined with the miracle of *Sgt. Pepper*. It moved into my adolescent soul, still there whenever I want to picture myself in a boat on a river...

Gay Linvill

I was 12 years old, had no money of my own, and so I struck a deal with my Mom to babysit my two younger sisters in exchange for *Sgt. Pepper*. I think she agreed to the deal in part because she was also curious about it. From the moment I first set eyes on the cover I was drawn into the rich, colorful world that The Beatles had created, a world that the music immediately propelled me into. Some critics have claimed that *Sgt. Pepper* is a concept album without a true, unifying concept. I heartily disagree. As Paul planned, *Pepper* liberated The Beatles from writing "Beatle" songs and gave them freedom to color way outside the lines. From the first buzzing of the crowd to the final ring out of the grand piano, The Beatles shared this freedom with us— taking us from a bandstand to a boat on a river with marmalade skies, to India, a music hall, and finally an impressionistic symphony that redefined the boundaries of popular music. Is *Revolver* superior musically? Arguably so, but it doesn't transport us to another place the way that *Pepper* does. Fifty years further down the river, *Sgt. Pepper* continues to move me, inspire me, and challenge me to push beyond what I believe I am capable of.

Bob Burris, Writer, Los Angeles

In June of 1967, I was twelve years old and living in Kewanee, Illinois. I had been a dedicated Beatles fan for over three years and regularly visited the few places in town that sold records. As I was browsing through the record section at Osco Drug, I noticed the new Beatles album, *Sgt Pepper's Lonely Hearts Club Band*. I took the record home and played it on my little battery-operated record player in the den of my house. As soon as I heard the crowd noise at the beginning of the title cut and looked at the colorful artwork and lyrics on the gatefold cover, I knew this was going to be something different. And it was. It was definitely The Beatles, and yet there was music on this record that was different than anything the band had done before. At the end of the album, I liked the reprise of the title cut, followed by a piece of music that was unlike anything I've ever heard, "A Day In The Life." It blew me away.

Michael Rinella

In 1985, I was in eighth grade and just learning about The Beatles. A fellow student in my chorus class brought in a cassette of *The Beatles 20 Greatest Hits*, and after hearing "Eight Days A Week" I was instantly hooked. I would visit my local record store and purchase every Beatles album I could find—ones my parents would buy for me, of course—and I assumed that everything would sound exactly like what I heard on that greatest hits collection. Imagine my surprise when I popped the *Sgt. Pepper* cassette into my tape deck. Instead of hearing "I Want to Hold Your Hand" or "Help!," unusual sounds and surrealistic lyrics blared out of the stereo speakers. At first I could not comprehend tracks like "A Day In The Life," "Lucy In The Sky With Diamonds" and "Being For The Benefit Of Mr. Kite!" And what was "Within You Without You" all about? As a 14-year-old in the 1980s, I simply could not relate to the psychedelic imagery and hallucinogenic qualities of some of the lyrics. It was all hippie stuff only "old" people enjoyed (old to an adolescent, anyway).

Thankfully, as I grew older, I realized that many of the album's ideas pertain to multi generations, as they are about broadening one's horizons and, to paraphrase a *Rubber Soul* track, starting to "think for yourself." While "She's Leaving Home" may be open to interpretation (why *is* she leaving home, exactly?), the conflict between parents and young adult told in that song is never-ending. "A Day In The Life" challenges listeners to rethink music itself, while "Within You Without You" states that we should "try to realize it's all within yourself no-one else can make you change." Becoming an independent thinker, examining generational differences, expanding one's very notions of pop music—all those timeless elements make up *Sgt. Pepper*. Now, I'm happy to say, I get it.

Kit O'Toole

In early 1964, The Beatles completely swept us off of our feet. Even at the tender age of 6, I was completely consumed by The Beatles, and this obsession has remained a reality for all of my life since. But when *Sgt. Pepper* came out in 1967, we younger kids were in agreement that we wanted our "Moptop Beatlemania Fab Four" band forever! Our impression was immediate. "What happened to our Beatles? What? They now have mustaches! Are you kidding me!" Remember, I'm barely 9 here! We were simply not done with our catchy short love songs yet! Yes, this is precisely how myself and many, if not most of the kids at my school responded initially. I remember it well. Of course, it was but a few short years later, the full value and impact of this landmark, incredible album was felt and its appreciation has lasted a lifetime! Certainly far longer than those initial innocent impressions of a 9-year-old. Where would we be without this amazing record? We can't even think of pop culture or musical history without it. That's the lasting impact of *Sgt. Pepper* it has deservedly earned. But mini-me didn't think so!

Perry Cox

In 1967, I was 16 and in love with The Beatles. My good pal Jon McGuffin brought his copy of the brand new *Sgt. Pepper* album to school and said, "I just got this, I'm loaning it to you for one night." I was thrilled, but my creepy stepfather hated The Beatles and we had a lousy record player. I ran to my pal Marc's house to find him asleep while watching Merv Griffin. I couldn't believe he wouldn't wake up for the new Beatles LP. I ran home and played the album on our lousy record player. My opera-loving stepfather walked in while I was listening to "She's Leaving Home." "It's got strings on it!," I said defensively, to which he replied, "Ugh!"

Stephen Bishop, musician, Los Angeles

I was eleven in May 1967. The Beatles had faded from view and popularity among my age group, save for the truly devoted. The Monkees had become the new innocent mop tops. There were a myriad of groups occupying space in the top 40 besides our beloved Fabs. The Beatles' "Penny Lane"/"Strawberry Fields Forever" single was different than any before, and I wondered what had transformed them so profoundly.

I first saw the *Sgt. Pepper* LP in downtown London at the Disc Shop. They had copies lining every wall around the store. I realized this LP must be important.

My best friend's parents would buy him every Beatles LP as it came out. I first heard *Sgt. Pepper* in the basement of his house on a portable stereo unit. I marveled that during the opening track you could cut the vocals completely and hear only the guitar solo using the balance control. I was also taken aback by the diversity of styles on the album.

I wanted the album so much after hearing and seeing my friend's copy. My opportunity came a few days later while grocery shopping with my mom. There was a mono copy by the checkout counter. I pleaded with my mom until she finally gave in. I took it home and played it at least five straight times as I merrily clipped away at the cut-out insert! I was a Beatles fan first and foremost once again.

Fred Young, London, Ontario, Canada

I heard *Sgt. Pepper* for the first time in the early 1980s when I was 12. There was nothing special about it to me. I think it would have been different if I was young at the time of its release and would have noticed the change in style and sound. I love "Lovely Rita" and "A Day In The Life" and most of the other songs, but I would not say it is my favorite album of The Beatles.

Thorsten Knublauch

I was 10 years old living in Newark, New Jersey, in June of 1967. When *Sgt. Pepper* was released, I was oblivious. Caught up in Top 40 radio, I didn't hear any of the songs from the album on AM radio. So, when I went off to summer camp in Hunter, New York that July, the last Beatles songs I'd heard were "Penny Lane" and "Strawberry Fields Forever." While at camp, an older kid, Marty Kessler (he must have been 15 or so), played me *Sgt. Pepper*. I'd never heard music like that, lyrics like that or sounds liked that. He also turned me on to The Doors, Janis Ian, Jefferson Airplane's *Surrealistic Pillow* and more great albums. But the crown belonged to this new adventure with all its risk and come hither seduction. I came home in August a changed boy.

My first day home, I went to the record store and came home with *Sgt. Pepper*. I devoured it. I read the lyrics on the back, looked at the pictures, drank in the bold colors and carefully inspected the iconic cover. I went from AM to FM, from mono to stereo, from 7" to 12" all at once. The next time I saw Marty was that December at the record store. He was buying *Magical Mystery Tour* and recommended I do the same. I did.

Lou Simon, Sirius XM Radio

I was 12 in June 1967 living in a suburb of Cleveland, OH when *Sgt. Pepper* came out. I bought a mono copy as the stereo version cost $1 more and that was a lot of money to me at the time! That summer everybody really kept on playing that LP as Johnny Rivers sang in "Summer Rain." 1967 was a great year – "Strawberry Fields Forever" and "Penny Lane" (someone brought the picture sleeve of the 45 to school and the teacher let us put it up on the bulletin board of our 6th grade classroom), *Sgt. Pepper*, "All You Need Is Love" and then *Magical Mystery Tour*! Such fond memories!

Nancy (Cuebas) Riley

So, *Sgt. Pepper* took me by surprise. I had barely recovered from the bizarre nature of *Revolver* when my buddy, Patty Dalme, purchased a new LP in which The Boys hardly resembled themselves on the cover. I was bewildered. Why (tell me why!), I thought, would The Beatles want to be anyone other than themselves? They were the toppermost of the pop-permost! Why assume a persona, especially the persona of an Edwardian-era band? The logic was lost on me. However, like every devoted fan, I craved a copy.

Through the fall, I waited, hinted, told Santa. Then, Christmas morning...voila! I ripped the wrapping paper off and clutched the album in my arms. After opening my other presents, I placed the record on the turntable. There was Ringo's jaunty "With A Little Help From My Friends," John's magical "Lucy In The Sky With Diamonds" and the thunderous "A Day In The Life." But strangely, amidst all the joy, I felt something was missing. That "something" was John. (Track by track, *Sgt. Pepper* is, of course, is a heavily McCartney LP. The sexy, gritty Lennon sound that drew me to the band in the first place was all but gone.)

Fifty years ago, in The Summer of Love, this innocent little girl from a staid Southern town longed for things to remain the same. I hadn't yet embraced the fact that the world was swiftly changing, and The Boys were changing. I still believed in Santa...and The Beatles from The Cavern Club.

Jude Southerland Kessler, Author

I have always loved *Sgt. Pepper*. Every time I hear the *Sgt. Pepper Reprise*, it drives me crazy with happiness. Although *Sgt. Pepper* may not be the best Beatles album, any Beatles anything is better than anyone else's anything.

Eddie Deezen (Richard "Ringo" Klaus)

JUDE

Rebecca bought *Sgt. Pepper* when it came out in 1967. She took it home and listened to the album day and night while her 5-month-old daughter danced in her playpen. Little did Rebecca know the seed she planted with this album would create a "monster" Beatles fan. Eleven years later her daughter's love for The Beatles and their music was rekindled by seeing their cartoons. *Sgt. Pepper* was the young girl's first Beatles vinyl album that she would buy in 1979 with her allowance. Many Beatles-related albums, dolls, books, magazines, posters, memorabilia, concerts and inspired events later, mother and daughter continue to enjoy the music of The Beatles and the opportunity to meet people who worked with them or just have a common interest. *Sgt. Pepper* truly changed the way of life for a mother and daughter forever. Thanks Mom!

Jennifer Sandi

I was driving my mother down a traffic-filled street in New York when WABC announced it would be playing the new Beatles album, *Sgt Pepper*. My heart stopped. I calmly told my mom not to open her mouth, that this was important to me. I clenched the steering wheel and tried to pay attention to the traffic while my brain was spinning to the beautiful streams of psychedelic Beatles music. When the album reached "She's Leaving Home," it struck a new chord in my brain. That song impacted me that day more than any other, because in a few short weeks, I, too, would be leaving home. Since February 1964 I had saved every penny with the goal of visiting London upon my graduation from high school, and now, with the lyrics of "She's Leaving Home" firmly planted in my head, it was soon to come true.

Whenever I hear any song from *Sgt. Pepper*, I think back to that day in 1967, when my plans added the theme song to my magical journey of meeting John, Paul, George and Ringo. But that is another story.

I did arrive home safely that monumental day with my mom and I still intact, and I also accomplished my goals in that amazing summer of 1967.

Leslie Samuels Healy, BeatleTripper

I was 14½ years old in June 1967. I had heard "Strawberry Fields" and "Penny Lane" on the radio. They were different. I had seen some photographs of the Beatles and noticed a transformation taking place. They were now looking bohemian, not the uniformed 'Mop Tops' anymore. The Beatles were evolving and taking us all along with them. My world was changing.

I needed to have a listening party of one with the Lads in my bedroom. From the very first sounds of *Sgt. Pepper*, I was being carried along on a marvelous musical journey with The Beatles. Mixes of many musical genres into one with profuse experimental sounds. Each song was so very unique. I would listen intently to each one while reading the printed lyrics on the back cover. I kept replaying "Lucy In The Sky With Diamonds," trying to decipher the meaning. The Beatles talking about LSD? If so, how radical and cool! I was 'in the moment' for each song. I played the album over and over. When my mom yelled for me to come to dinner, all I could do was yell "NOT NOW!!!"

My first listening of *Sgt. Pepper* was the most profound personal musical listening experience that I have ever had. Everything changed. Everything was beginning. Everything was ahead.

Ellen Berman, Artist, Los Angeles

In the summer of 1967, I was six years old. I don't remember seeing the Beatles on The Ed Sullivan Show, but my parents told me that I reacted like I had been electrified. As a result, my older brother and I were treated to *Meet The Beatles!* and a few singles here and there. So when I was six, I found myself in the unusual position of having been given some money by a relative, and against my parents' better judgment, bought *Sgt. Pepper* upon seeing it in the store. I knew even then that not only did it not sound like previous Beatles music, it didn't sound like anything I'd heard before. My favorite track, then and now: "A Day In The Life." Of course, it's still one of my desert island records, and like almost all of their albums, I never tire of hearing it.

Glenn Murphy

When I first listened carefully to Ringo's drumming, I was amazed at how much swing he had, almost as if he came from a jazz background. His drumming is so unique in the way he fits the perfect drum part to the song. No ego. *Sgt. Pepper* was revolutionary and more.

Denny Seiwell, drummer

AM radio and 45s. That's all that really matter to me in 1967. Well, those things and baseball cards. At nine years of age, it wasn't the Summer of Love for me. It was the Summer of The Monkees. My brother and I had the "A Hard Day's Night" LP and loved The Beatles, but the group was outgrowing us. They had mustaches! And while "Penny Lane" satisfied my pop tastes, "Strawberry Fields Forever" was too weird. *Sgt. Pepper* had so singles, so it was kind of ignored at my house.

I started buying more albums, but only bought Beatle singles. A friend of mine got *The White Album*, and I heard "Revolution 9." The Beatles had lost it. I stuck with Herman's Hermits and The Cowsills. In 1969 my brother came home with *Abbey Road*. He asked me to pay for half and I refused. The Beatles were old guys doing weird music. But after hearing it on our shared record player a few times, I had to reevaluate the band.

From there, I started working backwards and rediscovering The Beatles LPs. While *Sgt. Pepper* didn't have any singles, there were several great stand-alone songs, as well as the linked songs at the beginning and end. I had trouble getting into "Within You, Without You" and "She's Leaving Home," although I later grew to appreciate them. But the rest of the album knocked me out-- two years or so after it was released. So I have a bit of a time warp in my head. My Summer of Love and *Sgt. Pepper* experience didn't happen in 1967 when I was in third grade. But luckily it *did* eventually happen.

Tim Coulter

Although I was only six during the fall of 1966, I, like other Beatles fans, was anxiously waiting for the group's next LP after *Revolver*. When Christmas came without a new Beatles album, my older sister sat me down, pulled out The Monkees first album and said The Monkees were going to be the greatest band now that The Beatles had stopped making records. And besides, The Monkees were cuter. I hoped she was wrong, but I also liked The Monkees, so I accepted the idea that The Beatles weren't going to be around anymore.

A half year later I saw the *Sgt. Pepper* album cover in the window of a TV repair shop. The cover creeped me out. That stone bust looked like Lurch of The Addams Family. A lot of scary looking bald men. When I finally opened up the gatefold cover and saw them smiling, I was reassured that these new Beatles were the same ones pictured on my Flip Your Wig game.

Serene Dominic

I started to seriously listen to The Beatles in 1995, my high school sophomore year. This was the year The Beatles *Anthology* aired on ABC. My first Beatles CDs were *A Hard Day's Night*, *Help!* and *Anthology 1*. My next purchase was *Sgt. Pepper*, which was a significant departure. The music was so different from what I had previously heard that it took me several listens before I came to love the album. *Sgt. Pepper* showed me that the music of The Beatles was not just rock and roll, but rather encompassed styles and genres. The cover art is unlike any other album cover in history and proof that music releases are ideally owned in a physical format.

Scott Korf

We bought the mono *Sgt. Pepper* because we had an old clunky record player with only one speaker. I remember listening to the first track and thinking, "The Beatles are going back to rock 'n' roll." But as the album continued, you could tell they were doing something very different. It wasn't until years later that I heard the stereo mix on an eight-track tape. I listen to the stereo mix or the mono mix depending on my mood.

Steve Marinucci, contributor to Billboard, AXS.com

I was 16 and it was the end of June 1967 when I was first introduced to Billy Shears and the Band. My father, a career Marine, surprised me with what he described as "an interesting looking album" by – he thought – The Beatles. He had just purchased it at the Base PX. I remember being awestruck! These were The Beatles? Initially, all I could do was look at the cover. If I thought the Beatles' previously released albums were intriguing, then *Sgt. Pepper* was over the top. I analyzed every inch of the cover over and over again. The packaging, inserts, songs, instrumentation. Everything was magical to me. I played it, replayed it and continued to play it until I knew every lyric of every song by heart. Each listening brought another "discovery" in the form of a new sound or nuance, coupled with the wonderment of how The Beatles were able to create such an incredible work. Each time I played *Pepper*, it was as if time stopped. I was transported to an insanely surreal, wonderful, mystical, colorful, psychedelic world. How incredible to lay back in bed and imagine the fantasy world described in "Lucy In The Sky." From sentimental ditties to works that tugged at your heart, from mystical realms to wise notions about friendship, *Pepper* had it all. Fifty years later, when I play the album, I am transported back to that extraordinary summer. The fact that my Dad purchased it makes recollections even fonder.

Gene Flanagan

I was twelve when *Sgt. Pepper* came out at the start of my favorite summer. It had been a rough first year in junior high, as I had changed schools and homes five times before seventh grade. Music was becoming my trusted friend. I became a Beatles fan with *Beatles '65*, *Help!*, *Rubber Soul* and *Revolver*. My lifelong affair with music started with those recordings. I became a musician like millions of others.

I remember that whenever The Beatles changed musical styles and fashion, the world changed along to follow suit. They kicked the door open for all the great bands to follow. When I first saw and purchased their latest single, "Strawberry Fields Forever" and "Penny Lane," towards the beginning of 1967, I thought that this was the coolest and most amazing music I had ever heard. I couldn't have guessed what was to come that magical summer.

My brother had to repeat the album title to me a few times for me to grasp what he was saying! I bought the mono version as I didn't have enough for the stereo one. It turns out that was the one to have! It didn't matter, as all my cousins and friends had a copy, and it played continuously and everywhere I went throughout that summer of love. Every day of that summer became better than the day before as the songs weaved their way into our lives. I met new lifelong friends, even met my first girlfriend, and *Sgt. Pepper's Lonely Hearts Club Band* was the soundtrack to it all.

Even now when I hear it, those songs remind me of the days when everything was new, exciting and possible!

Ron Arnold, Musician, Los Angeles

My earliest memory from *Sgt. Pepper* was "Lucy In The Sky With Diamonds," which summoned simplistic temptations. As a young child, John's multicolored visions accelerated my passion for The Beatles. Decades later, that song would become almost a nursery rhyme for my daughter, Abby, who was drawn to the song's vivid images and begged to taste a marshmallow pie! John's celestial vocals attracted her in a most innocent manner and she continued to fall head over heels in Love, Love, Love.

Lanea Stagg, author

As evidenced by a 1964 photograph of me (age 2) donning a Beatles Halloween costume, I was "aware" of the Beatles at a very early age. But in terms of really "getting it," that kicked in around age 13, when a lot of kids develop their musical tastes, I suppose. Learning guitar at that same time upped the ante quite a bit.

In a sort of backward way, I was re-introduced to The Beatles by my affinity for Paul McCartney's new music and the renaissance of Beatlemania kicked up by the 1962-1966 and 1967-1970 collections.

Top-40 radio was a growing passion and my two biggest favorites of the day were McCartney and Elton John, who were then dominating the airwaves. I distinctly remember Elton's #1 single of "Lucy In The Sky With Diamonds" making a big impact on me, and one day a New York DJ played it back-to-back with the Beatles original. That definitely piqued my interest in going back and finding out what THAT was all about. *Sgt. Pepper* became an instant favorite and kicked off my quest to acquire a full set of Beatles albums (albeit the American ones) and the rest as they say ....

Ironically, the only thing I really didn't "get" was George's Indian flavored "Within You Without You." As a young teen that acquired taste had, well, not yet been acquired and I would often launch side two at "When I'm Sixty-Four." Today, the once overlooked track is one of my favorites of all the George Harrison compositions.

In recent years, it seems ol' *Pepper* has been supplanted by *Revolver* as many folks' nomination for "best" Beatles album. For me, that honor goes to *Abbey Road*, but Pepper never fails to strike me as anything less than utterly staggering with each successive play, as I'm sure it will continue to do so well past 2026, when I'm.....

Tom Frangione, Beatles writer/radio host

GARY AND TOM FRANGIONE

PHIL ROSS

113

I bought *Sgt. Pepper* at a Philadelphia department store in 1967. I remember sitting with it, unopened, looking at the sleeve and then reading the back cover's song lyrics, trying to imagine how they would sound. I remember the popping sound when I opened the gatefold for the first time. An explosion of color, all four sitting in their uniforms in front of a yellow background.

I remember pulling the record from the sleeve. More surprises. A red and white inner sleeve. A green cut out sheet. I've seen later pressings on Apple and later green, orange and purple Capitol labels. Every one of them looks wrong. That Capitol rainbow-edged black label is an essential part of the visual experience.

And the music. Even though the theme of the "new" band gets abandoned quickly, it really doesn't. It is a "concept album" because they say it is. As good as side one is, side two is better. "Within You Without You" sounded so impossibly exotic in 1967 and still feels the same today. I remember hearing "A Day In The Life" for the first time and the long decay of the final note seemed to last forever.

Stan Denski

I was living in Colorado Springs, Colorado in 1967. I planned on buying a stereo copy of *Sgt. Pepper* the day after its release to play on my new stereo record player (the kind with detachable speakers and a turntable that tilted out from the body of the case). I had saved up just enough money for a stereo copy, which always cost a dollar more than mono. But when I looked at the price tags on the *Sgt. Pepper* albums, I saw that the retail price had been upped a dollar so all I could afford was a mono copy. Without knowing it at the time, I was buying the world's greatest album and listening to it for weeks, months and years on end just the way The Beatles wanted me to hear it--in glorious mono! I even-

tually bought a stereo copy, but my first few hundred listens were the wonderful mono mix. From time to time, over the years, I have pulled out that mono copy and given it a loud listen. It was Fab then....and still is.

Sean Anglum

I was 12 when *Sgt. Pepper* was released. But it was less like a "record release" than if a cultural nuclear bomb had been detonated, with an immediate, permanent world-wide impact. My friend David and I were rabid Beatle fans and I recall vividly him rushing in with the album under his arm the weekend it came out. We put it on the turntable and listened to it non-stop for hours, pouring over the liner notes, studying the photos in rapt fascination. Little did I know that decades later, I'd have the honor of getting to know Sir Paul and having him relate the story of hearing Jimi Hendrix open his London show with *Sgt. Pepper* only days after the record had been released! Paul said he felt like that was the ultimate badge of honor.

Jim Wilson, Musician, Los Angeles

My mom bought me *Sgt. Pepper* as my junior high graduation gift. We listened to it on my folks' stereo console. She loved "When I'm Sixty-Four." *Sgt. Pepper* hit me as hard as *Meet The Beatles!* and *Introducing The Beatles* did: totally unique, absolutely life-changing.

Dan Lawton

I was only 13 years old in 1967. I persuaded a friend to lend me his brand new copy of *Sgt. Pepper*. That weekend things changed. I had been collecting Beatles stuff since 1963, but I had never really listened to the music before *Sgt. Pepper*, maybe being too young to appreciate it. I've been appreciating it ever since.

Garry Marsh

One of my favorite Beatles memories revolves around the release of *Sgt Pepper* to radio. Back then, there was a designated day when radio could begin playing a new release by an artist. Clearly, there was no artist more anticipated than The Beatles and especially *Sgt Pepper*. I lived in a small central California town and in 1967, AM radio was still king. I remember laying in bed, waiting for midnight and the birth of that special new day when radio could play *Sgt. Pepper*. At the stroke of midnight I began with my favorite top 40 station as they played a new Beatles song. But, it was still top 40 radio and playing an entire LP or even more than one song at a time didn't happen. I spent the next few hours with my transistor radio plugged in my ear, wandering up and down the radio dial stopping when I heard a new song that could be The Beatles.

Those who didn't grow up as first generation Beatle fans will never understand the absolute thrill of Beatles music heard by everyone almost simultaneously for the first time. The exhilaration of being part of something so part of the "now" was amazing! I spent the better part of that night remembering and piecing together this groundbreaking record. It was a glorious night to be a teenager in 1967.

Greg Sinclair

I wasn't able to buy *Sgt. Pepper* when it first came out. Instead, I had to settle for listening to some of its songs, such as "Lovely Rita," on WDRC and WABC. But once school ended in mid-June and I got an "OK" report card, my mom drove me to the Music Box in Hamden, Connecticut, where I bought my mono copy of *Sgt. Pepper*. I remember rushing out of the car and running to my bedroom to open the LP. I remember being mesmerized by not only the front cover, but also the portrait of the Beatles on the inside of the foldout cover. Pretty cool. Even before I put the vinyl disk on my record player I excitingly took the LP out to the backyard to show my dad the cover.

My dad took an interest in the LP after making a few remarks about their mustaches. He was a big music fan of 40 and 50's music, who thought Bing Crosby was all it. He let me play the LP on his high-fidelity stereo system with its Fisher amplifier, Garrard turntable and big 18" speakers. My dad listened to the album with me while studying the front cover and naming many of the faces in the crowd. At one point he remarked, "Too bad you didn't buy the stereo version, you would better appreciate the songs". Thanks dad.

Needless to say I played that LP all summer long and eventually wore it out on my crude record player with a needle that was worn out. So a year or so afterwards I ended up buying a new copy of the *Sgt. Pepper* LP, but this time in stereo. I'm glad to say I still have both LP's in my collection.

The June release of *Sgt. Pepper* coupled with the "All You Need Is Love" 45 a month later, made 1967 one of my best summers ever and one I'll always remember.

Tom Miller

Everyone has a story and music has provided the perfect platform for telling a story. In 1967, gas was 33 cents a gallon, the average price of a home was $3,840, American troops were ensconced in the Viet Nam war, discotheques arrived on the scene and The Beatles released *Sgt. Pepper*. It was a time when bands were experimenting with lyrics and sounds and as a twelve-year-old saving his allowance, I had to have this album. How wonderful to recall my grandfather taking me to Hecker's Record Store in Ephrata, PA to purchase this treasure! *Sgt. Pepper* was, and still is a timeless classic!

Thomas Grosh

Sgt. Pepper was released on June 2, 1967, but I heard most of the album a week earlier when WCFL Chicago DJ Ron Britain played an advance copy on stage at a May 27 concert featuring The Blues Magoos and Mitch Ryder. The acoustics were not the best, but what a treat to hear Sgt. Pepper before most of the world!

I bought my first copy for $3 at Sears. I had a small audio amplifier that I had built, a Heathkit, and a simple turntable to go with it, which required using a coin on the tonearm so it would track properly.

There was so much good music that summer, and what a way to start. How cool was it to have all the lyrics printed on the back cover--A Splendid Time Was Guaranteed for All!

Rich Tomera

The first time I heard Sgt. Pepper was probably in utero. I can't remember a time when I didn't know and love this music. I was born in 1985, eighteen years after the album's release. I came to the band through my father, who played his Beatles albums incessantly.

I remember writing about "I Want To Hold Your Hand" as part of a fourth grade assignment. And I recall singing "She Loves You" with several classmates after a sixth grade science fair. From middle school through college, I had my own musical preferences and though I never lost affection for The Fab Four, my focus shifted more towards Weird Al Yankovic, John Williams and the consumption and study of classical music.

I returned to The Beatles in grad school. A 2011 grant funded research for my first book, The Beatles & The Avant-Garde, and provided the foundation on which I've built a career as a professional Beatles scholar. Just as it was in my childhood, my life, in the words of my wife, "basically revolves around The Beatles."

Aaron Krerowicz, Beatles scholar/author

I was 14 and living in Salcoats, Ayrshire, Scotland in 1967. In those days, you had to wait an extra week or two after a record's release date to buy the record if you lived in a small town. Imagine my surprise when my uncle handed me Sgt Pepper on its release date fresh from London. For two solid weeks I played it to my friends before they could buy a copy themselves. Playing it each time I'd hear something new. It was amazing. Some of my friends didn't believe it was them because it sounded so different from anything they had heard before. I still have the same LP and it is played regularly, bringing back great memories of the summer of 67. Thanks Beatles and thanks Uncle.

John H. Auld

Hearing for the first Time
Sgt. Pepper's Lonely Hearts Club Band

I knew The Beatles had done it again
The new album, Sgt. Pepper, scored a big win
Mom said, save your allowance, do extra chores
Before you know it, Sgt. Pepper will be yours
Mom could be funny, showing some of her wit
As she knew, she had already purchased it
When we were done eating,
she said "I have something for you"
Go in your room, look to the right as you do
There was my Sgt. Pepper, in front of my face
On my player it went, with no time to waste
'Lucy in the Sky with Diamonds',
so magical and fun
I liked them all; too hard to pick just one
Then "Fixing a Hole", plus so many more
As I sang and danced all around the floor
With times changing for them and me too
The sky was the limit to what they could do

Terri Whitney, Author of "Any Rhyme At All"

I remember studying the *Sgt. Pepper* cover and thinking it was weird; trying to figure it out, wondering what it meant and who all the people were. They made a big impact on me very early on. Female, born 1961

It was a concentrated stimulus. The lyrics, the blending songs, the people on the cover, the insert. I was aware of it as an artifact, as a product. It reeked of symbolism, real or not. It was intriguing to me. Female, born 1954

The cover was part of the experience, the experience was more and more total. It created an environment. Who were all these people? People argued and discussed it. Female, born 1947

You were confronted with something you had to consider. There was a lot to take in. I was aware of it as a piece of pop culture, as something being presented to me. Female, born 1954

It was like approaching something forbidden that I wasn't prepared for; something leading me into forbidden territory. But it was the Beatles and I knew that ultimately it would be a good place, based on my history with them. Male, born 1957

Its biggest impact was that pop music could be a vehicle for thinking philosophically. Male, born 1950

I got *Sgt. Pepper* for my 12th birthday. My Dad and I looked at the cover and played it all the time in the living room. We loved it. My eight-year-old sister loved it too. It was a family experience. Female, born 1955

Even at twelve I was an "artsy" kid. I am still in the graphic design business. I went to music college, I went to art school. *Sgt. Pepper* sparked that in me. Male, born 1955

I was out with my parents, and they went into a store and left me in the car. So I turned the radio on and heard "Lucy In The Sky With Diamonds." The lyrics and the texture were mesmerizing. It was so different from the innocence of "A Hard Day's Night." Everything was getting serious. It seemed in tune with my getting older; their lyrics and my life seemed to parallel each other. Male, born 1953

[Listening to 'Within You Without You' was like] being in church and so you had to pay attention because it was important. Male, born 1957

Reading the words on *Sgt. Pepper*, you could see how words and music go together. It encouraged me to listen to the words by other artists. You knew that if it was arty you have to pay closer attention or you'd miss something. Male born 1948

It made me aware that things didn't have to be as they were. Female, born 1954

We were still interested in their personal lives and their girlfriends. There was lots of discussion about *Sgt. Pepper*—it was a big part of our lives. My friends and I would meet and hang out at the park on a Sunday afternoon, and we'd listen to the album. Female, born 1951

A Fan's Notes:

1967—It Really Was the Summer of ... Change

by Bill King (originally published in Beatlefan #107, July 1997)

A Beatles album named after a soft drink? I was a bit skeptical when my friend Chipper told me during the spring of 1967 that he'd heard on the radio that The Beatles' long-awaited next album would be called *"Doctor Pepper's Lonely Hearts Club Band."* I already knew the new album would be a little bit out of the ordinary, featuring a 1920s-styled number called "When I'm 64." (I'd read that in one of the teen magazines—which I didn't buy, but occasionally did peruse on the sly during my daily stops at Hodgson's Pharmacy, where they were located right next to the comic books that I did buy.) Still, Doctor Pepper seemed a bit of a reach, even for The Beatles. Fortunately, when the album in question finally surfaced in early June, the good doctor turned out to be a sergeant.

And, yes, the album WAS a reach, with music that lived up to the colorful, bizarre cover. But, I was fully prepared by the time I heard it because I didn't get a chance to buy *Sgt. Pepper* until about ten days after its June 2 release—after I'd read the Life magazine feature on "The New Far Out Beatles" and the making of the album. I took immediately to everything on *Sgt. Pepper* except "Within You Without You"—which would take a few decades to grow on me—and, like so many have said before, those songs provided a sort of soundtrack for a summer that was in many ways like no other.

At my 155 Hope Avenue home, as in rock music, change and new beginnings were the order of the day. I'd just finished 9th grade, which was part of junior high in my hometown of Athens, Georgia, and I was looking ahead with a mixture of fear and excitement to high school in the fall.

On top of that, our house, where we'd lived since I was four, was up for sale. I knew that, by summer's end, I would be moving from the area of town where I'd spent my entire life, leaving behind my regular haunts, neighborhood pals, my paper route—in other words, much of my insular little world. In the meantime, the world at large seemed to be getting out of hand. Just as summer vacation was beginning, war broke out in the Middle East. Within six days, Israel had defeated Egypt, Jordan and Syria and quadrupled its territory. The United Nations General Assembly went into emergency session (with coverage pre-empting regular TV).

Besides the Mideast conflict and the daily battle stories from Vietnam (a front page staple), it seemed like each afternoon's Atlanta Journal had another city erupting in race riots during that proverbial "long hot summer." First Boston, then Tampa, Dayton, Cincinnati, Newark, Detroit and more than a dozen other U.S. cities. By late July, LBJ had called out federal troops in Detroit and gone on national TV to appeal for calm.

There was a lot of other scary stuff in the paper. In Athens, 750 people were sealed off for the weekend in a downtown building in the nation's largest fallout shelter study. Not only was the Cold War still with us, that Sunday's front page blared the headline: "Red Chinese Explode First Hydrogen Bomb." A couple of days later, LBJ and Russian Premier Alexei Kosygin met for a summit in Glassboro, NJ, but parted with nothing between the two reigning superpowers resolved. Some problems simply weren't going to go away: Israel was being warned of the consequences if it refused to give up the conquered Old City of Jerusalem. Americans were being evacuated from the Congo as troops loyal to ex-Premiere Moishe Tshombe battled a president named Mobutu. And there were border clashes between Communist mobs and Hong Kong authorities.

There was very little coverage in the local papers of rock music's other major event that June, the Monterey Pop Festival, yet the editors seemed fascinated by the newly emerged hippies—sex, drugs and rock 'n' roll. They kept running bemused stories written as if about some curious primitive tribe discovered on the far side of the globe.

Most of the attention, of course, focused on San Francisco's Haight-Ashbury, where the scene was in full flower-power. In Atlanta, the Journal reported almost as a point of pride that the local hippie population (estimated at somewhere between 100 and 500) had held its first "love-in." (Within a couple of years, the thousands of long-haired kids from across the South crowding into the city's Bohemian "Tight Squeeze" district actually would resemble the Haight.) Meanwhile, in Athens, a university town, we'd had our own little colony of hippies near the neighborhood shopping district since mid-'66. There was even a hippie sanitation crew that had painted peace signs all over its

city garbage truck. They usually finished their rounds early and would spend the rest of the day cruising up and down the streets, waving and flashing the peace sign at amused residents.

Much to my delight, I found that the media fascination with the hippie world and psychedelia meant that hardly a week went by without a report on The Beatles. The second week of June saw an item on the designer and painter who had done the colorful new paint job on John Lennon's Rolls-Royce. They were feuding over who was responsible for (and the holder of the potentially lucrative commercial rights to) the psychedelic design. On Monday, June 19, there was a story about Paul admitting he'd used LSD (which he'd actually admitted the week before in Life magazine) and saying it had made him "a better, more honest, more tolerant member of society," though he warned, "I would like to make it perfectly clear that I do not advocate LSD. I don't want kids running to take it when they hear I have." Two days later, loyal Beatles manager Brian Epstein jumped into the fray to deflect some of this negative attention from Paul, saying he, too, had taken LSD. All four Beatles and Epstein would follow up a month later by taking out a full-page ad in the Times of London advocating the legalization of marijuana.

The worlds of foreign affairs and entertainment converged that week as Russia and four Eastern European nations pulled out of that Sunday's first global satellite TV broadcast because of the Middle East conflict. Our World was telecast to 26 countries on five continents at 3 p.m. EDT on June 25, with NET (precursor of PBS) carrying it live. Two years in preparation, it had international understanding as its theme and had contributions from the U.S., Japan, Mexico, Canada, Australia, France, Spain, Austria, Britain, Italy, Sweden, West Germany and Tunisia.

The segment on artistic excellence included Van Cliburn; Leonard Bernstein; and Franco Zeffirelli on the set of "Romeo and Juliet" in Rome, directing 17-year-old Leonard Whiting and 15-year-old Olivia Hussey (with whom I would fall in love from my cinema seat a year and a half later). Plus, the star attraction from Abbey Road in London: The Beatles recording a new song in a flower-bedecked studio before an all-star assemblage of friends and family.

I had only recently gotten my own television in my bedroom and I nervously set up in front of it with my little tape recorder and made my first home Beatles recording as "All You Need Is Love" blared out of the set. That little tape would get quite a workout between then and the release of the single three weeks later.

The Atlanta Braves (with Hank Aaron) were midway down the National League standings, Muhammad Ali (or Cassius Clay, as the papers still insisted on calling him) had a draft evasion conviction slapped on top of the unjust stripping of his heavyweight title. And, for a second-generation member of Arnie's Army, it was galling to see Jack Nicklaus win the U.S. Open.

We didn't get to the new Six Flags Over Georgia that summer, but other amusements passed the time. There was the country club pool. When I wasn't in the water or hitting the snackbar, I watched the bikini-clad high school girls parade the long way around the pool to answer those frequent phone-call pages.

There were movies, too. We began the summer with John Wayne and Kirk Douglas in *The War Wagon*; caught a double feature of *The Absent Minded Professor* and *The Shaggy Dog* at a local drive-in; introduced my youngest brother, Tim, to Disney's *Snow White and the Seven Dwarfs*; reveled in the mayhem of the latest 007 adventure, *You Only Live Twice*; and saw Jerry Lewis' *The Big Mouth*. Summer wasn't loaded with block-buster films like it is now. But, among the other flicks playing that summer were Clint Eastwood's *For a Few Dollars More*, Elizabeth Taylor and Richard Burton in *The Taming of the Shrew*, Michael Caine and Jane Fonda in *Hurry Sundown*, Elvis in *Double Trouble*, Lee Marvin in *The Dirty Dozen*, Robert Morse in *A Guide for the Married Man*, Jane Fonda and Robert Redford in *Barefoot in the Park*, Shirley MacLaine in *Woman Times Seven*, Robert Wagner in *Banning*, Hayley Mills (and, as the ads said, music by Paul "Beatle" McCartney) in *The Family Way*, Sidney Poitier in *To Sir With Love*, Dick Van Dyke in *Divorce American Style* and Jane Fonda (who'd obviously been quite busy) in *Any Wednesday*.

The summer wore on. The Monkees canceled a July 7 date at Atlanta Stadium. Mick Jagger and Keith Richards thought they'd have to serve time on drug charges. Blonde bombshell Jayne Mansfield was decapitated in a car crash in Louisiana. Bob Hope and Leonard Nimoy came to Atlanta for the annual July 4 Salute to America parade. Vivien Leigh died in London at 53. First daughter Lynda Bird Johnson bought a micro-miniskirt on Carnaby Street; her sister Luci gave the president a grandchild. Elvis and Priscilla announced they were expecting. And The Who and The Blues Magoos served as opening acts for Herman's Hermits in Atlanta.

On the Fab Four news front, the daily paper reported George Harrison was fined $16.80 for speeding 48 to 52 mph in a 30 mph zone in southwest London. NBC's Today show presented a still photo montage (including new shots of The Beatles) while playing "A Day in the Life," with commentary flashed silently on the screen while the music played. As the last chord boomed out, it read: "The end of the world?" George visited Los Angeles with Ravi Shankar and then toured San Francisco's hippie district with wife Pattie. Ringo and Maureen welcomed a new son, Jason.

My brothers and I made a nightly ritual of going to get frozen Cokes with my Dad at the EZ Food Shoppe. We read comic books (Batman and Superman were my favorites, though I liked to sample Spider-Man and Daredevil). I dragged out my old hand puppets and cardboard stage for a neighborhood Muscular Dystrophy Carnival. We spent our usual week in a cottage at Georgia's Lake Allatoona. The house had been sold and the dreaded move loomed, so I made the most of the time left in the cool, dark concrete basement that I loved so, briefly taking up model-making as I listened to the summer hits on my transistor AM radio.

What else was I listening to besides "All You Need Is Love"? Jefferson Airplane's "Somebody To Love," The Association's "Windy," Spanky and Our Gang's "Sunday Will Never Be The Same," Frankie Valli's "Can't Take My Eyes Off You," Every Mother's Son's "Come On Down To My Boat," Scott McKenzie's "San Francisco (Be Sure To Wear Flowers In Your Hair)," The Fifth Dimension's "Up Up And Away," The Doors' "Light My Fire," Petula Clark's "Don't Sleep In The Subway," Stevie Wonder's "I Was Made To Love Her," The Four Seasons' "C'mon Marianne," The Buckinghams' "Mercy Mercy Mercy," The Monkees' "Pleasant Valley Sunday," Aretha Franklin's "Baby I Love You," The Tremeloes' "Silence Is Golden," The Hollies' "Carrie-Ann," Nancy Sinatra and Lee Hazlewood's "Jackson," and Bobbie Gentry's mournful, memorable "Ode to Billie Joe."

We watched television, too, of course. Back then, summer replacement shows were commonplace, and that year we had George Carlin hosting the Away We Go replacement for Jackie Gleason, the London-based Picadilly Palace in place of Hollywood Palace, Our Place with the Doodletown Pipers and Burns & Schreiber and Jim Henson's Rowlf in place of The Smothers Brothers Comedy Hour, Rick Nelson hosting the beach-based Top 40 revue Malibu U, Vacation Playhouse (a collection of failed sitcom pilots), Roger Moore as The Saint and Frank Converse as a mysterious amnesiac in Coronet Blue. Plus, CBS' acclaimed four-hour documentary on the Warren Report.

Looking ahead, the networks were ceaselessly touting their new fall shows, which included future hits The Carol Burnett Show, Mannix, The High Chaparral, Ironside and The Flying Nun, along with forgettable fare such as Good Morning World, Cowboy in Africa, Garrison's Gorillas, Custer, The Second Hundred Years and Hondo.

In Atlanta, a low-budget new UHF TV station was preparing to take to the airwaves on Sept. 1. It was called WJRJ/Channel 17 back then and hadn't yet been bought by a billboard company owner named Ted Turner; you know it today as SuperStation TBS.

That summer wound up memorably. On Aug. 28, the TV news and papers reported Brian Epstein had been found dead the day before. On Tuesday, Richard Kimball finally caught up with the one-armed man in the conclusion of a two-part finale for The Fugitive. The next day, we moved across town to our new house.

That next week, the day after school started, the paper had an article about how The Beatles, shaking off Brian's death, were planning a Christmas TV special. It also reported their newfound fascination with an Indian guru, the Maharishi Mahesh Yogi. The following Tuesday, there was a story about a London bobby making Paul McCartney and his entire entourage clear the sidewalk while they waited for the psychedelic bus that would carry them on their *Magical Mystery Tour*.

It was only when I went to put these clippings in my Beatles scrapbook that I discovered (with a horror that still pains me) that it had gone missing in the move. That, I figured, was carrying new beginnings too far.

121

Sergeant Lonely Hearts Club Band In 1967 Germany

By Rainer Mores (born 1950)
Beatles Museum/THINGS in Germany

Let me take you down 'cause I'm going back to 1967 in West Germany. Forget all the communication possibilities nowadays and remember at the time we were looking for brand new information in weekly magazines and tried to hear Rock 'n' Roll and Beat news on some of the few radio stations where the Beatles single "Strawberry Fields Forever"/"Penny Lane" was played.

And so I'm telling you that we got the so-called news much later than the States or Great Britain. But the releases themselves came very close to those in other countries. It was quite normal to visit the record store and ask which new releases had arrived. Of course, with our small pocket money we tried to be the best customer because sometimes the seller had little gimmicks like the *Sgt. Pepper* beer mats (shown) he gave away.

I remember the first time when we read about this new Beatles album. It was in the one and nearly only magazine for young people in West Germany: Bravo. In the 20th issue (8th May 1967) the new Beatles album was announced as "Sergeant Lonely Hearts Club Band" with ten tracks (instead of 12). Better information appeared five weeks later (after the release of the LP!) in Bravo's 25th issue (12th June 1967), including the more complete title of the album, its release date in West Germany (Thursday, 8th June 1967) and the lyrics of seven of the twelve songs. The other five came the next week.

I wonder what went wrong. "Hör Zu" (a radio and TV magazine) released some LPs in West Germany under its own name. Rather than being on Parlophone, *Sgt. Pepper* was released as Hör Zu SHZE 401.

That weren't important yesterday. We were much more interested in this new music. After the albums *Rubber Soul* and *Revolver*, *Sgt. Pepper* was the third step to a new musical direction- and for many fans the uppermost level. Nearly all the Beatles songs through all these years weren't "dance floor" music at all. And *Sgt. Pepper* was an album to talk about. Before Saturday night parties came to an end and *Sunday morning creeping like a nun*, we discussed all the little clues we hoped to find in the songs and on the cover.

And in time you'll understand the reason why maybe there is not any clue you have to look for. You have to listen to the album and its songs. You should be *taking the time* to play them in the right order without skipping any of the little soundtracks of the sixties, which for many of us remains the best time we've ever had. *A splendid time is guaranteed for all.*

Das Schweigen ist gebrochen

Die Beatles haben endlich Einzelheiten über ihre nächste Langspielplatte verraten. „Sergeant Lonely Hearts Club Band" ist der kuriose Titel. Das Album wird wahrscheinlich nur 10 statt der gewohnten 12 Songs enthalten. Darunter sind „A Day in the Life" (ein John-Lennon-Solo mit 41-Mann-Orchester), „When I'm 64" (eine Paul-McCartney-Nummer im Stil der zwanziger Jahre) und „Meter Rita" (im typischen George-Harrison-Sound mit Sitar).

NEUERSCHEINUNGEN
UNTERHALTUNGSLANGSPIELPLATTEN
1

Sgt. Pepper's Lonely Hearts Club Band
The Beatles
Sgt. Pepper's Lonely Hearts Club Band ·
With A Little Help From My Friends ·
Lucy In The Sky With Diamonds · Getting
Better · Fixing A Hole · She's Leaving
Home · Being For The Benefit Of Mr. Kite ·
Within You Without You · When I'm
Sixty-Four · Lovely Rita · Good Morning
Good Morning · Sgt. Pepper's Lonely
Hearts Club Band · A Day In The Life
SHZE 401 DM 21,—
Stereo auch Mono abspielbar

Sgt. Pepper's Lonely Hearts Club Band-das Neueste der Beatles. SHZE 401-eine HÖR ZU Langspielplatte von HÖR ZU garantieren große Namen, gute Musik, beste Qualität. Fragen Sie den Fachhandel. Mehr über HÖR ZU Langspielplatten steht in HÖR ZU.

HÖR ZU
LANGSPIELPLATTE

Lonely Hearts in Italy
By Renato Facconi

Although I am Italian, I spent the summer of 1967 in Dublin, Ireland, trying to learn English and enjoy a holiday time. One day in June, I was invited to a "listening experience" held by a friend of mine, Luca de Gennaro. He presented the *Sgt. Pepper* album to an audience of people of all ages, including kids and people like me, a young lad of 17.

Listening to *Sgt. Pepper* for the first time was incredible—a strange experience. New sounds, new instruments, a stunning start and ending of the record, great songs, excellent production, and even a great colorful cover! It was the start of the flower power period and The Beatles, like most of the young generation all over the world, were changing.

I bought a copy of *Sgt. Pepper* and we all listened to the album over and over again. The more we played the disc, the more we enjoyed it. None of the songs had anything to do with the previous rock or pop productions and the music started to grow deeper and deeper in us.

When we came back to Italy a month later, we discovered that many people, especially the younger ones, were greatly impressed with the new Beatles album. Surely even in Italy, the first copies were sold immediately. An Italian record company, Carisch, issued a juke box single pairing "Sgt. Pepper's Lonely Hearts Club Band" with "A Day In The Life" (Parlophon PFC 7511), which was issued in December 1967.

With *Sgt. Pepper*, The Beatles completed their transformation from lovable mop tops to hippie artists. And yes, we loved and still do love those great lovable mop top hippie artists!

Sgt. Pepper in Belgium
By Dirk Van Damme

As evidenced by the popular magazines published in the sixties, Beatlemania spread from the U.K. to continental Europe, including my homeland of Belgium. Humo was and still is a weekly Belgium Dutch language magazine covering radio, television and music. In 1967, Humo, which based its charts on votes from 5,000 students in 240 schools, charted The Beatles single "Penny Lane" for 15 weeks, including three non-consecutive weeks at the top.

Shortly after *Sgt. Pepper* was released, Humo placed a color picture of The Beatles holding the album on its cover. Inside, the magazine ran a review of *Sgt. Pepper* under the heading "After Beethoven and Bach... The Beatles." Although Belgium readers did not know it at the time, the article, written by British journalist Chris Welch, had previously been published in the British magazine Melody Maker.

I started getting seriously interest in music in 1973 and discovered The Beatles through *Abbey Road* and hearing "Beware My Love" by Wings on the radio. Shortly after I bought *Sgt. Pepper,* but didn't think much about it. This has changed. I still get shivers down my spine when I hear "A Day In The Life" unexpectedly on the radio. While being in Liverpool in 2008 for the Liverpool Sound concert, I joked the day before the concert with an Italian friend that he would play that song because it was the 41st anniversary of the *Pepper* release, not realizing this really would materialize. But I was disappointed Paul gave the song an anti-climax by not playing it completely. The LP cover is such an iconic picture that I've been thinking for several years to make a large collage of it and hanging it on the wall.

HUMO

BEATLES

Week van 17/24 juni '67 ● Weekblad ● Radio en Televisie progr. ● 32e jaarg. ● Nr. 1397 ● 15 juni '67 ● 10 F

Sgt. Pepper Behind the Iron Curtain

by Михаил Гольцфарб

Dear Bruse! I hope, you will find my story somewhat amusing. It is about listening to the *Sgt. Pepper's Lonely Hearts Club Band* from behind the "Iron Curtain" for the first time. Back then, in the USSR, we could get some information on beat music from BBC and Voice of America broadcasts, that were being jammed by our special forces, but nevertheless, we managed to hear something. KGB tried to jam all radio waves that could be received from abroad.

A vinyl disc of Beatles could cost an average Soviet salary at that time. The discs were smuggled into the country. Buying them was not official, and they were rare, certainly. I had all early Beatles albums on tapes, and the quality was certainly compromised.

At that time I was a first year student of a Medical University in Chelyabinsk, a million-population-city in the Urals, near Siberia. It was winter holidays time, and my friend, also a Beatles fan, came to me from another city, where he studied. He brought this vinyl, which I took by my trembling hands. Just like a dream, I was holding a Beatles disc for the first time ever. Someone borrowed it to my friend for two weeks only.

The cover was amazing by itself. We literally studied every bit of it. And then, we put the precious disc to play. And here you go, something extraordinary, something really unusual to our ears is playing. This music differs dramatically from the previous *Revolver*, that I knew by heart by the time. What are they doing, those lovely guys, my idols? It was especially difficult to get so dear now "A Day In The Life." That day we listened to this album over and over, the second time, the third... And so it was, once and forever the music of my soul. The greatest album of all times! The Beatles Forever!

All the best, Mikhail Goltsfarb

The Single That Never Was

Who Am I To Stop A Good Rumor?
The Sgt. Pepper Packaging

The music was not the only memorable thing about *Sgt. Pepper*. The Beatles spent a considerable amount of time on the packaging. This was part of the group's desire to give as much value as they could to their fans purchasing the record. According to Paul, the group was aiming for "a great cover...packed with images." The final product achieved this goal, quickly becoming one of the most recognizable images of rock 'n' roll and sixties pop culture. It won a Grammy for best album cover of 1967, and in 1991 was voted the greatest album cover of all time by a distinguished panel of designers, photographers and critics assembled by Rolling Stone magazine.

The cover for Sgt. Pepper evolved from Paul's idea to present the group in an Edwardian sitting room in front of a wall of framed pictures of their heroes. The setting then moved outdoors. According to Paul, "I did a lot of drawings of us being presented to the Lord Mayor, with lots of dignitaries and lots of friends of ours around, and it was to be us in front of a big northern floral clock, and we were to look like a brass band." At the suggestion of London gallery owner Robert Fraser, Paul got artist Peter Blake involved in the cover project. McCartney credits Fraser and Blake for refining his idea:

"They changed it in good ways. The clock became the sign of the Beatles in front of it, the floral clock metamorphosed into a flower bed. Our heroes in photographs around us became the crowd of dignitaries...."

As for the dignitaries who would surround the band, a guest list was assembled by the Beatles and others associated with the project. Paul suggested people such as William Burroughs and Fred Astaire. George listed Indian gurus. John's want list included Oscar Wilde, Lewis Carroll, Edgar Allan Poe and, for shock value, Jesus and Hitler. Neither of the last two made the final cut. Ringo chose not to participate. W.C. Fields, Dion, Shirley Temple and Sonny Liston were among Peter Blake's suggestions making the grade. Paul's simple concept took on a life of its own. Ideas about the cover were discussed among the Beatles and Robert Fraser, Peter Blake and Blake's wife, American artist Jann Haworth. It was decided that the cover image should be photographed at an indoor set. Robert Fraser lined up Michael Cooper, a talented former Vogue photographer who was becoming popular with rock musicians such as the Rolling Stones, to take the picture at his Flood Street studio in Chelsea. EMI paid Fraser 1,500 pounds for his services (at the time $4,200), while Blake and Haworth only received 200 pounds ($560).

After obtaining photographs of the dignitaries who would form the crowd surrounding the band, Jann Haworth hand-tinted the black and white pictures to add color. Construction of the set, which took two weeks, began with the mounting of photographs onto hardboard sheets. Various three-dimensional items were added, including figures from Madame Tussauds Wax Museum (actress Diana Dors, boxer Sonny Liston and the Beatles themselves from an earlier era), a bust of T.E. Lawrence, dolls, plants and flowers. Also included were a Jann Haworth cloth doll of Shirley Temple wearing a shirt (owned by Adam Cooper, son of photographer Michael Cooper) proclaiming "Welcome the

Rolling Stones Good Guys," a portable TV (at the insistence of John, who was spending a lot of time watching the telly) and a bass drum fitted with the Sgt. Pepper logo, which was designed and painted by Joe Ephgrave, a fairground artist. "BEATLES" was spelled out in red hyacinth flowers. By having both the album title and the group's name appear as part of the image, there was no need to print any information on the cover.

The famous Sgt. Pepper satin uniforms worn by the Beatles were tailored by Berman's, a company that designed costumes for stage productions. George and Paul wore their MBE (Member of the British Empire) medals. The left sleeve of Paul's uniform sports a cloth patch of the Ontario Provincial Police (O.P.P.), which was given to Paul by a Canadian fan when the group was in Toronto on August 17 during their 1965 American tour. This memento, with its "O.P.P." initials, would later become one of many clues on the album cover that supposedly proved Paul was dead. People misread the initials as O.P.D. (Officially Pronounced Dead).

The Beatles held instruments not normally associated with a rock band: John (French horn); Ringo (trumpet); Paul (cor anglais); and George (flute).

The front cover photograph was taken on March 30, 1967. The uniqueness of image is best described by Rick Poynor in the Spring, 2000, issue of Eye, the International Review of Graphic Design:

"The Sgt. Pepper sleeve image is part collage, part sculpture, part installation, part studio shoot. Until it was photographed by Michael Cooper, with the living Beatles in their final poses, and then printed, it did not exist as a finished work."

Michael Cooper also took several pictures of the Beatles in their Sgt. Pepper uniforms. One of these color pictures was used for the open center gatefold and another for the back cover.

The inner gatefold sleeve was originally going to be a drawing done by a pair of Dutch artists, Simon Posthuma and Marijke Koger, known collectively as the Fool. Their psychedelic painting consisted of mountain peaks, birds, stars, comets and tiny images of the Beatles. Robert Fraser did not like the drawing and insisted that it not be used. He strongly recommended that the gatefold consist of a portrait of the band in their Sgt. Pepper uniforms. The Beatles, however, wanted to stay with the drawing submitted by The Fool.

Neil Aspinall helped push the group into following Fraser's advise. According to Aspinall, The Fool "hadn't somehow checked on the album size and their design was just out of scale. So they said 'Oh, OK, we'll put a border on it.' So now we had this design which was too small and a border being added just to fill up space. I said to the fellows, 'What are we selling here, a Beatles album or a centerfold with a design by The Fool which isn't even ready? Hadn't we better get a picture taken of the four of you, and stick that in so we can see who you are?'"

The Beatles changed their minds and the drawing by The Fool was replaced with a Michael Cooper portrait. Although their gatefold art was rejected, The Fool was commissioned to create a psychedelic design for the album's inner sleeve.

The back cover has a red background and a portrait of the band (with Paul's back to the camera) appearing in the lower center region. It was also a trendsetter with its inclusion of the complete lyrics to the songs—another first for the Beatles. Paul credits Gene Mahon, an ad agency designer hired to put the sleeve together, for coming up with the idea. Mahon, along with Al Vandenberg, had been responsible for selecting and supervising the enlargement of the photographs of the dignitaries on the front cover. It was also Mahon's

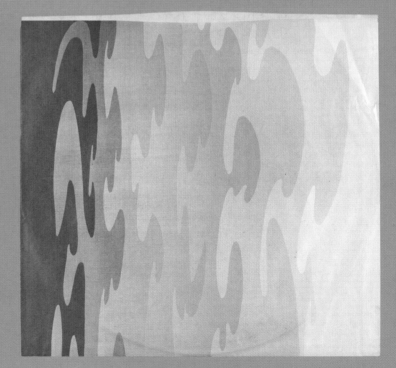

idea to conclude the text on the back cover with a line from "Being For The Benefit Of Mr. Kite!"—"A splendid time is guaranteed for all."

As part of the group's desire to give more to their fans, the Beatles wanted to include an envelope containing items such as stickers and buttons. EMI balked at this idea due to cost factors. A compromise was reached when the Beatles agreed to a cardboard insert containing cutout images of a moustache, a picture card of Sgt. Pepper, uniform stripes, badges of the Sgt. Pepper logo and of a bust of Sgt. Pepper, and a stand up of the Beatles in their Sgt. Pepper uniforms. The 12" x 12" green background insert is signed in the lower right corner by artists Peter Blake and Jann Haworth.

EMI had grave concerns about the *Sgt. Pepper* cover. While the Beatles had not considered the copyright issues involved in the use of photographs of famous people, EMI had visions of being sued by several of the dignitaries depicted on the cover. And there was no way the company was going to risk offending its customers in India by having Mahatma Gandhi on the cover of a rock album. The Beatles understood the concern over Gandhi and agreed to his removal. As for the other people, the Beatles pledged to contact and obtain their permission to be included on the cover.

EMI chairman Sir Joseph Lockwood also made the group indemnify EMI in the event of damages resulting from any legal action pertaining to the cover, which would be applied against the group's royalties. The maximum exposure for the indemnification has been reported at 10 million dollars and at 20 million pounds from different sources. In the summer of 1967, 20 million pounds was equivalent to 56 million dollars, which in 2017 adjusted dollars is worth over 470 million dollars.

Brian Epstein farmed out the task of obtaining clearances to former NEMS employee Wendy Hanson. While most of the individuals agreed without hesitation, there were a few glitches. Former Dead End Kid Leo Gorcey (who was on John's list) demanded $500 for the right of his likeness on the cover. Rather than set a precedent that could lead to financial bickering among stars ("If an ex-Dead End Kid is worth $500, then surely Marlon Brando is worth several thousand."), The Beatles refused to pay the fee and removed Gorcey from the cover image. Fortunately, his location on the top row made it easy to delete his face. Gorcey's unsuccessful demand for money to be included on a Beatles album cover did nothing to revive his career, which by that time had reached a dead end.

After receiving Ms. Hanson's request for permission to use her likeness on the cover to a Beatles album titled *Sgt. Peppers's Lonely Hearts Club Band*, a perplexed Mae West declined, asking what she would be doing in a lonely hearts club. The Beatles sent her a follow-up letter, signed by each member, in which they expressed their admiration for her and asked her to reconsider. This time she consented and is included with the act you've known for all these years.

Although no one sued EMI or The Beatles for including their likeness on the cover, a controversy developed regarding the plants above the word "BEATLES." The green leafed foliage looks suspiciously like marijuana plants, but is in reality peperomia. An in-joke possibly devised by a well-educated florist, though no one knows for sure. But for many people looking at the plants on the cover, there was no doubt in their minds—it was marijuana. Capitol president Alan Livingston knew better, but kept silent on the matter. His attitude was "Who am I to stop a good rumor that's helping sales of an album?"

SGT. PEPPER
CUT-OUTS
1. Moustache
2. Picture Card
3. Stripes
4. Badges
5. Stand Up

Sgt.Pepper

1.

2.

3.

4.

4.

PRINTED IN U.S.A.

Peter Blake/Jann Haworth

Who Taught the Band to Play?

by Max Gretinski

James Melville Babington (1854-1936) was a celebrated member of the Babington family, descended from Sir John de Babington, the Lord of the Manor of Babington, circa AD 1178. The Babington family was filled with notable members, including king's attorneys and abolitionists. In 1586 the family orchestrated the Babington Plot to overthrow Queen Elizabeth I, in order to replace her with her Catholic cousin Mary (Queen of Scots). This plot ultimately led to Mary's execution.

Being part of a long line of military men, James Babington served notably as a lieutenant in the 16th Queen's Lancers, an active cavalry regiment. Having established a reputation as a quick, capable officer, he was promoted rapidly and served under Sir Evelyn Wood – after which he returned to the Lancers to command the regiment. With a succession of promotions, his career was indeed getting better all the time. He served in India from 1896 to 1899, where perhaps he did find peace of mind waiting there. During the Second Boer War, Maj. General Babington command-ed the 1st Cavalry Brigade in South Africa. His victories there earned him a post in New Zealand in 1902. A few years after his departure from South Africa, the world's largest diamond was discovered there (1905) – but not by a woman named Lucy. Upon the outbreak of World War I, Babington commanded the 23rd infantry division, which trained for nearly a year and then shipped out to France. Many of the new volunteers were improperly equipped, but (never a thought for himself) Babington made sure that his soldiers received appropriate financing in order to be able to fight and survive.

The war ended in 1918, when Babington was sixty-four (but not losing his hair). Afterwards, he commanded forces in Italy prior to retiring as a Lieutenant General – having made the grade. During retirement, no doubt he took the time for a number of things that had not been important yesterday. He was highly decorated, including having been invested as a Knight Commander of the Order of St. Michael and St. George (KCMG). Lt. General Babington had one son.

Young adults in 1967 probably knew very little about the daring exploits of James Babington, but millions of them unknowingly saw his image, for it was Babington's portrait (commissioned in South Africa) from the book *Celebrities of the Army* (also available as a card) that Peter Blake and Jann Haworth adapted into their vision of Sgt. Pepper. Yet make no mistake, Pepper is not Babington. Just as great actors and actresses are able to convince us that they are elves or superheroes, Blake and Haworth used their artistic talents to bring forth a mythical sergeant that existed only in the imagination. James Babington was a real person with a celebrated life, but Sgt. Pepper is a work of art – a piece of magic, and we all owe the artists a debt of gratitude for bringing him to life. Certainly this is why a piece of original production art from the *Sgt. Pepper* cut-out insert sold at Sotheby's in 2012 for £55,250. When we hear the album, and when we see the image that Blake and Haworth created, we *believe* in Sgt. Pepper. We know that somehow he existed, performing his own daring deeds and teaching his band to play twenty, thirty, forty, fifty, sixty, seventy years ago today.

Sgt. Pepper

From a Photograph by

C. Knight.

MAJOR-GENERAL J. M. BABINGTON,

COMMANDING FIRST CAVALRY BRIGADE IN SOUTH AFRICA.

Recording History: Who Did What?

The Beatles decision to quit the rigors of the road after their 1966 North American tour gave the group the freedom to devote their full energies to what they considered most important—the music. The band would now have more time to write and record. As they would not be performing their new songs in concert, The Beatles were no longer limited to the standard two guitars, bass and rums lineup. They were free to create sounds in the studio without concern as to whether they or anyone else could duplicate them. The group's prior success had earned them the right to monopolize EMI's Abbey Road studios. Time and costs were no longer factors. They could record whenever they wanted and spend as much time as needed to get the sound they were looking for. There were no limits. The Beatles were no longer performers; they were now recording "artists" in every sense of the word.

When asked about the group's decision to quit touring, George Harrison responded: "It's not a matter of discontinuing performances—it's more a matter of spending more time on recording and, of course, writing. In 1967, recording will be the most important thing from our point of view so we're sure to spend a lot of time concentrating on that."

John expressed similar views: "We've always enjoyed recording sessions. I suppose we've enjoyed our first 1967 sessions on a different level to the 'Love Me Do' days. Every track you decide to tape is a real challenge. I don't mean to sound corny. But it's like painting something new and having a great big sheet of clean white paper and wondering what the finished job will look like."

The sessions for The Beatles new album started on November 24, 1966, and lasted nearly five months, ending on April 21, 1967. During that time, the group and Abbey Road engineers logged an estimated 700 hours in the studio. Recording costs grew to around 25,000 pounds (then equal to $70,000 and 50 years later in 2017 adjusted to over a half million dollars).

Two of the first three songs recorded during the sessions, "Strawberry Fields Forever" and "Penny Lane," were not included on the LP because they were issued as The Beatles first single of 1967. While Capitol Records in the U.S. successfully used hit singles to sell albums, George Martin and Brian Epstein frowned on the practice as they did not want to force people to pay twice for the same music.

Although *Sgt. Pepper* would later be recognized as rock's first concept album, it is not clear that this was the Beatles intent when they entered the studio in late 1966. Both "Strawberry Fields Forever" and "Penny Lane" were inspired by childhood memories (as recognized by the early childhood photos of John, Paul, George and Ringo featured on the back side of the single's picture sleeve), but it is unlikely that this was ever intended to form the basis for an entire album. The first songs recorded for *Sgt. Pepper* also have themes associated with northern England, but this may be a coincidence rather than a conscious effort. As the album evolved, childhood innocence was joined with drug references and relevant themes.

While different theories about the album's roots exist, Paul claims it emanated from the group's desire to break from the past and have musical freedom. In Barry Miles' *Many Years From Now*, Paul explains:

"We were fed up with being the Beatles. We really hated that...four little mop-top boys approach. We were not boys, we were men...[We] thought of ourselves as artists rather than just performers...Then suddenly on the plane [flying back to London from Nairobi, Kenya with Mal Evans on November 19, 1966] I got this idea. I thought, let's not be ourselves. Let's develop alter egos so we're not having to project an image which we know. It would be much more free. What would really be interesting would be to actually take on the personas of this different band...So I had this idea of giving the Beatles alter egos simply to get a different approach...It would be a freeing element. I thought we can run this philosophy through the whole album: with this alter-ego band, it won't be us making all that sound, it won't be the Beatles, it'll be this other band, so we'll be able to lose our identities in this."

As for the origin of the name, Paul believes it was a result of kicking ideas around with Mal Evans. Packets marked "S" and "P" for salt and pepper evolved into Sgt. Pepper, once again being a bit of a pun. The "Lonely Hearts Club Band" was a case of stringing words together to form something that flowed, but was also a bit bizarre. In Paul's words, "That'd be crazy enough because why would a Lonely Hearts Club have a band?"

Sgt. Pepper's Lonely Hearts Club Band

Recorded: February 1 & 2 (basic track) &
March 3 & 6, 1967 (overdubs) (Abbey Road Studio 2)
Mixed: March 6, 1967 (mono and stereo)

Producer: George Martin
Engineers: Geoff Emerick & Richard Lush

Paul: Lead vocal; bass guitar; lead guitar
John: Backing vocal
George: Backing vocal; guitar
Ringo: Drums
Outside musicians: James W. Buck, Neil Sanders, Tony Randall and John Burden (French horns)

Although Paul came up with the Sgt. Pepper concept prior to the start of the recording sessions, the band did not begin work on the song until February 1, 1967. That night, the Beatles ran through nine takes of the song (only one and nine being complete) to form the basic rhythm track. It consisted of Paul and George on electric guitars and Ringo's drums (recorded with heavy echo). Paul overdubbed his Rickenbacker 4001S bass guitar, which was directly injected into the recording console instead of through an amplifier. The following evening Paul's lead vocal and backing vocals from Paul, John and George were superimposed onto Take 9 and mixed down to form Take 10. The song remained in that form for a month while the Beatles turned their attention to other songs.

The group returned to the title track on March 3 for the addition of four French horns played by outside musicians, thereby transforming the mythical Sgt. Pepper's Lonely Hearts Club Band into a rocking brass band. Paul's fondness for brass bands would later lead him to produce a single by the John Foster and Sons Ltd. Black Dyke Mills Band ("Thingumybob" c/w "Yellow Submarine" issued on Apple 4 in the U.K. and Apple 1800 in the U.S. as part of Apple's initial releases in late August 1968). After the overdub recording of French horns was completed, Paul superimposed a stinging and heavily distorted lead guitar part on the same track as the horns. This was possible as the horns and lead guitar appear in different parts of the song.

Paul also came up with the idea of simulating a concert performance by the alter-ego band. Engineer Geoff Emerick remembers Paul saying: "Wouldn't it be good if we got the atmosphere? Get the band warming up, hear the audience settle into their seats, have the songs as different acts on the stage?"

On March 6 Paul's idea took shape with the addition of sound effects to the album's opening selection. The sound of the band warming up was taken from the February 10 orchestra session for "A Day In The Life.' Other effects were lifted from Abbey Road's tape archives. The crowd settling down for the concert is from Volume 28: Audience Applause and Atmosphere, Royal Albert Hall and Queen Elizabeth Hall. The applause and laughter is from Volume 6: Applause and Laughter, which consists of audience reactions from the 1961 George Martin-supervised live recording of the comedy show *Beyond The Fringe*. The screaming at the end of the song was also taken from the Abbey Road tape archives (and not the Capitol-recorded Beatles Hollywood Bowl concert as is often written). The *50th Anniversary Edition* contains Takes 1 (instrumental) and 9.

The attention-grabbing sound effects and French horns of the opening track cause some listeners to overlook the fact that "Sgt. Pepper's Lonely Hearts Club Band" is a great rock song. George Martin observed: "Anyone who thinks that Paul McCartney is not a great singer of rock 'n' roll only has to listen to his voice on this track. You can hear the gravel in it." This can be verified by listening to Paul's vocal track in isolation, where its full force is on display. His lead vocal is right up there was his previous efforts on "Long Tall Sally" and "I'm Down."

Paul's lead guitar, played on his Fender Esquire (right-handed model strung for left-handed musicians), is equally spectacular. Once again, it should be heard in isolation to fully appreciated. His playing is clearly inspired in style and tone by the incendiary guitar being played in the London clubs by Jimi Hendrix. McCartney, along with Ringo, had first seen The Jimi Hendrix Experience perform at the Bag O' Nails club on January 11, 1967. The entire group saw Hendrix perform at the Saville Theatre on January 29. When the group returned to the studio on February 1, they took a break from working on "A Day In The Life" to record the title track with Paul's Hendrix-style lead guitar. Jimi would return the favor. Within days of the album's release, Paul and George were in attendance at the Seville on June 4 when Hendrix opened his set with "Sgt. Pepper."

To add to the album's illusion of a continuous performance, the decision was made to eliminate the usual three- to six-second gaps between tracks by use of segues, cross-fading or split-second breaks between selections. In the case of the album's first two songs, there is a thematic as well as musical link. As the first song draws to a close, Paul sings "So let me introduce to you, the one and only Billy Shears and Sgt. Pepper's Lonely Hearts Club Band."

With A Little Help From My Friends

Recorded: March 29 & 30, 1967 (Abbey Road Studio 2)
Mixed: March 31, 1967 (mono); April 7, 1967 (stereo)

Producer: George Martin
Engineers: Geoff Emerick & Richard Lush

Ringo: Lead vocal; drums; tambourine
Paul: Backing vocal; piano; bass guitar
George: Backing vocal; lead guitar
John: Backing vocal; cow bell
George Martin: Hammond organ

The opening title track segues into the next song, "With A Little Help From My Friends," with screams from Abbey Road's tape archive and the group singing (as three ascending notes sung over George Martin's Hammond organ) "Bil—ly Shears," which serves as the introduction to Ringo's upcoming lead vocal. This segue passage was recorded as part of "With A Little Help From My Friends."

The delightful "With A Little Help From My Friends" was written by John and Paul for Ringo. An account of the writing of the song appears at pages 263-68 in *The Beatles* by Hunter Davies. It was written on the afternoon of March 29, 1967, at Paul's house at Cavendish Avenue in St. John's Wood. After John and Paul developed the chorus line and the melody, John came up with the idea of starting each verse with a question. Although many people, including Paul, believe the line "I get high with a little help from my friends" is drug-related, John insisted "It's really about a little help from my friends, it's a sincere message." When most of the lyrics were completed, John called Ringo and told him they would record the song that evening.

Although the drummer liked the song, he refused to sing the original lyrics to the opening verse. According to Ringo: "The original first verse to that was 'What would you do if I sang out of tune? Would you throw a tomato at me?' And I said 'I'm not singing that.'"

John and Paul quickly changed the line to "Would you stand up and walk out on me?"

That evening (March 29) the band recorded ten takes of the rhythm track with Paul on piano, George Harrison on guitar, John on cow bell, Ringo on drums and George Martin on Hammond organ. A reduction mix of Take 10 was made and bounced down to one track leaving three tracks open for overdubs, including Ringo's lead vocal and backing vocals by John, Paul and George, onto Take 11. Abbey Road studio paperwork shows that the song was initially called "Bad

Finger Boogie," but by the following evening it was given its logical title, "With A Little Help From My Friends." That night, the "Bil—ly Shears" vocals and timpani and snare drums were superimposed onto the segue passage. Additional overdubs included: Paul's bass guitar, George's distorted lead guitar and Ringo's tambourine, as well as more backing vocals by John, Paul and George. The song literally ends on a high note sung by Ringo with a little help from his friends. According to Ringo, "It took a lot of coaxing from Paul to get me to sing that last note—I just felt it was very high." The *50th Anniversary Edition* contains Takes 1 and 2 (instrumental).

"With A Little Help From My Friends" was one of the first *Sgt. Pepper* songs covered by other artists in the U.K., with the Young Idea hitting number ten and Joe Brown reaching number 32 in the summer of 1967. In addition, Joe Cocker scored a number one hit with the song in 1968, as did Wet Wet Wet 20 years later in 1988.

Lucy In The Sky With Diamonds

Recorded: February 28 (rehearsal) & March 1 & 2, 1967
(Abbey Road Studio 2)
Mixed: March 3, 1967 (mono); April 7, 1967 (stereo)

Producer: George Martin
Engineers: Geoff Emerick & Richard Lush

John: Lead vocal; guitar
Paul: Backing vocal; organ; bass guitar
George: Backing vocal; lead guitar; tambura
Ringo: Drums; maracas
George Martin: Piano (on early takes; not on master recording)

"Lucy In The Sky With Diamonds" was inspired by a drawing by John's son Julian, who was four years old at the time. In February 1967, Julian returned home from nursery school with a painting depicting one of his classmates, Lucy O'Donnell, against a background of stars in the sky. When asked by his father about his creation, Julian said it was "Lucy, in the sky, with diamonds." The phrase triggered memories of two of John's favorite books from his childhood, Lewis Carroll's *Through The Looking Glass* and *Alice's Adventures In Wonderland*.

Starting with the title to his son's painting as the chorus, John drew from passages of *Through The Looking Glass* ("A boat, beneath a sunny sky/Lingering onward dreamily/In an evening of July" and "Still she haunts me, phantomwise/Alice moving under skies/Never seen by walking eyes.") to form the dreamy first verse of his song:

"Picture yourself on a boat on a river/With tangerine trees and marmalade skies/Somebody calls you, you answer quite slowly/A girl with kaleidoscope eyes."

Paul contributed *Looking Glass* and *Wonderland*-inspired phrases such as "newspaper taxis." Although listeners spotted psychedelic drug references throughout the song, Paul insists that "In our mind it was an Alice thing, which both of us loved."

John's affection for The Goon Show also crept into the lyrics. According to member Spike Milligan, the "plasticine ties" of Goon Show fame merged with *Through The Looking Glass* to become "plasticine porters with looking glass ties."

The Beatles began work on "Lucy In The Sky With Diamonds" on February 28, 1967. Although the band was in the studio from 7:00 p.m. until 3:00 am, the session comprised solely of rehearsals, and no proper takes were recorded.

Thomas Thompson and photographer Henry Grossman were present at the session. Thomas observations, mixed with Grossman photographs and interviews with George Martin and members of the group, appeared in a story titled "The New Far-Out Beatles," which appeared in the June 16, 1967, Life magazine. Grossman's pictures appeared in other magazines, including Time. In 2008, Grossman's photographs from the evening were collected in a deluxe book titled *Kaleidoscope Eyes: A Day in the Life of Sgt. Pepper.*

The following evening, March 1, the band recorded the song with Paul playing the song's opening riff on a Lowery organ (with a bell stop) accompanied George Harrison on acoustic guitar (with George Martin on piano for the first six takes only), Ringo on drums and John's guide vocal and maracas. After the seventh and final take was deemed satisfactory, John's vocal on Track 4 was erased by the recording of George's tamboura, a droning Indian instrument, onto Track 4. The four-track tape was then mixed down to one track at 49 cycles per second (rather than the normal 50 cps) for additional recording. George's acoustic guitar was given a wow phasing effect during the mixdown (identified as Take 8).

The Beatles returned to the song the next evening adding overdubs to Take 8. Paul overdubbed his melodic bass guitar lines, and George added a guitar part played through a Leslie speaker onto one of the open tracks, Track 4. The two remaining open tracks were used to record two separate lead vocals from John, who is joined by Paul on the chorus. In his book on the making of *Sgt. Pepper*, George Martin explains the unique way the vocals were recorded:

"The vocals on 'Lucy' weren't recorded at normal speed. The first [on Track 2] was recorded at a frequency of [45] cycles, our normal frequency being [50] cycles. In other words, we slowed the tape down, so that when we played it back the voice sounded ten percent higher: back in the correct key, but thinner-sounding, which suited the song. It gave a slightly Mickey Mouse quality to the vocals. In fact, Paul was also singing on these two tracks, lending John a spot of harmony. I also added the odd bit of tape echo to the voices. The second voice track [Track 3] we recorded at [48½ cps], to see what that sounded like. 'Lucy' has more variations of tape speed in it than any other track on the album."

The song was mixed for mono on March 3, and for stereo on April 7. The verses start out using the vocals from Track 2, then blend the vocals from both Tracks 2 and 3 before finally switching to the vocals from Track 3. The song's chorus uses a blend of both vocal tracks.

Anthology 2 contains a unique mix combining elements of Takes 6, 7 and 8. Its basic track is Take 6, with tamboura added from Take 7 and vocals from Take 8. It contains John's guide vocal. The *50th Anniversary Edition* contains Takes 1 and 5.

After *Sgt. Pepper* was released, people noticed that "Lucy In The Sky With Diamonds" could be abbreviated as LSD. While the song certainly has its share of psychedelic drug imagery ("Everyone smiles as you drift past the flowers that grow so incredibly high"), John always maintained that it was unintentional, insisting that his son's painting was solely responsible.

The song's title and lyrical wordplay inspired other interesting titles, including "Judy In Disguise (With Glasses)," a number-one U.S. hit for John Fred & His Playboy Band which replaced the Beatles "Hello, Goodbye" at the top of the Billboard Hot 100 on January 20, 1968, and was a number three hit in the U.K. Fred, who was from Baton Rouge, Louisiana, intentionally parodied the song, changing "marshmallow pies" to "lemonade pies" and "kaleidoscope eyes" to "cantaloupe eyes." The song used sitar, while *Lucy* had tamboura.

Although "Lucy In The Sky With Diamonds" would have been a huge hit had it been released as a single, neither Parlophone nor Capitol pulled any songs from the album for release as singles until several years later. In 1974, Elton John recorded a version of the song that featured John Lennon (identified as Dr. Winston O'Boogie) on "Reggae guitars." The song was a number one hit in the U.S., selling over a million copies, and a top ten hit in the U.K.

Getting Better

Recorded: March 9, 21 & 23, 1967 (Abbey Road Studio 2)
Mixed: March 23, 1967 (mono); April 17, 1967 (stereo)

Producer: George Martin (March 9 & 21, 1967);
Peter Vince (March 23, 1967)
Engineers: Malcolm Addey, Ken Townsend & Graham Kirby (March 9, 1967); Geoff Emerick & Richard Lush (March 21, 1967); Peter Vince & Ken Scott (March 23, 1967)

Paul: Lead vocal; bass guitar; handclaps
John: Backing vocal; guitar; handclaps
George: Backing vocal; tambura; handclaps
Ringo: Drums; bongos
George Martin: Pianette

The inspiration for the title to "Getting Better" dated back to June 1964, when Jimmy Nicol served as the Beatles substitute drummer for five concerts while Ringo was suffering from tonsillitis. After each show, John and Paul would ask the drummer how he was doing. His standard reply was "It's getting better." According to author Hunter Davies, he was walking one morning with Paul when McCartney, commenting on the weather, said to Davies, "It's getting better." This caused Paul to reminisce about the Jimmy Nicol catch phrase from Nicol's brief tenure with the band. When Paul got home, he began work on the song.

Although Paul does not remember this incident, he does recall writing the music on his piano. In Miles' *Many Years From Now*, Paul described the tune as "an optimistic song." As for the opening verse's references to school teachers, Paul stated that he and John "shared a lot of feelings against teachers who had punished you too much or who hadn't understood you or who had just been bastards generally." While Paul's idea was to write an optimistic song, John provided the counterpoint. Paul recalls:

"I was sitting there doing 'Getting better all the time' and John just said in his laconic way, 'It couldn't get no worse,' and I thought, Oh, brilliant! This is exactly why I love writing with John."

John recalled providing some of the song's darker lyrics: "It is a diary form of writing. All that 'I used to cruel to my woman, I beat her and kept her apart from the things that loved' was me."

The Beatles began work on "Getting Better" on March 9, 1967. The initial recording had Paul on bass, John on electric guitar, Ringo on drums and George Martin on pianette, an early type of amplified piano that produced a sound described by Martin as "a cross between a harpsichord and a Fender Rhodes electric piano."

During the verses, Martin varied the sound by plucking the strings inside the keyboard rather than playing the keys as he did for the introduction and choruses. This was completed in seven takes. The instruments were then mixed down (in five attempts) to Track 1 of a new tape, leaving three tracks for overdubs on what was designated Take 12. The session ended at 3:30 a.m. The next evening the three open tracks were filled. Additional bass and drums were recorded on Track 2, and double-tracked on Track 3. The remaining track was filled with piano and George Harrison's tamboura.

The Beatles returned to the song on March 21 at a session attended only by Paul, John and George. A tape reduction mix was made to free up two tracks for the vocals. After a couple of unsuccessful tries, John informed George Martin that he wasn't feeling well. Martin, who thought John might feel better if he got some fresh air, took Lennon up to the roof of the studio and returned to the control room. When Paul asked about John, Martin informed him that John was up on the roof watching the stars. While Martin did not know why Lennon was feeling ill, Paul and George knew that John had taken a tab of acid. Realizing with horror that John was alone on a roof with no rails and in the middle of an LSD trip, the pair ran up to the roof to bring him back inside. According to Martin, this was the only time any member of the group was unable to work in the studio.

The group returned to the song on March 23. Paul's lead vocal, John and George's backing vocals and handclaps were double-tracked. The vocals were then mixed down to one track to open up a track, over which additional guitar was superimposed. The song was then mixed for mono. The stereo mix was made on April 17. The *50th Anniversary Edition* contains Takes 1 and 12.

Fixing A Hole

Recorded: February 9 (Regent Sound) & February 21, 1967 (Abbey Road Studio 2)
Mixed: February 21, 1967 (mono); April 7, 1967 (stereo)

Producer: George Martin
Engineers: Adrian Ibbertson (February 9, 1967); Geoff Emerick & Richard Lush (February 21, 1967)

Paul: Lead vocal; bass guitar; harpsichord
John: Backing vocal
George: Backing vocal; lead guitar
Ringo: Drums; maracas
George Martin: Harpsichord

"Fixing A Hole" was written by Paul, and contains what John described as "a good lyric." As was the case with several other songs from the album, people were quick to find hidden meanings in the lyrics that were never there to begin with.

The song's title and references to mind wandering led many people to conclude that the song was about shooting heroin. In Miles' *Many Years From Now*, Paul denies this. If any drug reference was intended, it was Paul's drug of choice at the time, pot. Paul's lyrics are an expression of his freedom to fix things as he chose:

"Mending was my meaning. Wanting to be free enough to let my mind wander, let myself be artistic....It was the idea of me being on my own now, able to do what I want. If I want I'll paint the room in a colourful way. I'm fixing the hole, I'm fixing the crack in the door...I'll take hold of my life a bit more."

Another misconception is that the lyrics are about Paul fixing the roof to his Scottish farm house. According to Paul: "It was much later that I ever got around to fixing the roof on the Scottish farm, I never did any of that till I met Linda. People just make it up!"

On February 9, 1967, the Beatles recorded the song at Regent Sound Studio on Tottenham Court Road in London. The session was booked at Regent because Abbey Road was unavailable. It marked the first time that the Beatles recorded a British EMI session at a studio other than Abbey Road. It was also the first Beatles session attended by Jesus, or at least a man claiming to be the son of God.

Paul recalls encountering a stranger at his gate prior to leaving his home for the studio. The man introduced himself as Jesus Christ. Paul thought, "It probably isn't. But if he is, I'm not going to be the one to turn him away." After sharing tea with the man, Paul invited him to the session if he promised to be very quiet. According to Paul:

"He came to the session and he did sit very quietly and I never saw him after that. I introduced him to the guys. They said, 'Who's this?' I said, 'He's Jesus Christ.' We had a bit of a giggle over that."

With "Jesus" in attendance, the Beatles recorded three takes featuring Paul's melodic bass and lead vocal, George's excellent guitar solo (on his Fender Stratocaster with his controls up very high), Ringo on drums and George Martin on harpsichord. Paul, John and George then added their backing vocals to the backing track.

The Beatles completed the song at Abbey Road on February 21. Take 2 was mixed down and renumbered as Take 3. Paul double-tracked his lead vocal and added more harpsichord. The song was then mixed for mono. The stereo mix was not made until April 7. The *50th Anniversary Edition* contains Takes 1 and 3.

She's Leaving Home

Recorded: March 17 & 20, 1967 (Abbey Road Studio 2)
Mixed: March 20, 1967 (mono); April 17, 1967 (stereo)

Producer: George Martin
Engineers: Geoff Emerick & Richard Lush

Paul: Lead and backing vocals
John: Backing vocals
Outside Musicians: Sheila Bromberg (harp); Erich Gruenberg, Derek Jacobs, Trevor Williams and Jose Luis Garcia (violins); John Underwood and Stephen Shingles (violas); Dennis Vigay and Alan Dalziel (cellos); and Gordon Pearce (double bass)

"She's Leaving Home" was inspired by a newspaper article in the February 27, 1967, Daily Mail about a seventeen-year-old runaway named Melanie Coe. Paul began the story line about the girl slipping out of the house and leaving a note for her parents at the top of the stairs. John provided the counterpoint lines giving the parents' view of the sacrifices they had made for their daughter.

Paul envisioned the song having an orchestral backing, so he called George Martin and asked him to score a string arrangement. Because Martin had already committed to a Cilla Black session, he told Paul he would have to wait. Paul, being anxious to record the song, contacted Mike Leander and asked him to write the score, not realizing that Martin would be hurt by his using someone else to write the arrangement. (Paul met Leander at a 1965 session during which Marianne Faithfull recorded a cover version of "Yesterday.")

While Martin was not entirely satisfied with Leander's score, he made only minor changes when the orchestral backing of harp and strings was recorded on March 17, 1967. The harp was played by Sheila Bromberg, who became the first woman to play on a Beatles recording. Paul sat in the control room while Martin conducted the orchestra. As was the case with "Eleanor Rigby," no Beatle played an instrument on the song. Although six takes were recorded, Take 1 was deemed the best.

Paul and John added their vocals, each double-tracked, on March 20. The song was mixed for mono at the end of the session. In order to make Paul sound younger, the track was sped up during the mono mix. This was not done when the song was mixed on April 17 for the stereo version, which runs at its recorded speed and is a semitone lower in pitch than the sped-up mono version. The *50th Anniversary Edition* contains instrumental Takes 1 and 6. The 2017 stereo remix runs at the same speed as the 1967 mono mix.

Being For The Benefit Of Mr. Kite!

Recorded: February 17 & 20 & March 28, 29 & 31, 1967
(Abbey Road Studio 2)
Mixed: February 21, 1967 (mono); April 7, 1967 (stereo)

Producer: George Martin
Engineers: Geoff Emerick & Richard Lush

John: Lead vocal; Hammond organ; harmonica (rehearsal only ?)
Paul: Bass guitar; acoustic guitar
George: Harmonica
Ringo: Drums; harmonica; tambourine; shaker bells
George Martin: Harmonium; piano; Hammond organ; glockenspiel
Mal Evans and Neil Aspinall: Harmonicas

The words to "Being For The Benefit Of Mr. Kite!" came almost entirely from an old poster John purchased from an antique store in Sevenoaks, Kent, on January 31, 1967, while the Beatles were there filming the promo clip for "Strawberry Fields Forever." The poster advertised the February 14, 1843, performance of Pablo Fanque's Circus Royal at Town-Meadows, Rochdale. Paul recalls the song being written from the poster, which John had hung on the wall of his Weybridge house: "We pretty much took it down word for word and then just made up some little bits and pieces to glue it together."

After John previewed the song to George Martin on his acoustic guitar, the two discussed how the song would evolve. John wanted to "smell the sawdust on the floor" and "taste the atmosphere of the circus." Martin envisioned a "hurdy-gurdy sound." When John stated that he loved the sound of the music to the children's show The Magic Roundabout, Martin mentioned that he was thinking of the "pipy-sounding" organ played by a dwarf in Disney's animated Snow White. After realizing that it would be impractical to import a steam organ into Abbey Road Studios, Martin decided to start with a harmonium and build from there.

The Beatles began work on the song on February 17, 1967, with John on guide vocal, Paul on bass, Ringo on drums, George Martin on harmonium. Because the harmonium is powered by pumping feet, the rehearsals and seven takes of the song left Martin exhausted. "I remember only too well pumping with my feet at that bloody harmonium for hour after hour, trying to get it right, and being absolutely knackered, heart going at about 130 beats per minute." It was worth the effort as Martin's harmonium playing "established a vaguely circusy atmosphere to the song straight off." John overdubbed his lead vocal (in the process erasing his guide vocal) onto

Take 7. This was then mixed down during Takes 8 and 9, with Take 9 being deemed the better mix. John then added another lead vocal onto Take 9. Paul and George Martin may have re-recorded their bass and harmonium parts, wiping out their original performances.

On February 20, George Martin and Geoff Emerick created the swirling "circus atmosphere" sound effects that would later be added to the song. Martin's original idea was to use tapes containing calliope music. When he discovered that the only steam organ recordings readily available were military marches such as Sousa's "Stars And Stripes," he came up with the idea of transferring segments of the marches to tape, chopping up the tapes, tossing them into the air and reassembling the tape strips in random order. This created a "chaotic mass of sound" in which it was impossible to identify the actual tunes, but was clearly the sound of a steam organ. The final result was the fairground atmosphere John was looking for.

The Beatles returned to the song on March 28, superimposing additional instruments onto Take 9. Mal Evans played bass harmonica, joined by George Harrison, Neil Aspinall and Ringo on harmonicas. For the instrumental break following the line "And of course, Henry the Horse dances the waltz," John envisioned a swirling sound. This was achieved by Martin playing chromatic runs on a Hammond organ. John added the "oom-pawpaws" sounds by hitting chords on a Lowery organ, while Ringo tapped a tambourine and Paul added a guitar solo. All of these parts were played an octave lower and taped at half speed, so that when the tape was run back at full speed, the instruments were not only faster, but also in the correct key. The next evening, the calliope sound effects created on February 20 were added. The song was completed on March 31, with the addition of another organ part and a glockenspiel. That evening, the group supervised seven mono mixes, during which extra calliope sound effects were added from the calliope tape during the middle and end sections, and John's vocal was treated with ADT. Remix 4 was selected as the best. The stereo mix was made on April 7, also with added calliope sounds and ADT on John's vocal.

Anthology 2 contains the first two takes of "Being For The Benefit Of Mr. Kite!," both of which quickly break down, along with Take 7, which was used as the rhythm track for the finished master. It consists of the live performance of John's guide vocal (later erased) backed by George Martin on harmonium, Paul on bass and Ringo on drums. The *50th Anniversary Edition* contains the speech before Take 1, and Takes 4 and 7.

Within You, Without You

Recorded: March 15 & 22, 1967 (Abbey Road Studio 2)
& April 3, 1967 (Abbey Road Studio 1)
Mixed: April 4, 1967 (mono and stereo)

Producer: George Martin
Engineers: Geoff Emerick & Richard Lush

George: Lead vocal; tambura; sitar; acoustic guitar
Neil Aspinall: Tambura
Members of the Eastern Music Center of Flinchley, London:
Tambura; tabla; svaramandal; dilruba

Outside Musicians: Erich Gruenberg, Alan Loveday, Jullien Gaillard, Paul Scherman, Ralph Elman, David Wolfsthal, Jack Rothstein and Jack Greene (violins); Reginald Kilbey, Allen Ford, and Peter Beavan (cellos)

George Harrison's initial offering for *Sgt. Pepper* was "Only A Northern Song," which was recorded on February 13 and 14, 1967. When George Martin decided that the song was not good enough for *Sgt. Pepper*, he gently broke the news to Harrison and suggested that he come up with something better. "Only A Northern Song" would be resurrected for the *Yellow Submarine* cartoon film.

Harrison's second attempt to have one of his compositions on *Sgt. Pepper* yielded better results. "Within You, Without You" was written at Klaus Voormann's house in London, one evening after dinner. According to George: "I was playing a pedal harmonium in the house when the song came to me. The tune came first, then the first sentence...*we were talking*...I finished the words later."

George Martin recalls George auditioning the song for him on acoustic guitar: "The tune struck me as being a little bit of a dirge; but I found what George wanted to do with the song fascinating. It was cosmically different—weird! The lyrics touched on what you might call metaphysical: the inner meaning of life, and all that kind of thing. And it was deeply anti-establishment."

To complement the serious nature of his lyrics, Harrison decided that the song should be played by Indian musicians. The backing track consists of three tambouras, tabla, swarmandal and dilruba, and was recorded in one 6½-minute take on March 15, 1967. Harrison and Neil Aspinall each played tamboura, along with musicians from the Eastern Music Circle of Finchley, London. On March 22, two additional dilruba parts were superimposed onto Take 1, which was mixed down and numbered Take 2.

"Within You, Without You" was the last *Sgt. Pepper* song to be completed. In a case of East meets West, the April 3 session began at

7:00 p.m. with George Martin conducting eight violinists and three cellists. Playing with the previously-recorded Indian instrumental track proved quite a challenge for the classical musicians, who were pushed to keep up with fast-paced dilrubas. Once a satisfactory performance was captured on tape, Harrison added his lead vocal, sitar and acoustic guitar. Although it was 3:00 a.m. when the recording was completed, Harrison wanted to carry on with a mixing session. Several mono mixes were attempted until the session ended at 6:30 a.m. The next evening (April 4), the song was mixed and edited for mono and stereo during a 7:00 p.m. session that ended at 12:45 a.m. According to Martin, "We did a lot of technical things, like artificially double-tracking the strings to give them more body." At Harrison's request, some laughter was added at the end of the song.

George was the only Beatle to participate in the recording of the song, which John described as "one of George's best songs." The *50th Anniversary Edition* contains Take 1 (Indian instruments only).

When I'm Sixty-Four

Recorded: December 6, 8, 20 & 21, 1966 (Abbey Road Studio 2)
Mixed: December 30, 1966 (mono); April 17, 1967 (stereo)

Producer: George Martin
Engineers: Geoff Emerick & Phil McDonald

Paul: Lead vocal; piano; bass guitar
John: Backing vocal; guitar
George: Backing vocal
Ringo: Drums; chimes
Outside Musicians: Robert Burns, Henry MacKenzie and Frank Reidy (clarinets)

"When I'm Sixty-Four" is the oldest song on the LP in multiple ways. The tune was written by Paul when he was 15 or 16. And, with "Strawberry Fields Forever" pulled from the lineup for issuance as a single, it was the first song recorded for the album that ended up on the album. George Martin is certain the song was written by Paul with his father in mind—"a kind of nostalgic, if ever-so-slightly satirical tribute to his dad," who had played in a dance hall band during the twenties and thirties. Paul thought the tune was "too vaudevillian," so he wrote his lyrics "very tongue in cheek" with "Goon Show humour."

The Beatles began work on the song on December 6, 1966. The initial rhythm track consisted of Paul's guide vocal, accompanied by Paul on bass and Ringo on drums with brushes. In the next round, Paul overdubbed piano, Ringo re-recorded his brushwork

and John added guitar. Paul returned to the studio two days later to record his lead vocal onto Take 2. On December 20, Paul, John and George added backing vocals, and Ringo contributed strategically placed chimes. The song was then given two reduction mixes, with Take 4 deemed the best. The final touch the next day added George Martin's score with two clarinets and a bass clarinet onto Take 4.

Mono mixes were made on December 21 and 29, but Paul was not satisfied with the results. For the December 30, 1966, mono and the April 17, 1967, stereo mixes, Paul requested that the tape be sped up, which raised the key from C major to D flat. This made Paul's voice sound thinner and higher. Although Geoff Emerick and George Martin think Paul wanted the tape sped up to make him sound younger, Paul claims he wanted to lift the key to make it sound more "rooty-tooty." The nostalgic vaudeville sound of "When I'm Sixty-Four" sets it apart from the psychedelic and mystical sounds of the album's other tracks. George Martin describes the song as "an affectionate satire regarding old age from a young man's point of view." The *50th Anniversary Edition* contains Take 2.

Lovely Rita

Recorded: February 23 & 24 & March 7 & 21, 1967
(Abbey Road Studio 2)
Mixed: March 23, 1967 (mono); April 17, 1967 (stereo)

Producer: George Martin
Engineers: Geoff Emerick & Richard Lush

Paul: Lead vocal; piano; bass guitar; comb and paper
John: Backing vocal; acoustic guitar; comb and paper
George: Backing vocal; acoustic guitar; comb and paper
Ringo: Drums; comb and paper
George Martin: Piano

After breaking out of the love song mold with "Paperback Writer," Paul sometimes took on the role of a novelist—creating characters such as Eleanor Rigby for a song. "Lovely Rita" was yet another creation of Paul's fertile imagination. He got the idea when he learned that, in America, traffic wardens were called meter maids. He found the term amusing. To him, "maid had sexual connotations, like a French maid." Rather than be antagonistic towards the person who had written the parking ticket, Paul found it more fun to imagine the meter maid as "a bit of an easy lay." He came up with the name Rita because it rhymed with meter.

After the album was released, a London traffic warden named Meta Davies claimed she was the inspiration for the song, having placed a parking ticket on Paul's car in St. John's Wood. According to Meta, Paul arrived just as she was sliding the ticket under the windshield. She claims Paul removed the ticket and noticed her name, telling her that it would be a good name for a song. Paul doesn't remember it that way, but admits he was given the ticket. He recalls working on the words during a nighttime walk near his brother's home in the Wirral near Liverpool.

The Beatles began work on "Lovely Rita" on February 23, 1967. The basic rhythm track, consisting of all four Beatles performing live with Paul on piano (with tape echo), John and George on acoustic guitars and Ringo on drums, was completed in eight takes (half being false starts). Take 8 was mixed down to a single track, with the tape machine running at 48¾ cps, to form Take 9. Paul then added his bass to Take 9. The following evening Paul recorded his lead vocal with the tape machine running at 46½ cps, causing his voice to sound faster and in a higher pitch when replayed at the normal speed of 50 cps. The song was given two reduction mixes, designated Takes 10 and 11.

The group returned to "Lovely Rita" on March 7 to add backing vocals, which were recorded with heavy tape echo. According to Martin, the session evolved into a free-for-all during which the boys "resorted to a choir of paper and combs, as a mock brass section... [blowing] through combs covered with regulation-issue EMI toilet paper, to create a bizarre, kazoo-like sound." John, aided and abetted by the others, added a variety of vocal shenanigans, including moans and sighs, to flesh out the song's ending.

The finishing touch was added on March 21 by George Martin, who was elected to fill the song's middle eight with a piano solo. The piano was recorded at 41¼ cps, thus allowing Martin to play the desired notes at a reasonable speed and providing a fast-paced solo upon playback at 50 cps. The sound of the piano was further altered by the placement of a piece of editing tape on the recording machine's capstan. This caused the tape to stretch as it rolled past the recording head, providing an old-fashioned honky-tonk sound. Later that evening, the song was mixed for mono with the tape machine set at 48¾ cps. The stereo mix was made on April 17. The song's original extended piano opening was edited down during these mixes. The *50th Anniversary Edition* contains Take 9.

Good Morning, Good Morning

Recorded: February 8 & 16 & March 13, 28 & 29, 1967
(Abbey Road Studio 2, except February 16, Studio 3)
Mixed: April 19, 1967 (mono); April 6, 1967 (stereo)

Producer: George Martin
Engineers: Geoff Emerick & Richard Lush

John: Lead vocal; rhythm guitar
Paul: Backing vocal; bass guitar; lead guitar
George: Backing vocal; guitar
Ringo: Drums; tambourine
Outside Musicians: Barrie Cameron, Alan Holmes and David Glyde
(saxophones); John Lee and ? (trombones); ? (French horn)

As the Beatles were no longer limiting their writing to love songs, inspiration came from a variety of sources. "Good Morning, Good Morning" sprang from a Kellogg's Corn Flakes commercial ("Good morning, good morning, the best to you each morning") and contained a reference to the British TV situation comedy *Meet The Wife*. John often composed with the TV on very low in the background. The Kellogg's jingle grabbed his attention, and he wrote it into the song.

Although John, in his Playboy interview, dismissed the song as "a throwaway, a piece of garbage," it is much more complex, both musically and lyrically, than the commercial behind it. In his book on the making of *Sgt. Pepper*, George Martin explains the song's strange structure. He also provides insight into John's state of mind in early 1967, describing the song as: "an ironic, not to say sarcastic look at that suburban life-style. Its lyrics make sharp little digs at the whole suburban deal: 'Everybody knows there's nothing doing, Everything is closed it's like a ruin, Everyone you see is half asleep...I've got nothing to say but it's OK, Good Morning...' That just about summed up how he felt about his way of life at the time."

The rhythm backing for "Good Morning, Good Morning" was recorded on February 8, 1967, in eight takes, with George's rhythm guitar and Ringo's drums each given a separate track. John's lead vocal and Paul's bass were added to the remaining empty tracks on February 16. At this stage, the song contained none of the "Good morning, good morning" backing vocals, horns or sound effects that would later give the song its unique sound. The *50th Anniversary Edition* contains both Take 1 (an instrumental breakdown) and the unadorned Take 8, highlighted by Ringo's excellent drumming and Paul's hyperactive yet melodic bass playing. At the end of the song, John and Paul can each be heard saying "Good morning."

Take 8 was given two reduction mixes at the end of the February 16 session, with Take 10 being the best. The song remained in this form for nearly a month until a March 13 session added the horns, which were played by the members of a Brian Epstein-managed band then known as Sounds Inc. George Martin's score (translated from John's guidance on guitar) consisted of three saxophones, two trombones and a French horn. Two of the sax players, Barrie Cameron and Alan Holmes, were holdovers from the original group when it was called Sounds Incorporated. The horns provide punch, giving the song a hard-driving sound.

The Beatles returned to the song on March 28. After John recorded his lead vocal, a reduction mix was made (Take 11) to free up a track, which was overdubbed with backing vocals by John and Paul, and stinging lead guitar by Paul on his Fender Esquire.

To give the song even more atmosphere, a tape of animal sound effects was prepared towards the end of the session and added to the beginning and end of the song the following evening. The sounds came from the Abbey Road tape archives, specifically Volume 35: Animals and Bees and Volume 57: Fox-Hunt. In homage to the Kellogg's rooster, a crowing cock opens the song, followed by the horns and John and Paul's "Good morning, good morning" vocals. Towards the end, the rooster returns, followed by cats, dogs, horses, sheep, lions and elephants (in order of appearance). The sounds escalate to a fox hunt, complete with pursuing bloodhounds and galloping horses. According to Geoff Emerick, the order was carefully planned. "John said to me during one of the breaks that he wanted to have the sounds of animals escaping and that each successive animal should be capable of frightening or devouring its predecessor!" (The effect is reminiscent of the railroad crossing, barking dog and moving train sounds heard at the end of the Beach Boys' *Pet Sounds* album.) The song ends with a clucking hen that would later be used to blend with the sound of Harrison bending a guitar string at the introduction to the "Sgt. Pepper" reprise.

During the reduction mixes of the song, ADT was added to John's lead vocal, the horns and Paul's guitar solo. Initial mono and stereo mixes were made on April 6, with additional mixing and cross-fading completed on April 19. It was during this final mixing session that Martin came up with the idea to match the sound of the clucking chicken with the bending guitar notes at the beginning of "Sgt. Pepper's Lonely Hearts Club Band (Reprise)." While this is well executed in the stereo version of the album, the mono version sounds awkward and jerky.

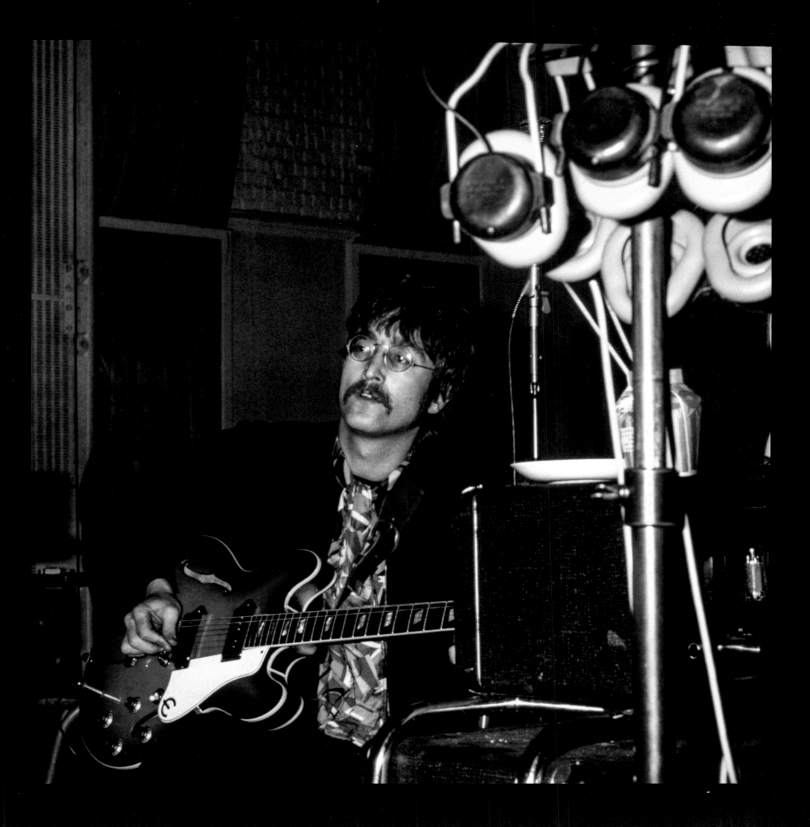

Sgt. Pepper's Lonely Hearts Club Band (Reprise)

Recorded: April 1, 1967 (Abbey Road Studio 1)
Mixed: April 1, 1967 (mono); April 20, 1967 (stereo)

Producer: George Martin
Engineers: Geoff Emerick & Richard Lush

Paul: Lead vocal; bass guitar
John: Backing vocal; Hammond organ
George: Backing vocal; lead guitar
Ringo: Drums; tambourine

George Martin credits Neil Aspinall with the idea to record a reprise of the album's title track. The producer recalls Aspinall suggesting: "You've given a concert. Why don't you wrap up the concert with another version of "Sgt. Pepper"? When everyone agreed it was a great idea, the act you've known for all these years reconvened at Abbey Road on April 1, 1967.

For the second version of the title track, the group was going for a high-energy live sound. The session took place in Studio One, which normally was reserved for orchestral recordings. The cavernous room enhanced the live feeling of the song, giving it, in George Martin's words, an "electrifying, football stadium atmosphere." The basic track consisted of the band performing live, with Paul singing a guide vocal backed by his bass, George on his Epiphone Casino, John on Hammond organ and Ringo on drums. The band recorded nine takes, with Take 9 considered the best. All four Beatles then added their voices, erasing over McCartney's guide vocal, with Ringo also tapping a tambourine. Between the "two" and "three" during Paul's count-in to the song, John can be heard saying "bye" in a dreamy voice. The song was further embellished with audience sound effects (applause and laughter). The mono mix was completed at the end of the session, which ran from 7:00 p.m. until 6:00 a.m. the following morning. The stereo mix was made on April 20.

For the reprise of "Sgt. Pepper," the lyrics were changed to inform the listener that the show was getting very near the end. Lines such as "We're sorry but it's time to go," "We'd like to thank you once again" and "We hope you have enjoyed the show" came directly from Paul's end-of-concert stage banter, as exemplified by Paul's comments from the band's August 23, 1964, Hollywood Bowl performance: "This next song will have to be our last one for this evening...sorry....We'd like to thank everybody here tonight for coming along, thank you very much....And we all hope that you've enjoyed the show. Have you enjoyed the show? Good, great."

A comparison of the opening and closing versions of "Sgt. Pepper" brings to mind the philosophy of NASA after a series of budget cuts. The reprise, economically recorded in a single session, is "faster, better, cheaper." *Anthology 2* contains Take 5, a high-energy performance complete with Paul's rough guide vocal. The *50th Anniversary Edition* contains Take 8.

A Day In The Life

Recorded: January 19 & 20 & February 3, 10 & 22 (Abbey Road Studio 2, except February 10, Studio 1)
Mixed: February 22, 1967 (mono); February 23, 1967 (stereo)

Producer: George Martin
Engineers: Geoff Emerick; Phil McDonald (January 19 & 20); Richard Lush (February 3, 10 & 22)

John: Vocals; acoustic guitar; piano (final chord)
Paul: Vocals; piano; bass guitar; piano (final chord)
George: Congas
Ringo: Drums; maracas; piano (final chord)
Mal Evans: Counting measures; alarm clock; piano (final chord)
George Martin: Harmonium (final chord)
Outside Musicians: Erich Gruenberg, Granville Jones, Bill Monro, Jurgen Hess, Hans Geiger,D. Bradley, Lionel Bentley, David McCallum, Donald Weekes, Henry Datyner, Sidney Sax and Ernest Scott (violins); John Underwood, Gwynne Edwards, Bernard Davis and John Meek (violas); Dennis Vigay, Alan Dalziel, Francisco Gabarro and Alex Nifosi (cellos); Gordon Pearce and Cyril MacArthur (double bass); John Marston (harp); Basil Tschaikov and Jack Brymer (clarinets), Roger Lord (oboe), N. Fawcett and Alfred Waters (bassoons), Clifford Seville and David Sandeman (flutes), Alan Civil and Neil Sanders (French horns); David Mason, Monty Montgomery and Harold Jackson (trumpets); Raymond Brown, Raymond Premru and T. Moore (trombones); Michael Barnes (tuba); and Tristan Fry (timpani and percussion)

The album's final selection is *Sgt. Pepper's* most memorable song. "A Day In The Life" began its life with John's wonderful opening line "I read the news today, oh boy." The second verse grew from John's appearance in the movie *How I Won The War*, while the other verses were loosely based on newspaper stories. The opening verse was inspired by an article in the January 17, 1967, Daily Mail about the car accident that killed Guinness heir, Tara Browne. John told biographer Hunter Davies:

"I didn't copy the accident. Tara didn't blow his mind out, but it was in my mind when I was writing that verse. The details of the accident in the song—not noticing traffic lights and a crowd forming at the scene—were similarly part of fiction."

Paul remembers his contribution differently: "I was not attributing it to Tara in my head. In John's head it might have been. In my head I was imagining a politician bombed out on drugs who'd stopped at some traffic lights and he didn't notice that the lights had changed. The 'blew his mind' was purely a drug reference, nothing to do with a car crash."

The third verse, which Paul recalls writing with John, came from an article in the January 7, 1967, Daily Mail about 4,000 potholes in the streets of Blackburn, Lancashire.

Paul had a separate tune ("Woke up, fell out of bed....") that he and John wanted to link to the verses. They came up with the line "I'd love to turn you on," knowing that it was a drug reference, but perhaps ambiguous enough to allow for a denial. In 1968, Paul admitted that the song was deliberately provocative, "But what we want to do is turn you on to the truth rather than on to pot." The conservative BBC failed to see the ambiguity and banned the song.

The initial recording session for "A Day In The Life" took place on January 19, 1967. The group rehearsed the song with John on piano, Paul on Hammond organ, George on acoustic guitar and Ringo on congas. By the time they were ready for a proper recording, they had reworked their instrument assignments. Take 1 was beautiful in its simplicity, consisting of John's heavily echoed lead vocal, backed only by his Jumbo acoustic guitar, Paul on piano, George Harrison on maracas and Ringo on congas.

Paul thought the song should have something special coinciding with and following the line "I'd love to turn you on," which appears twice in the song. His suggestion was to add 24 bars each time, and have Mal Evans count them accompanied by Paul banging away on piano. Mal's voice was given greater amounts of echo each measure, reaching critical mass at the count of 20 before becoming buried behind Paul's piano, which grew more frenzied and dissonant towards the climax ending. To mark the end of the first 24-measure gap, Evans set off an alarm clock. Although not originally intended to be part of the song, it fit well with Paul's lyrics "woke up, fell out of bed" and so was retained.

Paul's middle section was also present from the start, although it had no vocal. All of the instruments were recorded on Track 1, and John's vocal on Track 4. Four takes were recorded this way, with Takes 1, 2 and 4 completed, and Take 4 being the best and treated with overdubs. John added another two sets of echo-laden vocals onto Tracks 2 and 3, with Paul inserting some heavy piano chords on Track 3 during John's second additional vocal. The group called it a night at 2:30 a.m.

The next evening, three reduction mixes were made from Take 4 with the instruments on Track 1 bounced down to the new tape's Track 1, and the best parts of all three of John's vocals, along with Paul's additional piano, bounced down to Track 2. In some sections, two or three of John's vocals were bounced down to create a double-tracked effect. This was done on the last word of each verse and on the line "I'd love to turn you on." These mixes were designated Takes 5, 6 and 7, with Take 6 deemed the best. Paul then added his bass, and Ringo added his drums onto Track 3. Paul also added some piano to Track 4 and made his first attempt at his vocal for the "Woke up, fell out of bed" segment, which begins after the sound of the alarm clock. This was superimposed onto Track 2, which also had John's vocals in the other parts of the song. Paul's vocal, like John's, was treated with repeat echo. At the end of the middle section, Paul flubs the lyrics and lets out an expletive.

On January 30, while the Beatles were in Sevenoaks, Kent, for the shooting of the promotional film for "Strawberry Fields Forever," George Martin supervised a rough mono mix of Take 6. This mix was used to prepare an acetate of the song for demonstration purposes. Although the surviving acetate is fascinating in its own right, the Beatles recognized there was still much work to be done.

On February 3, Paul and Ringo simultaneously re-recorded their bass and drum parts on Track 3, erasing their parts from January 20. While there was nothing wrong with Ringo's original drumming on the song, the new performance, dominated by tricky tom-tom fills, bass drum and cymbals, is clearly superior. During this re-recording of bass and drums, tambourine and maracas were also added, most likely played by John and George Harrison. Once this was completed, Paul re-recorded his vocal for the middle section, this time without repeat echo, on Track 2, wiping out his earlier effort. After Paul sings "I noticed I was late," John adds some panting sounds. Finally, Paul added his series of vocal "ahhh"s that begin after he sings "I went into a dream" and lead into the last verse. Paul's vocal was treated with repeat echo to give it a dreamlike quality. (John sang a falsetto harmony vocal behind Paul that is barely audible.)

Although much had been accomplished, there was still the matter of filling the two 24-bar segments. Paul approached George Martin with the idea of using a symphony orchestra. Although Martin balked at the cost of bringing 90 musicians into Abbey Road, he realized that with an orchestra, he and the Beatles "could make a lovely sound." In order to control costs, Martin decided half a symphony orchestra would do just fine.

Armed with Paul's idea "to create a spiraling ascent of sound," Martin began work on his orchestral score. First he decided to have the strings echo John's wavering voice on "I'd love to turn you on" by playing a slow semitone trill that would gradually increase in frequency and intensity. This would be followed by the dissonant orchestral climb envisioned by Paul. Musicians were instructed to begin playing on their lowest note as quietly as possible and work slowly up the scale to finish at the end loudly playing their highest note. Martin wrote out reference notes at each bar to give the musicians an approximation of which note should be played at a particular time. To achieve the desired dissonant sound, Martin instructed the musicians not to play as a cohesive unit, but rather to play as individuals. Each symphony member was told to ignore all others, "to go your own way" and "make your own sound."

The orchestral session took place on February 10. At the request of the Beatles, George Martin and the orchestra members wore formal evening wear. The session took on a party atmosphere, with several of the Beatles friends, including members of the Rolling Stones, Marianne Faithfull, Donovan, Graham Nash (then of the Hollies) and Mike Nesmith of the Monkees, in attendance. Many of the 40 symphony members got into the spirit, wearing carnival novelties provided by the Beatles. David McCallum, leader of the London Philharmonic (whose namesake and son starred in the TV series *The Man From U.N.C.L.E.* and recorded for Capitol), wore a large red clown's nose. Violinist Erich Gruenberg wore a gorilla's paw on his bow hand. The two bassoons were adorned at their top ends with balloons, which went up and down when the instruments were played.

George Martin and Paul conducted the orchestra with Geoff Emerick posted in the control room behind the recording console. Two four-track recorders were synchronized for the session. While one machine played the previously recorded tape, the second four-track machine recorded the orchestra. Four takes were performed, with each take being recorded on a separate track. A fifth take was then recorded onto Track 4 of the previously recorded tape. This gave Martin five sets of orchestral backings, effectively increasing the number of musicians from 40 to 200.

While the orchestral pieces were stunning, the song still needed a suitable ending. Martin believed that after the spiraling climb of the orchestra, the song needed to be brought back down to earth with a loud resonant chord. His initial idea was "to make a chord of people singing." After the symphony musicians left, the Beatles and a few of the remaining guests attempted to give the song its dramatic ending. The singers hummed into microphones for four takes before getting through the exercise without bursting into laughter. Three overdubs were then made over the fourth vocal edit piece to fill out the remaining three tracks. What seemed like a good idea at the time failed to pan out as the singers could not hold their notes beyond 20 seconds.

After four mono mixes were attempted on February 13, the Beatles returned to the song on February 22 to record the song's climatic ending. This time the final E major chord was played by John, Paul and Ringo, and Mal Evans spread over three pianos (the Steinway upright, the Steinway grand and the Challen "jangle box"). This was recorded three times. The sound was further bolstered by George Martin playing a low buzzing note on harmonium. The chord was sustained for 53½ seconds, although it was faded out about 10 seconds earlier on the final mixes. After the edit piece was completed, the song was ready for mixing and editing. Two four-track tape machines, one with the Beatles performance (plus the orchestra on Track 4) and the other with the four orchestra performances, were synchronized. The song was mixed for mono with the sustained chord edited to the end of mono Remix 9. Although nine stereo mixes were made that evening, the stereo master was not completed until the following night, when the ending chord was edited to stereo Remix 12.

Anthology 2 contains an interesting sampling of parts of "A Day In The Life" at different stages of the song's development. The track opens with studio talk, the testing of the alarm clock and John's "sugar plum fairy, sugar plum fairy" count-in to the song from Take 1. This leads to Take 2, which features John's lead vocal backed by his acoustic guitar, Paul's piano, George Harrison on maracas and Ringo on congas. As John sings "I'd love to turn you on," Mal Evans' echo-drenched voice is heard counting the 24 measures that would later be filled with the orchestral buildup. The track then switches to an acetate made of Take 6 on January 30, which contains Paul's first attempt at singing the "woke up, fell out of bed" segment, complete with expletive after he flubs the lyrics. After returning to Take 2 for the final verse, the *Anthology 2* edit switches to a new mix of the song's orchestral climb which abruptly stops at the top without the song's chord finale. The track ends with Paul commenting about the use of the orchestra:

"The worst thing about doing this, that we're doing something like this, is they'll think of it. At first people said a bit suspicious...you know, 'Come on, what are you up to?'"

Even George Martin had concerns that he and The Beatles "were being a bit pretentious, a bit clever-clever." He gained confidence in the album after a visit from Capitol president Alan Livingston, who found "A Day In The Life" fascinating. The *50th Anniversary Edition* contains Takes 1 and 2, the orchestral overdub session, the hummed last chord (Takes 8-11) and the last chord.

Inner Groove Additions

Recorded: April 21, 1967 (Abbey Road Studio 2)
Edited and mixed: April 21, 1967

Producer: George Martin
Engineers: Geoff Emerick & Richard Lush

The Beatles: Random chatter and funny noises

Although it's hard to imagine anything following the incredible ending of "A Day In The Life," The Beatles had a few surprises in mind. The end of the second side of the British album contains two unique finishing touches.

On April 21, 1967, The Beatles decided to record some nonsense gibberish to fill the album's run-out groove. People having turntables with an automatic return arm would hear the gibberish briefly, but those without this modern feature would hear the random sounds over and over again until manually lifting the arm from the disc. For this recording, the Beatles made funny noises and nonsense statements. The tape was then chopped up and randomly spliced together.

According to Barry Miles, this "recording" session took three separate three-hour blocks to complete, during which time Mal Evans kept the boys supplied with bottles of Coke and Scotch. It mercifully came to an end around 4:00 a.m.

Although the random sounds had no intended meaning, when the disc was spun backwards, listeners heard an obscene message: "We'll f*ck you like Superman." Paul insists that was purely unintentional. He recalls the group selecting a tape segment that sounded like "Couldn't really be any other."

At the group's request, a high-frequency tone was inserted between the end of the final chord to "A Day In The Life" and the run-out groove gibberish. This was done at the same pitch as a police dog whistle to perk up the album's canine listeners. While

Mark Lewisohn credits the idea to John, George Martin recalls Paul mentioning his sheep dog Martha and requesting that something be added that only a dog could hear. The Sgt. Pepper special issue of The Beatles Book reported that the note was pitched at 18 kilocycles, which is above the general limit audible to the human ear.

Although the random gibberish was reduced to tape, the high-pitched tone was not added until the British lacquers were cut by Harry Moss (mono on April 28 and stereo on May 1). In America, Capitol did not add the high-pitched tone or gibberish. The U.S. album ends with the long, fading final chord of "A Day In The Life."

The reason for Capitol leaving off these extras may have been dictated by the way the company mastered its albums rather than artistic considerations. EMI typically created one master metal part, which was then used to create the mothers and stampers to press the records. EMI also used its mothers to go backwards and create new sub-masters, which in turn created more mothers. Capitol did things differently, cutting between 20 to 30 masters for each Beatles album. This meant that Capitol's cutting engineer would need to duplicate the high pitch and inner groove gibberish 20 to 30 times as opposed to Harry Moss doing that only one time.

Alternate Running Order

George Martin's initial running order for the album differed from the sequencing that eventually came to be. While Side Two remained unchanged, the initial order for Side One was as follows: "Sgt. Pepper's Lonely Hearts Club Band," "With A Little Help From My Friends," "Being For The Benefit Of Mr. Kite!," "Fixing A Hole," "Lucy In The Sky With Diamonds," "Getting Better" and "She's Leaving Home." It has been reported that the order was changed to better accommodate the program breaks on 8-track tapes. It is fortunate that the running order was changed before the album was mastered as the sequence we've known for all these years is superior to the earlier order.

Additional Recordings

The Beatles recorded three songs during the *Sgt. Pepper* sessions that did not make it onto the album: "Strawberry Fields Forever," "Penny Lane" and "Only A Northern Song." The first two were issued on a single in mid-February 1967, while the third later appeared in the *Yellow Submarine* cartoon film and on its soundtrack album. The group also recorded an experimental piece that was never intended for the album.

Strawberry Fields Forever

Recorded: November 24, 28 & 29 & December 8, 9, 15, 21 & 22, 1966 (Abbey Road Studio 2)
Mixed: December 22, 1966 (mono); December 29, 1966 (stereo)

Producer: George Martin
Engineers: Geoff Emerick & Phil McDonald

Note: For the first part of the December 8 session, Dave Harries served as producer and engineer until Martin and Emerick arrived

John: Lead vocal; guitar; piano
Paul: Mellotron; bass guitar; bongos; backing vocals on Take 1
George: Guitar; swarmandal; timpani; backing vocals on Take 1
Ringo: Drums; maracas
Mal Evans: Tambourine
Outside Musicians: Tony Fisher, Greg Brown, Derek Watkins and Stanley Roderick (trumpets); John Hall, Derek Simpson and Norman (cellos)

John wrote "Strawberry Fields Forever" while in Almeria, Spain, for the film *How I Won The War*. The song's title comes from Strawberry Field, a Salvation Army home for orphans located near John's childhood home. John recalled going to parties there and took the name as an image. The song, with its childhood references, is in many ways an extension of his reflective "In My Life," but more thought provoking. In a little over three years, Beatles singles had grown from "Yeah you, got that something, I think you understand" to "Living is easy with eyes closed, misunderstanding all you see." In his 1980 Playboy interview, John explained some of the song's lyrics:

"So the line says, 'No one I think is in my tree, I mean it must be high or low.' What I'm saying, in my insecure way, is 'Nobody seems to understand where I'm coming from. I seem to see things in a different way than most people." Not only was John seeing things differently than most people, but now he was expressing it in his songs. The line "It's nothing to get hung about" comes from a childhood expression used by John. When his aunt Mimi criticized his behavior, John would respond, "It's nothing to get hung about," meaning his conduct didn't merit the death penalty.

Upon returning to England, John recorded demos of the song at his Weybridge home. An edited sequence of these demos with guitar and vocals is on Anthology 2. The intimate demos allow the listener to envision how the song sounded when John auditioned it for George Martin at Abbey Road on November 24, 1966.

The Beatles first attempt at "Strawberry Fields Forever" sounded totally different from anything the group had ever recorded. The song opens with John's dreamy lead vocal and Paul on mellotron, a new electronic instrument capable of duplicating the sounds of stringed instruments. The finished recording is an exquisite blend of mellotron, guitar, slide guitar and creative drumming topped with John's double-tracked lead vocal and beautiful backing harmony vocals by John, Paul and George. Although Take 1 is a truly remarkable performance, John was not satisfied, and this early version of the song remained unreleased until its legitimate debut on Anthology 2.

The Beatles returned to "Strawberry Fields Forever" on November 28 to record a totally different arrangement. In its second incarnation, the song opens with a mellotron introduction and the order of the lyrics is different. The melody for the mellotron opening had been in John's head for years. In The First U.S. Visit, filmed in February 1964, John can be heard playing a brief segment of the melody on a melodion. This equally compelling and fascinating version of the song, featuring mellotron, guitars, pianos, bass, drums and maracas, was completed on November 29, with Take 7 being mixed and used to cut four mono acetates. Anthology 2 contains the mono mix of Take 7, along with an expanded instrumental edit piece tacked on the end.

About a week later, John decided the group should have another go at the song. On December 8, the band started on the new version's backing track, which was considerably faster than the previous arrangements and full of additional percussion, including timpani, bongos and tambourine. Takes 15 and 24 were edited to form Take 25, which was mixed down to one track and subjected to considerable overdubbing the following night. Ringo added percussion parts, while George contributed a swarmandal (an Indian harp-like instrument with 21 to 36 strings). Backwards-recorded cymbals were also superimposed.

On December 15, four trumpets and three cellos played by outside musicians were added, and the four-track tape was mixed down into Take 26. John then added two separate lead vocals. Additional vocals and piano were overdubbed on December 21. The completed Take 26 is a fast-paced heavy-sounding extravaganza, light years beyond the delicate original version of the song.

The following day John informed George Martin that he liked parts of the two most recently completed versions of the song. George Martin recalls: "He said 'Why don't you join the beginning of the first one to the end of the second one?' 'There are two things against it,' I replied. 'They are in different keys and different tempos. Apart from that, fine.' 'Well,' he said, 'you can fix it!'"

Miraculously, Martin and Geoff Emerick solved the problem by speeding up Take 7 and slowing down Take 26. This resulted in both versions running at approximately the same speed and having the same pitch. The first minute of Take 7 was then edited to Take 26 (minus its instrumental introduction) to form the finished master.

Remix sessions for "Strawberry Fields Forever" took place on December 29 and 30, with a mono tape copy of the finished master made on January 2, 1967, along with a mono tape copy of "When I'm Sixty-Four," supporting reports that "When I'm Sixty-Four" was originally slated to be the flip side of "Strawberry Fields Forever." The 50th Anniversary Edition contains Takes 1, 4, 7 and 26.

In the fall of 1969, the song's fade-out ending caught the attention of those looking for clues of Paul McCartney's rumored death. John supposedly could be heard saying "I buried Paul," but his actual words are "cranberry sauce."

Penny Lane

Recorded: December 29 & 30, 1966 & January 4, 5, 6, 9, 10, 12 & 17, 1967 (Abbey Road Studio 2 except January 10 & 12, Studio 3)
Mixed: January 25, 1967 (mono)

Producer: George Martin
Engineers: Geoff Emerick & Phil McDonald

Paul: Lead vocal; piano; bass guitar; harmonium; tambourine
John: Backing vocal; piano; guitar; congas; handclaps
George: Backing vocal; guitar; handclaps
Ringo: Drums; hand-bell; handclaps
George Martin: Piano
Outside Musicians: David Mason (piccolo trumpet); Ray Swinfield, P. Goody, Manny Winters, Dennis Walton (flutes and piccolos); Leon Calvert, Freddy Clayton, Bert Courtley and Duncan Campbell (trumpets and flugelhorn); Dick Morgan and Mike Winfield (obos and cor anglais); Frank Clarke (double-bass)

Paul's "Penny Lane" was the perfect song to link with John's "Strawberry Fields Forever." Like John's contribution to the single, "Penny Lane" was named after a real place in Liverpool. In Barry Miles' Paul McCartney Many Years From Now, Paul recalls:

"It was childhood reminiscences: there is a bus stop called Penny Lane. There was a barber shop called Bioletti's with head shots of the haircuts you can have in the window and I just took it all and altered it up a little bit to make it sound like he was having a picture exhibition in his window. It was all based on real things.... John came over and helped me with the third verse, as was often the case. We were writing childhood memories...."

Although "Penny Lane" did not generate three separate versions, it still took the band nearly three weeks to complete. Paul began work on the song on December 29, 1966, recording six takes of the basic piano track until he was satisfied. Two additional piano tracks (one played through a Vox guitar amplifier with reverb and the other played at half-speed and then played back at a faster speed to obtain a different sounding texture), a harmonium (also played through a Vox guitar amplifier), tambourine and percussion were added to fill out the four-track tape, which was then mixed down to one track the following evening to accommodate the addition of Paul's lead and John's backing vocals. On January 4, 1967, John added another piano part and George recorded his lead guitar. The following evening, Paul added another vocal track. On January 6, Paul's bass, John's rhythm guitar and Ringo's drums were recorded, along with John on conga drums. After another reduction mix, John and George Martin added additional piano parts. The group supplied handclaps and Paul, John and George added background vocals. The 50th Anniversary Edition contains Take 6 and vocal overdubs.

The first of three classical instrument overdub sessions was held on January 9, with four flutes, two trumpets, two piccolos and a flugelhorn played by outside musicians. The next evening scat harmony vocals and a hand-bell were added to the tape. On January 12, outside musicians added two trumpets, two oboes, two cor anglais and a double-bass.

The final crowning touch was added on January 17 by David Mason, who was brought in by Paul to play the song's distinctive lead trumpet parts in the middle eight and at the end of the song. Paul had seen Mason's performance of Bach's Brandenburg Concerto No. 2 in F major on the BBC2 television series Masterworks on January 11. Mason recalls:

"I took nine trumpets along and we tried various things, by a process of elimination settling on the B-flat piccolo trumpet. We spent three hours working it out. Paul sang the parts he wanted, George Martin wrote them out, I tried them. But the actual recording was done quite quickly. They were jolly high notes, quite taxing, but with the tapes rolling we did two takes as overdubs on top of the existing song."

At the end of the January 17 session, three mono mixes were completed, with the final mix, Remix 11, being considered the best. A tape copy of Remix 11 was made and sent to Capitol for use as the master tape for the single. After further review, it was decided that the song could be improved, so additional mixes were made on the evening of January 25. The third and final mix, Remix 14, was copied to tape for use as the finished master for the single.

The primary difference between Remix 11 and 14 is that Remix 11 has Mason's seven-note B-flat piccolo trumpet solo at the end of the song, whereas Remix 14 does not. The tape of the new finished master was sent to Capitol, but not before the label had pressed promotional copies of the upcoming single (Capitol P 5810) using Remix 11 and sent them to distributors, radio stations and reviewers. Thus, when the song received its pre-release air play in America, listeners heard the version with the trumpet solo at the end. The trumpet solo ending was not commercially released until Capitol's 1980 Rarities album (Capitol SHAL-12060), which edited the ending solo onto a stereo mix of the song. The complete mono mix with the trumpet solo used for the original Capitol promotional record was finally made available on the *50th Anniversary Edition*.

Anthology 2 contains a new edit and mix of the song combining and highlighting various elements of the many overdub sessions. Of particular interest is Paul's single-tracked vocal, the cor anglais and trumpets on the bridge and the extended B-flat piccolo trumpet solo at the end. At the song's conclusion, Paul can be heard saying, "A suitable ending, I think." And who are we to argue?

Only A Northern Song

Recorded: February 13 & 14 & April 20, 1967
(Abbey Road Studio 2)
Mixed: April 21, 1967 (mono)

Producer: George Martin
Engineers: Geoff Emerick & Richard Lush

George: Lead vocal; organ; guitar
John: Piano; tambourine
Paul: Bass guitar; trumpet
Ringo: Drums
Group: Tape effects, noises, percussion, glockenspiel

Although initially recorded for the *Sgt. Pepper* album, George's psychedelic-sounding "Only A Northern Song" did not make the cut. The band and George Martin preferred his "Within You Without You," so the *Pepper* reject was relegated to the *Yellow Submarine* cartoon film and soundtrack album.

Only A Northern Song is a humorous jab at Northern Songs, a publishing company that was partially owned by John and Paul, although George's target was majority owner Dick James. According

to George's lyrics, "It doesn't really matter what chords I play, what words I say...as it's only a Northern song." As George was under contract to the company, his tune truly was only a Northern song.

The band recorded nine takes of backing tracks on February 13, 1967. Instruments included George on organ, John on piano, Paul on bass, Ringo on drums and all sorts of weird sound effects. The following evening, Take 3 was mixed down three separate times forming Takes 10-12. Two George Harrison lead vocals were added to Take 12, and the song was mixed for mono for demo purposes. Apparently not satisfied with the Valentine's Day mix, the group came back to the song on April 20, wiping out previous overdubs on Take 3, and adding bass, guitar, trumpet (reportedly played by Paul) and glockenspiel. Vocals were then added to Take 11, which was a Take 3 reduction mix from February 14. On April 21, the revised Take 3 and the revised Take 11 were mixed together in sync to form a very strange discordant-sounding mono master.

For *Anthology 2*, producer George Martin and engineer Geoff Emerick created a stereo mix that features vocals with different lyrics from the February 14 session. The *Yellow Submarine Songtrack* album from 1999 contains a true stereo mix of the master recording made possible by state-of-the-art digital technology.

Carnival of Light

Recorded: January 5, 1967 (Abbey Road Studio 2)
Mixed: January 5, 1967 (mono)

Producer: George Martin
Engineers: Geoff Emerick & Phil McDonald

The Beatles recorded an *avant-garde* piece on this evening after Paul completed his vocal overdubs for "Penny Lane." According to Paul, Barry Miles asked him to provide an experimental 15 to 20 minute recording for the January 28 and February 4, 1967 event at London's Roundhouse Theatre known as A Million Volt Light and Sound Rave (also known as the Carnival of Light Rave). With McCartney leading the way, the group created a fragmented and abstract sound collage mixing distorted instruments, percussion, sound effects, feedback and random voices (John and Paul screaming phrases like "Are you alright?" and "Barcelona!"). This experimental recording, running nearly 14 minutes, was never intended for the *Sgt. Pepper* LP or any other record. Geoff Emerick recalls George Marin's reaction when the session ended: "This is ridiculous, we've got to get out teeth into something a little more constructive."

We Hope You Have Enjoyed The Show!

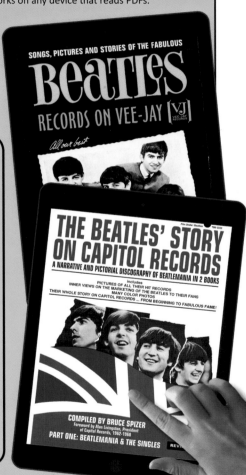

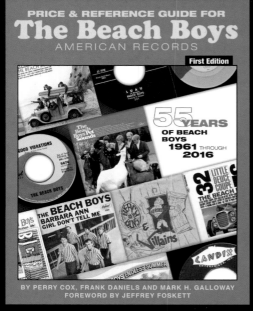

HAPPY 50TH ANNIVERSARY
SGT. PEPPER'S LONELY HEARTS CLUB BAND!